THE FIRM BOND

THE FIRM BOND

Linking Meaning and Mission
In Business and Religion

by Robert Lawrence Kuhn
and George Thomas Geis

PRAEGER

PRAEGER SPECIAL STUDIES • PRAEGER SCIENTIFIC

New York • Philadelphia • Eastbourne, UK
Toronto • Hong Kong • Tokyo • Sydney

Library of Congress Cataloging in Publication Data

Kuhn, Robert Lawrence
  The firm bond.

  Bibliography: p.
  Includes index.
  1. Industrial management—Moral and ethical aspects.
2. Organizational behavior—Moral and ethical aspects.
3. Commitment (Psychology) I. Geis, George T. II. Title.
HD38.K77   1984   658   84-8354
ISBN 0-03-063639-6 (alk. paper)

HD
38
.K77
1984

Published in 1984 by Praeger Publishers
CBS Educational and Professional Publishing
a Division of CBS Inc.
521 Fifth Avenue, New York, NY 10175 USA

© 1984 by Praeger Publishers

456789 052 987654321

Printed in the United States of America

on acid-free paper

DEDICATION

To my parents, Lee and Louis Kuhn; to my wife, Dora; to my children, Aaron, Adam and Daniella — who are the core of my life.

R. L. K.

To my mother, Anne, and to my wife, Penny, who continually teach me about commitment.

G. T. G.

PREFACE

"Don't mix business and religion!"

That advice, given for generations, we ignore. Business and religion are precisely what we *do* mix; we tell the truth and take the consequences.

Morality is not the issue (Don't misunderstand. Morality *is* an issue; it's just not our issue here.) We do not judge "Right" or "Wrong." What counts is what works, and what works is understanding organizations: how to make members and employees more committed; how to make groups and companies more productive.

We mix ecclesia and commerce in an unusual brew, very different from the common expectation. We use religious organizations and religious commitment to probe the deep structure of *organizations* and *commitment*.

What we learn from religion, we apply to business. How, we ask, can corporations improve the dedication of employees and executives? Whatever makes adherence in religion so potent should make allegiance in business more meaningful.

We do not leave the circle incomplete. What we learn from business, we apply to religion. The principles derived we spin back to their source. Although religious organizations are not our primary audience, what we have to say may strengthen members and ministers. We hope so. The things of God draw our profound concern; they command our deepest respect.

A word about the Bible. This remarkable document appears in many of our case histories. Though attitudes about it differ, and interpretations may belie its original intent, the Bible is the cornerstone of Judeo-Christian society. To many it is literal truth, historic and prophetic as well as salvational and spiritual, the direct revelation of God. To others it is morality and grace, the inspired teachings of righteous men. To still others it is wisdom and virtue, the pinnacle of early literature. To all it is important, the foundation of western civilization.

The Firm Bond is about organizations and commitment, not the Bible and theology. But since religious organizations play a crucial supporting role, we state our *belief* in the Bible as the written record of mankind's relationship with God. The Bible, in our opinion, has special relevance for the modern world.

vii

This book is about something distinctly human: *personal commitment*, the psychic knot tying individuals and institutions, the primal force sustaining the structure of society. Our concern is people and organizations; we seek meaning and fulfillment for the former, mission and success for the latter.

We write from experience. We write of groups and organizations, congregations and companies — clusters of human beings professing common missions and goals.

Emotions show. The examples are real; the people we know. Though form is disguised, substance is not. (All cases are composites.) This is no place for academic aloofness. Business and religion run the gamut of human struggle, and we seek insight into both.

Our experience is dual, our backgrounds diverse. Each of us, at different times in different groups, has been both participant and observer, each caught in compulsion, each dispassionate in analysis. Sometimes we were hot, burning with organizational fervency; sometimes we were cool, inquiring with professional precision. At all times we were committed.

Having felt the pulse of various groups, we note the presence of a repetitive beat. A striking signal emerges from clutter and noise. Each organization, when viewed from within, considers itself at least somewhat unique; but these same organizations, when observed from without, suddenly manifest remarkable similarity.

Corporation, foundation, university, hospital, government, church — though cultures may differ, issues do not. Fundamentals affect them all: goals, strategy, structure, resource allocation, control systems, employee policies, politicing, leadership, succession, change — the list is long and the commonality strong. In every case, from company to congregation, *management* plays the crucial role.

We help managers understand common concerns by cutting across divergent groups. Our objective is to clarify problems and define solutions. What issues are shared by both business and religion? A dominant theme, developed with variations, is the *commitment connection* between individuals and institutions.

To get what we want, we must see what we need. We must augment reality, expanding vision and bringing into sharp focus this bond between group and member, employee and company.

How do we magnify the commitment connection? We use a "special lens,"[1] and and we look through it in both directions. *Religious organizations* become our "lens," and *religious attachment* our "magnifying glass." What we see is an enlarged picture of the member-group bond, a pulsating portrait in three dimensions, one that gives managers new tools to increase employee dedication and company productivity.

We live in an age of crosscurrents, a⌐
seemingly contradictory trends spiral ⌐
society is more scientific; on the other, ⌐
technology invades our businesses and⌐
ple is the main topic for organizational ⌐

Both in theory and practice, the focus ⌐
companies deal with personnel occupies mu⌐
While understanding human resources is a m⌐
sultants, it is also central to the growth, if not⌐
American business. How firms attract, train, allocate, ⌐
tain, and account for its people is a major matter for sen⌐
ment. Managing personnel, according to surveys, is the centra⌐
chief executives.

Are these crosscurrents strange bedfellows, mingled ineptly ⌐
the electric confusion of a tightly wired world? Or is the phenomenon
a real one, a new mix? Do technological advance and human concern
feed each other positively, with the growth of one eliciting need for the
other? Does the ascent of rational analysis trigger an equal and opposite reaction that is "distinctly human"?[2]

This book is founded on experience and aimed at practitioners. It
has antecedents in academic research, but it stresses sharp relevance
and easy access. The business-religion connection is vital. The varied
stories portray how people and organizations interact when pulled by
profits and position or when driven by eternity and morality. (When
hearing our interest in having business learn from religion, a well-
known media evangelist remarked, "It's about time — religion has
sure learned enough from business!")

Even if we do not all go to Church, we are all in a "church." This sense
of belonging and community is the cornerstone of social life. What we
seek, as individuals and as institutions, is rooted in religious experience.
Life within organizations, any organization, has spiritual overtones.

Mission is the heart of group existence just as *meaning* is the soul
of group participants. Each is driving energy and directing force. Mission and meaning, the two are related — groups seek to achieve objectives; members strive to fulfill purposes — the soundness of the relationship determining the tightness of the bond.

Personal meaning and *company mission* are the two poles of our
axis. What one does affects the other, intimately, repetitively, consistency. Strong employee commitment, at all corporate levels, correlates highly with long-term company achievement. Personal fulfillment and organizational success are clear and commanding targets,
with religion our guide and business our goal.

Although this book is not designed as a scholarly treatise, we
believe it to be rigorous and coherent. In Part I we use personal

to build a model of commitment (inductively); in Part II we
onal histories to apply the model of commitment (deductively).
ffer managers a fresh framework to build employee strength,
hieve our objective. If we breed cross-fertilization between
ess and religion, we make our mark.

The essence is simple. The critical linkage forms between *personal
aning* and *company mission*, and it is this *firm bond* that becomes
ur working definintion of commitment.

Robert Lawrence Kuhn
George Thomas Geis

CONTENTS

PART I
LINKING MEANING AND MISSION

CHAPTER ONE

FIRM COMMITMENT:
WHAT IT'S ALL ABOUT

Bradley Collins had it made: good family, easy money, no sweat. Sitting pretty, this Brad, or so you'd think.

Work, if that's the word, was smooth. His father ran a very successful, privately held company that promised financial returns forever. At the plant every morning Brad's body showed late, his heart not at all. He seemed to be chasing and cruising. Yet something else was going on. Underneath the blustery image was a creative spirit burning to break free.

Brad imagined himself a writer. Fat chance. He had majored in English in college, but never received top grades. It was now five years since graduation, and he had brooded enough. It was time, he decided, to give fantasy a fling.

For years he had been working on scripts for television. The tube, he figured, had a voluminous appetite for scripts. Trouble was, it wasn't hungry for his. He wrote constantly: every morning before work, most evenings after work. All scripts sent out on spec; all scripts sent back in time — most unread, many unopened. Countless hundreds of hours expended; countless dozens of rejections received.

Then, out of the blue, a fluke — a surprise catch. Brad made an instant decision. The check, for $5,000, would be his grubstake. He could live on it for a year. But could he sell another script?

One year would have to be the time limit. Although self-imposed, it was no less real. He would try crashing the tight Hollywood scene. He knew no one, he had no inside pull. All odds said he didn't have a prayer to make a sale, much less make a living. If he couldn't crack the sacred circle in 12 months, he would return to his father's firm. There would be no choice; his young family needed support.

Brad rented a small cubicle in a blemished building. The stains he ignored; the location he adored. The old barn was owned by a major production studio, and several secondary writers, television writers, were stabled there. Just entering that windowless hovel was ecstasy. His fingers tingled in anticipation of attacking the typing keys. Create the

3

atmosphere, he told himself, then the reality. He was among writers, *real* writers. It was, he imagined, like being in the bullpen, warming up, waiting to be called to the mound in relief.

Brad closeted himself there every day. His keyboard hummed with plots and characters; pages sizzling with action and snap flew out of the infernal machine. But nobody noticed; the janitor was more involved in studio productions.

The year was grinding on. Brad was writing his guts out and not earning a dime. The five grand was about out; the family Buick was up for auction.

Then a chance encounter, a classic "break." A hack producer asked Brad to "brighten up" his dull script. The producer, officing next store, was lazy and desperate. His still-born film was lousy, but the color of his dough was green.

Brad read avidly through the script, bad as it was. Just a rip-off, and a poor one, of a popular foreign flick. Lots to be done; he would earn that fee.

Then the clash. Everthing Brad recommended cutting the producer loved; everything Brad wanted to add the producer hated. Yet the offer was still dangled: "Five Big Ones, kid, just do the fix."

Brad refused the offer and the money. Turned the hack down flat. Either he would be a real writer or no writer at all.

For Brad, success or failure was not as important as doing what he really wanted. If he failed, at least he'd have tried, at least he'd given his best. Brad Collins was *driven*. Devotion to his dream was white-hot.

There are thousands of Brad Collins in the world. The fact that the vast majority fail without a sputter in no way inhibits more from rising. That is the human spirit and the American way.

What happened next is completely irrelevant. The point is made: attitude, not outcome, is our concern. True commitment thrives independent of external results. But the real story is a real kicker.

The person on whom "Brad Collins" is based *did* sell a script just after the close of that test year, and a couple more the second year. (At a high school reunion some years later, an old English teacher would ask with incredulity, "Do you really earn money *writing*?")

Within 12 years Brad had created, produced, and written over a dozen television series, including some top-rated ones. In characteristic style he turned down a huge guarantee from a major studio and took the risk of opening his own firm, putting all his assests right on the line.

He struggled for years with payrolls and cash flow in addition to scripts and scenes. But the risk produced enormous returns — as much as an oilfield strike — when a series became a number one hit. But once again, success, though it feels so nice, is not the issue. Outlook and intent are what we seek.

Dedication, ever present, never changed. With all his Hollywood success and public praise, Brad is still a writer, happiest when tucked away with his typewriter. He still works 15-hour days, writing in early mornings, producing in afternoons and evenings. He is juggling 20 shows at the same time, each at different stages of production — watching daily filmings from the set, managing ever-delicate creative staffs, pitching powerful network execs — electric eyes sparking the whole time.

Recently he refused a million dollars to write two movies for a major studio because he didn't like one of the themes. Instead, he wrote a couple of TV episodes — for which he gave himself union minimums.

"I am terribly overpaid," Brad reflects, "not in relationship to the industry but to the world. Maybe I contribute to the public good by giving people some escape and relaxation. I guess we all need it. But I have no illusions about my intrinsic 'worth.' Though some in Hollywood are possessed by their own importance, there is little of lasting value here. I do what I enjoy, and I am happy when I make others happy. If Congress passed a law cutting my income by 95 percent, I'd still be up a 6 A.M. tomorrow, doing the same thing with the same fever."

MUSIC MAKING

Fever. Devotion. Dreams. The struggle to find meaning, to transcend imposed limitations, to express one's soul. That's the start of our story.

"Many people die with their music still in them," lamented Oliver Wendel Holmes. Only the fortunate few play out their music.

Of these few, some (such as Brad) compose their own symphonies and conduct their own orchestras. Others find organizations where they can perform their "meaning music." They, to be sure, are the lucky ones.

Organizations. Group goals. Collective objectives. Institutional purpose. That's the other part of our story.

"Most organizations live with their mission still in them." Not vintage Holmes, but true nonetheless. Only rare companies become concert halls for creative spirits, drawing out career-long performances of personal meaning tone poems. Most companies are noisy beerhalls, drowning out any attempt at tender melody or resonant harmony.

Personal meaning, organizational mission, and the turf where they meet — that's the terrain we explore.

GOING FOR BROKE

Philip Walker began as a broker. He was 27 and Metropolitan Real

Estate was the most prestigious firm in town. When Walker received word he had been hired, a few nervous days after his somewhat stilted interview, he was thrilled. He felt as if he had been admitted to a corps as elite as the Green Berets. He laughed as he recalled Groucho Marx's line that he wouldn't want to join any group that would have him as a member. Nevertheless, he basked in his newfound, albeit parochial, status with Metropolitan.

Philip Walker had a natural talent for selling. Radiating high energy and amplified by company power, Walker flew through three banner years. Real estate was right; Metropolitan was the high flier; and Walker had the touch. Rolling off a six-figure income was heady stuff for him. Still shy of 30, he was making more in four months than he had ever made in a year. Yet, in spite of his superb performance, Walker stood in awe of Metropolitan's superstars, especially his branch manager, Terry Rogers.

Rogers was a polished professional, always impeccably dressed, always ready with a firm hand, smooth words, and cool head. He was the epitome of the Metropolitan image. Walker virtually idolized his boss and looked to follow him up the corporate ladder. When Rogers announced his resignation, Walker was stunned.

Although Rogers was on a fast track at Metropolitan, the track wasn't fast enough. Ambition had expanded in the heat of success. When Phiro & Daniels, a second-tier real estate company, offered him their presidency, the appeal was instant and the offer was accepted.

Within two months, Walker also left Metropolitan and joined P & D — thanks largely to Roger's persuasive powers. More than charisma was pulling Walker, himself now a seasoned salesmen. Rogers put together a sweet package, including a branch managership, a larger than normal base salary, plus freedom to continue personal selling.

Two years and one real estate collapse later, Rogers was struggling to keep P & D afloat. The problem, in retrospect, began when the first-tier alumnus took the reigns. As part of his strategic plan, Rogers was determined to upgrade the company's image to reflect quality, to recreate the model that had been so successful at Metropolitan. The effect was immediate. High quality came, but so did high overheads. The breakeven point — that critical fulcrum of financial balance — skyrocketed.

Cutting overhead and undermining company countenance was an anathema to Rogers. Vision and pride required another solution, and only one, he concluded, was available. Sales had to be increased — dramatically. For this he needed Walker.

When Rogers called in his associate, he first reminisced about their banner days at Metropolitan. Then he made the pitch: "I want you to be my sales manager." The post would be full time, and the managerial responsibilities would augur a career shift. Together,

Rogers assured Walker, they could complete P & D's transformation to elitism, and maybe give their alma mater a good run for its money.

It was a time of tugs and pulls for Walker. The opportunity for advancement was ego flattering and the salary increase attractive. The relationship with Rogers — the comaraderie and equality — resonated with long-standing emotions. Yet, there was a flip side, one not so flattering or attractive. Becoming full-time sales manager would mean no personal sales, and no personal sales would mean being cut off from clients. Clients were ultimate security in this business. With active customers tucked under his wing, Walker could go anywhere should P & D go under. Giving them up would be bridge-burning.

But financial security was not the only factor to consider. Walker had competing motivations. What about Phiro & Daniels? Walker identified deeply with building a company that matched or even exceeded the quality and character of Metropolitan, and he knew that many of his associates at P & D shared his dream. Others now relied on him, having bought into his vision. Sure, Walker wanted to improve his personal station in life, who doesn't? But there was more here than personal materialism and independent ego. Walker's sense of self had merged with his firm's forward direction. Personal meaning was overlapping company mission.

Walker's moment of truth centered around *commitment*, decisions of personal *meaning* given the context of P & D's company *mission*. Walker's dilemma triggers some basic questions, and thus provides a backdrop for the issues of commitment.

COLORING COMMITMENT

Commitment draws us all; we are attracted by its mental magnetism. But what, really, is *commitment,* and ordinary enough word with common-sense understanding?

As human beings we belong to various groups. Whether economic, political, social, or religious, these groups compete constantly for our loyalty and our attention. Which groups we choose and how we allocate energy to each affect our lives intimately. Little else makes such matter. The power of groups is immense.

How do people go about making these allocation decisions? Why do they exert effort to support company policy? Why subjugate individual desire to collective need and make sacrifices for nonpersonal goals? What considerations are given, what points weighed? What are the factors that build organizational ties? What are the antecedents of commitment and how do they perform their magic? Neither financial considerations nor social conventions, however influential, explain everything. The formula for organizational glue has other essential ingredients.

What is this bond between people and groups? What is it about human nature that extends the boundaries of self beyond self, stretching one's skin to encompass others, merging individual identity into amorphous mass, melding *I* into *we* and ego into crowd? What is the subtle and complex interplay between organizations and members? How does each sculpt and mold the other? And what are the dynamics when the organizational knot begins to unravel?

Our focus is managers — of all kinds, at all levels, in all groups — and we view them on both sides of the organizational lens. On the one side, these administrators have the authority and responsibility for building corporate strength and employee cohesion; and on the other side, they themselves feel the pressures and tensions of company association and career ambition.

What makes people give all, putting out to accomplish company programs? Why strain to work in concert with others? These are fundamental executive questions. To give subordinates such stimulation is to move the company aggressively forward. This directed thrust develops a firm's competitive capacity. To build strong market position in a turbulent industrial environment, a tight, tough team is essential.

Just how sensitive to commitment are business effectiveness and production efficiencies? If effectiveness involves "doing the right thing," what role does personnel commitment play in influencing company goals? If efficiency involves "doing things right," what is the value of employee commitment in improving company performance?

What, also, are the pathologies of commitment? What happens when blinding zeal degenerates into savage inhumanity? And what can such pathologies tell us about the rational functioning of commitment?

Finally, how can the dynamics of commitment be unleashed for both personal fulfillment and group well-being? What can an organization do to maximize individual commitment and mobilize it to accomplish collective purpose? How can a "personal commitment strategic plan" be designed to achieve one's own goals? When are tradeoffs necessary, and how are they best made?

In dissecting these questions, we mark our starting place and ultimate objectives. But first, we define the essential terms.

DEFINING COMMITMENT

Scholars studying organizational commitment have not always agreed on definitions, much less measurements.[1] Some writers frame commitment in terms of "strength of individual involvement" with a given organization, stressing acceptance of values, willingness to allocate effort, and desire to maintain membership. Others view commitment in terms of "intent to maintain the group," targeting the impulsion to support the organization because it provides what the person needs. Still others see commitment as emotional, a sensate attachment to an organization, an affective allegiance to its goals and values — totally apart from any material gain or worth that an individual may drive from the association.

We propose a structural definition. *We define commitment as the link between personal meaning and organizational mission.* Commitment is the emotional lines of force that attract individuals to institutions, the psychic energy that maintains physical presence and mental membership. It is the strength of the meaning — mission link which determines the power of the attachment.

Metaphors for commitment come easy: The interpersonal glue that produces group stickiness? The master knot that ties together independent strands? ("Knot" rather than "glue" may be a better metaphor for the firm bond, since ideally one should be "tied," not "stuck," to an organization.)

Commitment can be described as "purpose with action," an internal compulsion of the individual to achieve an external objective of the group. It is the "strong force" that holds people in the organizational nucleus. It is the human essence that endows groups of people with centripetal focus and agglutinizing strength. The coherent commitment of individuals generates the cohesive attraction of groups.

Commitment signals emotional attachment, and the continuum runs the gamut from extreme self-sacrifice through blasé detachment to fierce adversarial attack. All ranges of personal meaning can be present, including nonmeaning.

THE SPECIAL LENS

The book has an organizing principle, a way of looking at the world. We believe that organizational characteristics in general, and commitment in particular, can best be studied in their purest form. This is our operating paradigm, our conceptual prism.

We define "pure form" as those environments where what we seek is readily apparent, where its manifestation is overt and its presence powerful. In such situations the target characteristics stands out and, though exaggerated, can be massaged and manipulated. It is one way to examine an intangible.

What kinds of organizations do we require? Ones where the desired attribute appears in strongest and most dominant mode, where the "signal" of the target trait is highest relative to the "noise" of all other traits. Once this pure form is isolated and analyzed, then the emerging understanding can be applied. Manifestations of the characteristic in other environments, though not as overt, can then be investigated.

Organizations exemplifying the pure form of the characteristic are the special lens, and it is through them that we look. What kinds of organizations are the special lens needed for scrutinizing commitment?

ORGANIZATIONS: KINDS AND TYPES

Classification is a creative task. The process of grouping and splitting may trigger some insights. The structural scheme in Table 1.1 is both exhaustive and terse.

TABLE 1-1. ORGANIZATION TYPES

1) Ideological
2) Collegial
3) Creative
4) Bureaucratic
5) Social

There are five categories. With then we subsume all kinds of organizations from all sectors and for all purposes. No attempt is made to justify the precision or rightness of the categories, since such precision or rightness does not exist. The categories are presented for simplicity. Our object is to select a prototypical organization, the pure form, for commitment.

Ideological: Organizations where missions and goals dominate; associations founded on philosophical and conceptual ideas; often a search for the ideal and the ultimate; classic examples are religious and political movements.

Collegial: Organizations where members are peers and partners; the grouping of associates and equals; professional organizations (doctors, lawyers, accountants); trade and job associations; academic faculties; government bodies (house and senate).

Creative: Organizations with artistic or intellectual focus — music, art, writing, advertising, media (television, movies);

intellectual institutions — universities, think tanks, research departments, scientific laboratories; the inherent independence of creative and innovative personnel.

Bureaucratic: Organizations with strict systems of reporting and controls; where lines of authority and formal structures of communication dominate; hierarchial or pyramid-type structures; traditional corporations, government agencies (federal, state, local).

Social: Organizations with personal, fraternal, or societal objectives; clubs and community endeavors; civic, and charitable organizations; special interest groups; the fulfillment of personal and social needs.

PURE FORM CHARACTERISTICS

Table 1.2 is another leap of faith. In it we select the dominant characteristics for each category of organization. The selection is intuitive; the foundation is experience and insight; the evaluation belongs to the reader.

TABLE 1-2. ORGANIZATION TYPES: PRINCIPAL CHARACTERISTICS

1) Ideological	→ Personal Commitment
2) Collegial	→ Peer Interaction
3) Creative	→ Personal Expression
4) Bureaucratic	→ Group Structure
5) Social	→ Common Community

We seek the pure form. According to our paradigm, this would ease analysis since we could study the chosen trait in relative isolation.

What we learn from studying the pure form, where the target characteristics are most cleanly dissected, we can then apply to all organizations. The pure form, in this context, becomes our dissecting scalpel — the instrument we use to delineate structure and highlight detail.

Accordingly, if we were to study peer interaction, we might choose law firms, accounting firms, and group medical practices as the pure form substrate for our analysis. If we were interested in personal expression, we might choose opera companies, creative departments of advertising agencies, high technology R & D labs, and think tanks. What we would learn in these collegial and creative organizations we could then apply to all organizations, from profit-making corporations to government agencies. The same procedure — studying a chosen characteristic in pure form first — can be applied to all group characteristics. This our framework.

THE PURE FORM OF COMMITMENT

Where is commitment best exemplified? Where is it readily isolated and analyzed? Although a critical component of all organizations, commitment appears most prominently and vigorously in *ideological* organizations — environments of religious and political passion. Here attitudes of mind are more singular, more linear, more focused.

Futhermore, to enhance the effect, we look toward the far end of the scale, toward those religious and political settings where collective mission subjugates individual meaning, where party fidelity swamps private desire, where sect purpose crushes personal freedom. Here, at the extreme outposts of ideological organizations, we dig for concepts and cases. These situations, tailor-made to examine commitment, we label "total organizations."[2]

Why are total organizations ripest for examining commitment? For one, they are both "closed" and "ideological." Closed oganizations are impermeable, and often this is intended and enforced. Commitment, therefore, is both cause and effect, cause at the beginning, effect after a time. (Both "closed" and "ideological" are required for full impact. Many political movements are ideological but not closed — commitment to them need not be potent. Prisons, on the other hand, are closed but not ideological — few inmates evidence commitment.)

We utilize total organizations — arenas of powerful religious fervor — as the analytical framework within which we examine commitment. The objective, remember, is *not* to study these situations per se; rather, we use them to elucidate the essence of commitment, which we will then apply to companies and institutions of common kind.

Religious belief enflames human emotion; with ultimate things at stake, unusual things are done. One bible college, for example, stopped playing basketball against another school, when it discovered that its rival was run by another religion. (Can't play ball with the devil, you know.) A Congessional Medal of Honor holder sent back his medal because his new religion taught against war. Such stories are endless, the convictions profound.

Religious belief generates mankind's strongest, most soul-stirring feelings. How many thousands of missionaries and saints have sacrificed their lives in pursuit of their visions! How many millions give their time and their money to aid the poor and preach the Word! How much of mankind's culture — music, art, literature, morality, justice, customs — is founded on religious values and inspired by religious principles! For better or for worse, for good or for evil, religion promotes the pinnacle of human achievement and evokes the height of human emotion.

What might we see under the magnifying glass of religious organizations? Can, for example, the attitudes of a minister in a sect shed light on the effectiveness of a manager in a company? Can understanding the devotion of church members improve the dedication of factory workers?

The psychic processes involved in the two situations are very much the same. Religion and business run parallel universes; just because commitment is more obvious in the former does not mean that it is less important in the latter. The nature of religious commitment is merely a cleaner, more overt form of the same phenomenon, the same magical mental force that binds individuals to institutions and energizes goal-directed action. Understanding what commitment means in extreme religious organizations helps us understand what it means in all organizations. (Specific religious examples, please note, do not reflect general religious attitudes. Biblical theology personifies ultimate human aspirations; its message is mankind's highest hope.)

OVERVIEW

How is the book structured? Where are we, and where are we going?

In Part I we examine the components of commitment, the pillars that form its foundation — personal factors (primarily "meaning"); organizational factors (primarily "mission"); and experience factors (primarily the interaction between "meaning and mission.") These elements are combined at the culmination of Part I to construct a "commitment model" (Chapter 5).

In Part II we use the model to describe how commitment can be built and broken; how the bond between individuals and institutions can be formed and severed. The book concludes with chapters showing how understanding commitment can help individuals and improve institutions.

In both parts, points are portrayed through case and example. Real people in real organizations, from business and religion, energize *The Firm Bond*.

CHAPTER TWO

PERSONAL MEANING:
WHAT TURNS YOU ON

"I hope I die before my husband," confided Betty Arnold softly, "else no one will know I ever existed."

Betty would never have uttered such words 20 years ago when, as a vivacious teenager, she was voted the girl most likely to succeed by her high school graduating class. But at age 37, after almost two decades of being wife and mother, her personal world view had turned inward.

During early adulthood, Betty had attended a fundamentalist bible school in Oklahoma. Church and college teaching had cast her with a set and structured role as a woman. The husband must rule his wife, it was taught, as Christ ruled the church; and although Christ seemed to give this church a great deal of flexibility, the same freedoms were forbidden for wives.

The doctrine was applied in ways strange and specific. Women, for example, were permitted to work only 20 hours per week if not married, and only in babysitting and baking if they were. Anything more, it was reasoned, might encourage "a competitive spirit." Betty certainly didn't want to catch that dread disease and always conformed. Her calling was clear: her purpose in life was to be wife and mother and no other activity was acceptable or even thinkable. Betty was content. She had dedicated her life to God.

College faculty busied themselves regularly in matchmaking and nuptial preparation, and Betty had felt considerable pressure to marry a pleasant enough young choral director named Alan. On their wedding night, before the act of physical consummation, Alan was required to give his suit pants to Betty. She was obliged, according to church custom, to try them on. "If they don't fit," went the catechism, "don't wear them." Only then were they allowed sexual relations.

Betty was a very talented musician with potential well exceeding Alan's. As a young girl she had been a fine pianist and excellent violinist, and was often invited to play chamber music with her teachers. In her junior year Betty won the first-violinist seat in her high school orchestra; and in her senior year she was named associate conductor — the first female in the school's history to have that position.

It was a time of family turmoil when Betty accepted the post in defiance of her parents, one of the leading church families in the state. Being a conductor, it seemed, would put her in a position "over men" — she would be telling men what to do — an overt violation of church dogma. After two tearful months, she resigned the position amidst school snickering that "women were too emotional for conducting." Later that semester Betty turned down a music scholarship at a major midwestern university. She matriculated the following fall at the bible college.

During and after college, the church awarded her special permission to perform at certain "allowable and controlled times," but they were only at informal occasions. Although she practiced in private, she rarely played in public. When she did play at those "allowable and controlled times" — say during the Wednesday Women's Bible Lunch — she was careful not to play too well; her ever-present pastor, she was concerned, might think she was spending too much time on herself and not enough time on her family. "God has plenty of musicians," he once admonished her, "but Alan has only one Betty."

The years sped by and her practicing slowed down. Betty had no quarrel with any of this; family values must always, she firmly believed, take priority in her life. Her mission and fulfillment rested in serving her husband and children. But when the youngest of the three Arnold children entered school, when for six hours the house was still, restlessness began to set in.

Alan, meanwhile, with more ambition than talent, worked hard in his profession. His advanced studies led to a good position at the bible college as well as to some performance opportunities with the church choir. Betty, as a faithful wife, accompanied her husband on the choir tours, basking, as she was taught, in his reflected glory. No matter that she, with little effort and no practice, could sense the music better than he — Betty was always supportive and never critical.

A church wife was not usually permitted to work with her husband in business, "lest some think her his equal." Alan, however, largely in response to what he considered to be Betty's irrational outbursts of recent date, suggested that she begin helping him with some demonstrations. He was holding seminars on performance techniques for choir directors and frankly needed the aid. He was sure that all she needed was a change of pace, and that seeing her husband make public presentations would enhance her respect for him.

During several of the seminars, Alan used his wife at the piano to illustrate his "gravity downbeat" technique for conducting, a concept so amateurish that Betty couldn't help but wince behind her plastic smile. She had been too ashamed to even tell Alan of her two-month conducting career, now so very long ago.

One day, in one of Alan's few seminars presented outside the church, Betty blurted something out. It was just a comment about counterpoint, no more than a couple of words, but the clear impression was that she was correcting her husband, and worse, that she was right. Alan, nonplussed, cut her short; he feared the reaction of church members perhaps present. They would think he "couldn't control his wife" — not a minor offense — and he had to show who was boss. He had a good job and such gossip might jeopardize it.

As luck would have it, there were no church members in attendance that day. There were present however, a sharp group of women, including the program organizer not known for her subservience to men. At the conclusion of the little talk, they approached Alan and Betty. Alan, of course, was expecting the syrupy fountains of praise that commonly gushed from church women before church leaders. He put a slightly condescending grin on his face and stood a step in front of his wife.

"Why don't you get the hell out of your wife's way?" growled the program organizer with excessive loudness. "At least *she* won't embarrass *you!*" The woman went on to extol Betty's raw talent and musical sensitivity, completely ignoring any mention of Alan or his silly seminar. Other participants chimed in, dazing Alan and exciting Betty.

The women articulated what Betty dared not. She craved personal achievement and recognition beyond the family. Family was of course vitally important, and she certainly was not abandoning the Church, but she could no longer uncritically accept all its teachings.

Betty now felt that her individual development had been stunted. Opportunity had been foreclosed[1] on her prematurely and the chance to build her career stripped away. She felt cheated out of youth. Perhaps she wouldn't have changed all that much, but it was that lack of choice and personal control that now churned frustration.

Her change was not sudden. Though she began to practice intensely and enrolled in a music theory course at a local university, there was not a day when pangs of guilt and doubt didn't mix with fear of discovery and church disgrace. "Women not content at home," went a favorite church aphorism, "will find scorn on the street." Of religious fear, however, she knew nothing. She believed wholly in the Bible and accepted Jesus as her Savior. She would read often of Sarah and Deborah, Ruth and Esther. There was nothing she was doing not pleasing to God.

Betty Arnold's experiences in the closed system of a total organization magnifies what happens frequently in corporate life for both men and women. In the course of the adult life span, developmental needs and awareness emerge that can have dramatic impact on individual commitment to the major institutions in one's life. Youthful idealism of early adulthood can be replaced by the frenetic goal shifting of midlife. Regrets over past planning can establish need priorities that in turn can draw new patterns of commitment and dominate behavior.

Betty's desire to become her own person[2] and fulfill her potential is an example of what happens when developmental needs erupt. Closely akin is the emergence of entrepreneurial drives within an unaccommodating corporate structure. How does one deal with such people and pressures? The easy answer — Get rid of them! — deprives the company of innovative potential. On the other hand, strategies that allow for the expression of such needs promote mutual benefit for employee and organization. These will be explored later.

WHAT YOU'RE ALL ABOUT

Classifying people is the easiest thing to do fast and the hardest thing to do well. Psychologists like to devise systems to help us, to make personality assessment snappy, to put people into simple boxes we can understand. It is said that there are as many theories of human personality as there are theorists (and maybe more, since theorists often change their minds).

The touchstone of truth has long been sought. Freud looked to unconscious processes and biosocial instincts of self-preservation and sex. Neo-Freudians kept Freud's basic picture of human personality as a battleground between primal instincts and social values. Some, however, proposed different candidates for the critical instincts. Adler posited the need for "superiority" as a primal force, thus popularizing the "inferiority complex." Jung, drawing heavily from physics and mysticism, saw the libido or primal force as a general life energy that socially binds individuals to the whole of the human race. (Jung also developed the introvert-extrovert scale.) Frankl emphasized the search for meaning, claiming ultimate answers are the root motivation of man. Erikson proposed a life-cycle approach, with distinctive "psychosocial crises" at different stages of one's life.

Humanists, such as Maslow and Rogers, emphasized individual growth motivation and stressed the importance of "self-actualization." Behavior theorists, such as Skinner, saw human personality resulting more from environmental factors than psychic events. Human personality can be analyzed, they proclaim, only in terms of the interplay of human action and environmental consequences.

Enough of personality theory. There are others, of course, but enough. Human personality is complex, that's clear. Although each theory has something to tell us, none has a monopoly on truth. (We should always beware the "Cosmic Concluder;" unhappily, or happily, there is no magic key.)

Our interest in human personality is more focused. We center on aspects of personality that an individual brings to an organization, and how these personal traits influence the style of commitment. We choose twelve "personal factors" in three classes. We generate them inductively by the twin engines of insight from case histories and findings from organizational research. How do these variables influence commitment? The mechanisms emerge in our examples.

PERSONAL TURN-ONS

Desire breeds motivation. If we want nothing, we do nothing. For the want of water, food, or sexual partners, rats will traverse electrified grids until their feet run raw. For want of things similar in character, people will do just about anything.

Different people desire different things. In building a model of commitment, in establishing a pragmatic union between individuals and institutions, we must understand the human side of the linkage.

Following are some general categories of human desire. We intend no value judgment. It is not that some desires are "good" and some are "bad"; all are real, and that is all that matters here. In exploring the categories, remember that each is expressed, at one time or another, to a greater or lesser degree, by every one of us. All compete constantly for our attention and control, and all are involved in building and breaking the firm bond.

Our approach is to look at ourselves in various ways, from various perspectives. It is the composite, we stress, not the components, that really turns us on.

Figure 2.1 lists some personal factors that influence organizational commitment. The list is neither exhaustive nor infallible. More important factors may be left out, and less important factors put in. All variables, however, relate to commitment, and all will appear in upcoming cases. We define three classes of variables[3] describing personality: *meaning-related* needs; *security-related* needs; and *other* personal variables descriptive of the individual. All, remember, influence commitment.

MEANING-RELATED FACTORS

Transcendence: The need to go beyond the corporeal limitations of individual humanness; a deep interest in an ideal world and how to create it; a profound concern for the nature of ultimate reality. Companies that match corporate objectives with executive ideology

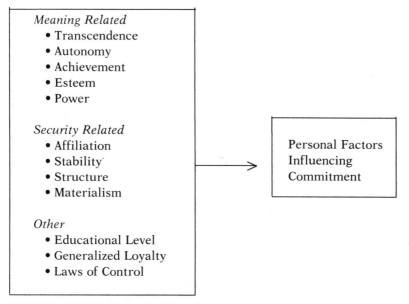

Meaning Related
- Transcendence
- Autonomy
- Achievement
- Esteem
- Power

Security Related
- Affiliation
- Stability
- Structure
- Materialism

Other
- Educational Level
- Generalized Loyalty
- Laws of Control

Personal Factors Influencing Commitment

FIGURE 2-1 PERSONAL FACTORS INFLUENCING COMMITMENT

optimize commitment. Such coherence is more easily obtained in not-for-profit institutions such as religious organizations, charities, hospitals, foundations, and the like. Some innovative firms — often high tech — offer excitement in company products and flexibility in company structure. Businesses can alienate personnel by being insensitive to religious convictions. Employees who believe in some higher order will often be more dependable on the job (though "head in clouds" can sometimes lift "feet from ground").

Autonomy: Independence from authority and external control; the capacity to do what you want when you want. Entrepreneurs would rather work 60 hours a week for themselves with less pay than 40 hours a week for someone else with more pay. Creative and innovative types, increasingly important in an information and science-based society, demand autonomy and freedom in work conditions, and managers must find ways to accommodate and encourage them.

Achievement: The desire to complete tasks and reach goals, whether assigned by another or set by oneself. Accomplishment carries its own reward — and it can dominate all others, irrespective of other benefits no matter how large. Job satisfaction can correlate more with finishing work than with increasing pay. Entrepreneurs as a group are motivated far more by achievement than by power or money; they would rather finish the job in an old garage than direct operations from an eight-window corner office.

Esteem: A sense of personal worth; prominence and recognition among friends, respect and admiration among peers. Some people will do anything for accolades and acknowledgment. The craving for fame can be an addiction (so much so that when celebrities are forgotten, they can become suicidal). Star status fascinates us, epitomized by the line, "I don't care what newspapers say about me as long as they spell my name right."

Power: Control and authority over people, groups, and things; the capacity to influence ideas and dominate events. Political leaders, government officials, military generals, newspaper editors, university presidents do not earn high salaries by today's standards; though many are motivated by lofty ideals, others trade off materialism and wealth for power and influence.

SECURITY-RELATED FACTORS

Affiliation: The social sense of belonging; the desired association in organizations and groups. Club memberships; fraternal societies; common interests drawing people together. Many men and women live for their avocation, whether active or spectator sports, card games, recreational activities, or simply socializing with friends at the "club." "Acceptance" is important here; whether it be the Blue Bloods of Boston or the Bowling Team of Brooklyn, belonging to groups can be serious business.

Stability: The comfort of calm; maintaining routine; keeping of the status quo; staying the course. The elimination of surprise and the attenuation of change. Some people value constancy and surety above all else; they are "risk averse" and would never switch jobs for a 50 percent increase in pay if there were even a 5 percent chance of getting sacked.

Structure: Dependency on others; looking beyond self for solutions to one's problems, answers to one's questions, and provisions for one's needs. Where one fits in the social order is of primary concern. The need for organizational position, ratified by title and benefits, is common in large companies. Some are uncomfortable with new forms of governance without clear lines of authority.

Materialism: The desire for wealth; the security money can bring, the things money can buy. Bonds in the bank and stocks in the safe. Homes, cars, furniture, clothing, jewelry, electronic toys, and the like are things that we have; trips, travel, shows, dinners, entertainment, and the like are things that we do — all are in the spirit of materialism and represent the trappings of wealth. A doctor who buys exotic cars may well be more motivated by materialism than a corporate president who builds his business.

OTHER PERSONAL FACTORS

Educational Level: The nature and extent of formal education; the quality and quantity of academic experience. Research findings have shown that, other things being equal, individuals with higher levels of education tend to be less committed to organizations and more committed to professions.[4]

Generalized Sense of Loyalty: A desire to continue supporting groups with which one is associated; a "sticker," not a "quitter." This variable has roots in one's cultural and family background, with a good dose of individual temperament thrown in.[5]

Locus of Control: Whether one's behavior is determined internally or externally. People with an internal locus of control see themselves as active "origins," feeling that they direct personal events from within. Those with an external locus of control see themselves as passive "pawns," feeling that chance, powerful people, and forces beyond their influence determine individual occurrences and life course.[6]

BACK TO BETTY

Betty Arnold's mind is a virtual battlefield. Reawakened achievement needs — sprinkled generously with autonomy and esteem needs — war with her continued desire for affiliation and structure.

Being wife and mother had provided Betty with coherent meaning, a transcendent purpose that received potent social support in the closed system of her church organization. These roles are still important to her, but an internal clock — almost a time bomb — has been ticking within. Personal meaning must now include other avenues of expression. Achievement, autonomy, and esteem needs cannot be ignored. Betty has determined to redesign her life, to shift the locus of control inward.

All this is set against the backdrop of her strong generalized sense of loyalty which is reflected in her continued commitment to family and church. This force is powerful and persistent and cannot be dismissed. Her dedication to Christ has not changed, but her renewed reading of the bible casts fresh perspective on opportunities for women.

The university studies she is beginning could well signal movement toward increased commitment to music as a profession. How she balances this out with her traditional roles is yet to be determined.

Undoubtedly, the transition to internal locus of control has had multiple triggers. For one, different needs are spawned at different phases of life. With the children off to school, an increase in discretionary time encourages self-reflection in this artistic yet un-fulfilled individual. For another, Betty is receiving strong external support, given by such people as the program organizer and, we can imagine, professors and students at the university.

Some of the personal factors we use to explore commitment, such as generalized loyalty, are relatively stable over time. Many of them, however, are subject to change. What was vitally important to Betty at age 22 may no longer drive her at age 37. New meaning-related needs have emerged in her midlife, so that the ingredients that provided a full life mix in early adulthood no longer seem sufficient.

HOW YOU GONNA KEEP THEM DOWN ON THE FIRM?

Rob Gorden began working for InfoSystems right out of high school. He started as a computer operator, with little more than enthusiasm in his head. But with company growth and personnel shortage Gorden was advanced quickly into applications programming, the entry level for the career-oriented programmer.

That was eight years ago. Gorden was ambitious and energetic, with a natural aptitude for logic and design. Soon he was doing systems programming, a distinct step up in the caste system of the computer world. Gorden was thankful for his opportunities. But the passage of time had transformed appreciation into appetite; he had learned much but wanted more. Education, that is, not money.

Infosystems was a small shop, fielding a total of eight computer-skilled employees. Almost all of Gorden's training had been informal and on-the-job. It was provided in-house by Al Nichols, one of the company's two owners. Nichols was a real bull on learning, and thus, ironically, induced the sequence of events that follow.

Rob Gorden had started talking seriously about going to school, even entertaining the idea of taking a degree in computer science. When he made his final decision to enroll he couldn't wait to tell his mentor. But when he did, he found displeasure on Nichols's face.

There was no way the boss wanted one of his best employees out there in the world, taking the coursework, mixing with people, building his mental muscles. Nichols began to stew. Exposure to other companies is the blood that attracts the head-hunting sharks, those firms paid to steal other companies' top workers.

"That's a lot of time with your nose in a book," said the older man trying to sound helpful, "none of that stuff will ever help you in the real world."

Nevertheless, Gorden began the program, but on a part-time basis. He didn't hide the fact from Nichols, and made every effort to ensure it would not affect his work time or performance. One course was hardly a degree, and Gorden was hardly a scholar, but the seed had taken root and the high school graduate was on his way up.

In his second quarter of studies, Gorden enrolled in two courses, both at the intermediate level. Many a night the books remained open well past midnight. He was late for work only twice, and only a few minutes each time, but just before finals he got word that the boss wanted to see him.

Nichols came right to the point. Now, he reasoned, was the last time he could strike from a position of power. He expressed strong concern that Gorden's activities were outside company interests and were in fact interfering with his work product. Gorden asserted that his classes were both helping him in his present programming and preparing him for greater service, but logical response did not smooth emotional objection.

Gorden's point, of course, was precisely what Nichols feared. Combining talent and training with ambition and exposure makes one very desirable employee — for competitors! Data processing was known for its high turnover rates; there was little employee loyalty in the industry. InfoSystems was a good firm, but hardly High-Tech Heaven. In less than a year, Nichols realized, Gorden would be unable to apply what he was learning; frustration would set in and he would move on. The time to lock the door is before it ever opens.

Nichols's first appeal was to Gorden's sense of work ethic and company loyalty; but almost immediately he showed true colors by demanding that the courses be dropped, implying that demotion or even dismissal could result if Gorden carried on. Losing the kid would be a problem, reasoned Nichols, but his "academic enthusiasm" was spreading like an infectious disease, and soon other employees would be taking courses and becoming exposed to other employment opportunities.

Gorden responded by saying he would consider his boss's desires but only after completing the quarter. The next day, having never before even imagined leaving InfoSystems, Gorden made an appointment with a job-placement firm specializing in data-processing personnel. He'd ask about salary, too; money was now important.

This story is common, the outcome inevitable. Nichols was attempting to transform his company into a total organization, constructing a closed system in order to isolate employees from the world of greener-grass opportunities characteristic of data processing. InfoSystems had been the only company Gorden knew as an adult worker. He was quite happy there. His employer had misinterpreted his desire to do college work as his first step out the door, and in the process created a self-fulfilling prophecy.

Now it is not without basis that employers fear employee education. When key people go after advanced degrees, the likelihood of their leaving the firm increases. Thus, in Gorden's case, there was legitimate concern. Over time he would probably start identifying more with the profession of systems programmers and less with the one company called InfoSystems.

An extreme reaction on the part of an employer, however, is most likely doomed to failure. Nichols blew it from the beginning, setting up an adversarial relationship that sabotaged what had been a fine boss-employee relationship. It may be possible that because of job inertia, fear of the unknown, or a complaint personality, an employee would choose to bow to such constricting pressures. In most cases, however, resentment will build as opportunity loss is perceived by the employee — and resentment that ferments carries dangers not worth the risk. A corporate underground, frustrated and suspicious, can severely undermine corporate commitment.

When a company makes strategic investment in training to build the human capital of key employees, the return to both company and individual can be triple digit. The challenge is to develop creative human resource strategies that simultaneously support employee educational needs and maximize their organizational commitment.

Nichols had at least an even shot at Gorden. With encouragement from his boss, the kid would have worked his heart out for InfoSystems. As for the future, who knows? Perhaps Gorden could have expanded the scope of company operations into complementary areas, using new skills and old loyalty.

Attitudes toward education may differ, but when it's weak it's always a problem — even when it shouldn't be. Consider the ghetto fighter.

THE STREET-SMART EXECUTIVE

Norman Jackson, a power player, had worked his way up from the back alleys of New York to become senior manager of a major industrial company. Singlehandedly, he had turned around several perennially losing divisions. As a result, he became a rising star in the company firmament, as well as its highest ranking black.

Employees just busted gut for the guy. An amorphous group became a tight team, with Norman their hard-driving coach. Every division he took over became determined to go from cellar to playoffs in a single season. All of them made it, some quicker than others. A "failure" was taking two years instead of one.

Norman's firm had high designs for him. They decided to groom their candidate for top-level management with the help of an elite educational program at a first-rate graduate school of business. The fact that Norman had never even graduated from high school seemed, well, "academic."

This executive was as smart as he was tough, but his business sense was intuitive and managerial, not analytical and financial. In the business school, his achievement record was one of the highest. But his formal education was one of the lowest. (Half the class had doctor's or master's degrees.)

During the first few weeks of the course, Norman cut a dominant figure, leading complex business discussions with strength and perception. But then came the first tests in economics and computer science. Norman's scores were poor and his confidence was shaken. Enthusiasm eroded. Leadership plummeted. He no longer took an agressive role; he sank back in his seat and submerged into obscurity.

Norman had a problem, of course, but it was not the one he thought. The poor grades were meaningless. What counted was self-appraisal. He had grossly misjudged his strengths and weaknesses. Nobody expected him to compete with physicists in computers and economists in finance. Norman was being sent to such a high-powered program because he was *already* a sucess at what mattered in the real world. He was an outstanding manager, and in order to make it all the way up the ladder in modern times, he needed some technical skills, some familiarity with the frontiers of business thinking. He wasn't being paid, however, to be a technician. He was an executive with vision and fortitude, and he would have to preserve and appreciate his own assets.

A few weeks later Norman was back in the thick of things. He had been working extra hard and started pulling decent grades. And how much more he was learning than his classmates!

Some time later he was walking with two associates on the streets of New York when he met his former finance teacher, a man of international repute.

"Professor Cohen," said Norman, on the defensive but with ego restored, "I'd like you to meet Mr. Jerry Kelly and Dr. Henry Schwartz — both of whom are smarter than I am."

"Maybe," smiled the professor, "but I bet they both work for *you*."

WHITHER THOU GOEST I WILL GO

William Hendrichs had just inherited $100,000, but he was not happy. Money in the bank was causing conflict in his head. How should he use his fortune, a sum five times his annual salary? The largest number that had ever graced his account before was under $2000, and that was in preparation for marriage two decades ago.

Personal needs were numerous. Outstanding debt existed on the washing machine, and the car required replacement. Hendrichs and his wife had always wanted to buy their own home. More important, they had not been able to provide orthodontia for their three children, whose distorted smiles were a source of gnawing guilt. College costs would begin within two years, and even at the state university, the fees were dizzying.

On the other hand, Hendrichs had recently received a letter from his church, an exclusivist denomination founded in the nineteenth century that was beginning to have some impact in the twentieth. Hendrichs was a devoted member and took seriously the pleas for members to give generously to support the church's missionary work. To give to God was the greatest blessing one could have.

How often in the past had Hendrichs yearned to respond with substance! He had prayed to have means to give. But now that the money materialized, would God expect him to give it all? The bible taught that a true Christian must sacrifice all earthly possessions for the Kingdom. But the bible also taught, he reminded himself, that he who does not provide for his family is worse than an infidel. And what about his own desires — the home, a new car, a trip to Hawaii, even some clothes? It had been years since he last bought a suit.

Given his sense of group loyalty, Hendrichs's action was predictable. He knew where his priorities were and what he had to do. To deny conviction would deny life. Transcendence and loyalty overwhelmed materialism. It was no contest.

Hendrichs gave $80,000 to the church; the remainder would be used for his children's dental work and first college expenses. He felt good. Church and family needs would always come first. His own had to come last, which meant, of course, not coming at all. When a friend asked his wife why her husband gave away so much of his inheritance, she responded: "I expected him to do it; that's just how he is. Where his treasure is, there his heart is also."

CULTURE AND COMMITMENT

East versus West: the collective, group orientation of oriental culture versus the individual, personal propensity of Western society has been a common theme in recent management literature and the popular press. The central idea is that American culture espouses the value of self-expression and self-determination, while Japanese culture places a much higher value on loyalty to the group, whether at home or at work.

Although cultural differences of primary loyalties surely exist (whether for self or group), vast individual variance can be found among Westerners. The closed systems of total organizations require, by their very nature, first and absolute claim to loyalty. Closed systems demand high commitment. Organizations and their goals must be placed before individuals and their needs. Any deviation threatens the group's reason for being. Whether such organizations in fact receive undivided commitment from members often depends on, among other things, the degree to which the member brings along generalized sense of loyalty. William Hendrichs, as we saw, had it in spades.

One well-known software company noted the surprising number of new programmers who were ex-members of a quasi-religious sect noted for its tightly closed system. These programmers displayed strong attachment to their company and fierce dedication to their work. Stories were told of employees sleeping in parking lot trailers instead of going home. We are *not* surprised. Computer programming requires intense commitment, hundreds of hours dedicated to codes and systems, with a powerful charge for successful completion. For those who have lost the vision (or abandoned the dream) of transcendent religion, the process of programming (not the content), is a rather close substitute. If group loyalty is an integral part of the programmer's personality structure, the dynamics for forming another firm bond are still in place.

LOYALTY TO INSTITUTIONS

When dedication to an institution is abiding, enduring, and unquestioning, conflicts can run deep. Marriage is such an institution, perhaps the most important in human life.

The fact that marriage is called an "institution" is more than a play on words. There is substance here. Marital bonds are often our strongest, and when they're severed it's never fun. Divorce is hard for many; for some it's impossible.

Andy Poche was in shock. His world had been quaked. After 20 years of marriage, his wife Jo had announced that she was divorcing him. Jo told him he was insensitive and cruel. He was not giving her enough room for personal growth. It was time, she said, to break out of this family prison.

Andy was a guidance counselor. Friends and clients alike had always viewed him as a sensitive and caring person, and they had told him so regularly.

"Andy, there's got to be another man," said a buddy over a beer. Andy broke into tears. It was a couple of minutes before he could talk.

"It would be easier for me if there were," Andy responded when he finally regained composure. "I've done everything from probing Jo's best friend to tracking her when she goes out. There is no one else. What's she's doing doesn't make any economic sense. It's emotionally disturbing to the children. But she is doing it for only one reason — I'm not sensitive enough.

"She had been talking this way for the past year, but I never thought I'd hear the word 'divorce.' To me that's the ugliest word in the English language."

Andy was devastated and riddled with self-doubt. The very essence of what he thought himself to be, of what he stood for, was under assault. He had always viewed the family as sacred, as a total system that was closed and unbreakable. Commitment to one's spouse was complete and absolute. Divorce, as far back as anyone could remember, was unknown in his family. Family was the core of his self-identity. To lose here was to lose all.

Andy saw marriage as an institution that would always have his loyalty, independent of what it returned to him. He couldn't understand how his wife could measure her marriage relationship, find it wanting, and decide to break the sacred trust.

LOYALTY TO ORGANIZATIONS

For some, loyalty to organizations isn't contingent on return; organizations are sustainers of ego and to flout them undermines the foundation of life. For most, group membership must bring enough benefit to warrant continuance. For the rest, organizations exist to be used. There is little if any loyalty to institutions, unless such "loyalty" richly serves personal interests.

Len Barclay was director of an engineering research center at a major Eastern university. His position put him in contact with many business executives and he frequently received requests for research and consulting services. Barclay almost always had a choice whether to classify a project as a "research project" for the university center, or as a "consulting assignment" for his private company. To dub a project as "research" and run it through the university would build the center and help the university. To call the project "consulting" would be personally lucrative to Barclay.

His actions evinced his priorities. Virtually every opportunity that became available was "clearly" a "consulting assignment." It was true that Barclay ran conferences for the center and managed a laboratory, but his main motivation was having a platform to build his consulting business. The research reputation of the center diminished until Barclay was asked to either rejoin the faculty on a full-time basis or relinquish control of the center.

TRANSCENDING POLITICS

In total systems it is common for members to concede to the organization full responsibility for life and work. Only one real choice is ever made: the one to make all future "choices" by organizational wisdom. This means that every important individual decision is determined by hierarchy and structure, power and policy.

Harry Roberts was a valued employee of an aggressive and growing church. Its doctrinal beliefs were standard in the conservative Protestant tradition, but its missionary zeal was exceedingly strong. There was real energy in this church, and its vision enlivened its members. Most gave credit to the dynamic first president who had died two years ago, leaving in his wake some uncomfortable political jockeying.

Roberts was not concerned with politics, being far removed from the goings-on above. But one day he realized that several church departments were seeking to convince him to transfer their way; little remarks were passed here and there, the headhunter game gone internal.

It was his skills in project management, coupled with an easygoing personality, that made Roberts a prize catch. A hard worker, he accomplished his tasks with competence and conviction.

Prior to joining the church he had been a successful advertising salesman for a medium-sized agency. In "Satan's world" he had been as competitive as hell, never turning away a chance to better himself at someone else's expense. But that changed when he made his emotional allegiance to God. In short order he was called to church headquarters, where he compiled an enviable record of making his superiors look good and not feeling bad in the process. Everyone liked Harry Roberts.

To work at the church's corporate offices, in proximity to the High Council, was viewed by members as being on a par with going to Heaven. Yet Heaven was supposed to be perfect, and the conflict among departments of church operations, rumored for some time, was now breaking into the open. Roberts knew God was working here, but the bickering was disillusioning. As but one disturbing example, media and pastoral control departments were virtually in a state of war over which should control the prime evangelistic campaigns. In a celebrated case — "celebrated" at least on the underground grapevine — a Pastoral manager tricked a Media executive into drinking well beyond the sanctioned "one luncheon drink" and well within the view of several rather chatty church members.

Roberts had been working for the printing division for two years when, amidst the growing turmoil, he was made a clandestine offer to join the accounting department. Though discreet, the offer was direct. Money and power, the classic appeal in executive recruiting, was never discussed; continued participation in God's Mission was all that counted.

"We've done the audit," began the accounting second-in-charge after exhausting the small talk at their not inexpensive lunch. "Printing won't be around next year — we've seen to that. They're incompetent; we're going to go outside — but we'd like to save you."

Roberts was stunned. Loyalty to his department was strong. He recalled the recent closed-door meeting in which the director of printing gave broad hints that the High Council was considering a "big change" in the senior management of accounting — and since everyone knew that the brother of the director's wife was a permanent member of the fabled High Council, his information was considered reliable. How, Roberts wondered, could church people deal with each other so crudely?

"Is it my decision whether to take this new job?" Roberts asked the accounting manager.

"Sure," was the comforting answer, but the smug grin was unnerving.

Roberts always viewed his place at the church's corporate headquarters as being determined by its leading officials, whose decisions in turn reflected God's Will. His growing awareness of the jousting and jockeying for political position didn't shatter this conviction. It only made it more an act of faith.

Church politics is not strange, no more so than the same squabbles in business, academia and government. But when the mission is transcendent, internal conflict can be more readily accepted by members; after all, how can minor personality problems compare with ultimate salvation and eternal life? Such transcendence is the remarkable, vitalizing force of bible-believing churches.

Two weeks later Roberts was called in by his boss at printing and told that he was being transferred to accounting. Roberts was unsure what had transpired, but felt confident that the decision was God's. The next day it was announced that the brother-in-law of the director of printing was suspended from the High Council after having been seen in public drunk. Roberts was saddened, sure, but he gave God thanks that he could continue to serve in the most important work in the world.

INSIDE-OUTSIDE

Some people feel they can direct their lives; others feel they cannot. Some take charge actively; others think they are forever running uphill.

Do you sense you have control over your circumstances? Are you able to point where you want to be, project what you want to do? Or do you feel at the mercy of destiny and the whim of chance, with little ability to affect pace or outcome? The former attitude represents an *inside* locus of control, while the latter characterizes a person with an *outside* locus of control.

Employees of closed systems often exemplify the far end of the scale, much closer to the outer than the inner locus. They affirm by their compliance the legitimacy of organizational assumption of private decision making. While such control is more potent and rigid in total organizations than in traditional corporations, the general importance of this personal variable in determining individual commitment should not be underrated.

Locus of control is one of the personal factors at work on the individual side of the individual-institution bond. It is highlighted by the magnifying glass of total organizations in which members often abdicate self-direction of their lives. Thus, having studied locus of control in such pure form environments, we can apply what we've learned to all group environments. A similar analysis could be made of the other personal factor variables. Each is incomplete in itself, merely one part of the whole, an element in understanding the firm bond.[7]

We now jump to the other side of the bond. We examine how key *organizational* variables affect personal commitment.

CHAPTER THREE

COMPANY MISSION:
WHERE THE GROUP GOES

Don Stevens edged forward on his eighth-row seat. He had waited outside three hours, since 5:00 AM, for that choice location; but such was
no matter since he had been waiting six months, ever since coming to
Harvard, to hear the legendary Holy Father Huang Yu Yun.

High anticipation filled the great hall. Walls that normally resonated
with classical sounds from the West would today reverberate with contemporary sounds from the East. Yesterday it was one of the finest orchestras from Germany; today it is one of the greatest prophets from
China. Yesterday entertainment; today eternity.

Huang Yu Yun was a mysterious figure, known only from his
dynamic writings and faithful followers. His teachings he called
"Cosmic Synthesis," and he claimed to bring together the best of the
world's religions: Buddhism, Hinduism, Christianity, even a little
Judaism. His devotees he labeled "Called Ones," and the promises he
made them were not small — protection from "Wrath Divine" and
rulership over "Earth Reborn" were only a hint of Reward. Though
never claiming he was the messiah, Yun's official biography was as a
polished mirror for his giveaway tract, "Finding the Savior" (pur-
ported circulation over ten million). Every question asked in the tract
was answered in the bio. It was a perfect match, and little surprise.

Their Boston "Cosmic House," as Father Yun's local congregations were called, was buzzing with activity and bursting with growth.
Though founded only 11 months ago, they had already moved twice to
handle the rush of questers and curious. Called Ones were coming
from all universities in the area, new proselytes were showing up daily. Stevens had been attending "House" for four months. He first had
learned of Father Yun back in Connecticut where his success in
science, made college easy entry. For five years admission to Harvard
had been his goal. Now it seemed so trivial.

It was Monday morning and Stevens would have to miss an important class in physics; his professor, a stickler for attendance, was

introducing a new section in quantum mechanics. Always a compulsive student, Stevens' stomach should have been churning from such neglience. But academics had no meaning now, not with eternity on the table.

Speculation was feverish at Cosmic House. Upcoming was the "Inspirational," Yun's self-proclaimed public appearances. Father Yun, it was rumored, would electrify the faithful. He would portray the Coming Kingdom in vivid detail. He would enumerate global responsibilities that Called Ones would be awarded. He would forge the future.

This was no Sunday morning service. Yun's busy schedule had to be accommodated. Waiting for the Holy Master to appear, Stevens felt pulses of guilt about skipping that class. Then, remembering eternity, he felt even more guilty for having any hesitancy about attending the Inspirational. Today he would learn about Realms and Dimensions of Spiritual Spectra, about the ultimate unfolding of the universe — including his own part in it! The best his physics professor could explain were partial elements of physical reality. Father Yun would deal dogmatically with *all* reality.

The Holy Father began, as was his custom, by quoting the accepted scriptures of his host country. He paraphrased an analogy from the New Testament about small beginnings that yield enormous growth. "God always works by the principle of the 'mustard seed.' Consider the majestic sequoia of California. It starts a seed a fraction of an ounce. Yet it can reach 270 feet and weigh 6,200 tons. That's growth! 600-billionfold growth. . . . If God can do so much with a seed of which He has many, what will He do with His Called Ones of whom He has few?"

Yun waxed eloquent. He showed that although the Cosmic Synthesis started out small, it would grow until the time of Great Turmoil and Planetary Consternation. Our cosmic Master, he trumpeted with thundering power, will then intervene dramatically and give to His Called Ones authority for governing the Earth.

Then followed, in Yun's stylized staccato cadence, specific positions Believers could assume. Such detail! The local head of the Cosmic House, called the "Guardian," might be made city mayor. A gardener among the Called Ones could handle park planning. An architect could manage urban renewel. A scientist could take over the university. And these honors, Yun gave his assurance, would be the barest beginning of blessings. Authority would continue to expand until the entire universe was subsumed.

A rush came over Stevens as if dosed by drugs. Where, he wondered, could he fit in? Might he head up Harvard? Perhaps he would be "American Chief Scientist"? He had little competition in Boston Cosmic House.

But whatever his position, Don Stevens was surely part of something moving, something on the roll. His career path was not insubstantial but Yun's vision overwhelmed it all. The Holy Father was so convincing, so certain, and the sprouting of Cosmic House was clear confirmation. Cosmic Synthesis was an organization with *momentum* — it had the "Big MO" — and compared to it everything else seemed stuck.

ORGANIZATIONAL FACTORS

The momentum of a group is a critical element influencing commitment. It is included in "progressiveness," the category that defines degree of movement, the presence or absence of organizational motion.

In this chapter we deal with the institutional side of the individual-institution bond. What characteristics of the organization affect member commitment? Some factors are presented in Figure 3.1. (The list is neither precise nor exhaustive; if it proves representative and descriptive we are satisfied.) We set the factors into two classes: *mission-related* and *other*.

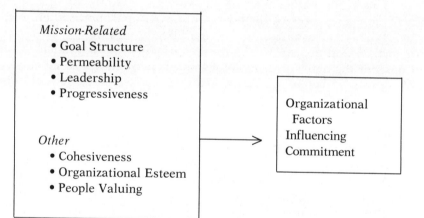

FIGURE 3-1 ORGANIZATIONAL FACTORS INFLUENCING COMMITMENT

MISSION-RELATED VARIABLES

Goal Structure: The nature and essence of group goals, whether visionary or pedestrian, comprehensive or limited, theoretical or practical, attainable or illusory. What is the planned position for an organization, its grand design, its purpose, its mission?

Permeability: The openness of group boundaries; the ease of passage inside out and outside in; the degree to which an organization desires members to interact with external elements. Does the group maintain a life-style different from general society, and does it shield members from interference?

Leadership: The character and strength of senior management, whether sharp or bland, individual or collective, democratic or dictatorial, logical or emotional, permanent or transitory. The style of the chief, the charisma of the boss. How dominant is the organization's leader, and what would be the impact of change?

Progressiveness: The presence or absence of forward motion; the dynamic sense of momentum, whether the group is growing or holding, moving or stuck. The innovative character of the organization, the willingness to explore and take risks. Is the group going ahead, and at what pace?

OTHER ORGANIZATIONAL FACTORS

Cohesiveness: The strength with which an organization adheres together; the unity and coherence of the group. Whether the agglutinizing force is internal or external, desire or coercion. How strongly does the organization pull together; how tightly do members support group goals?

Organizational Esteem: The internal sense of organizational worth, whether appreciated by outsiders or only by insiders; the collective confidence in intrinsic value; the degree to which members feel proud of group association. Do members boast or hide their affiliation?

People Valuing: The extent to which people are recognized and treated as organizational assets (to be maximized and developed), and not as organizational expenses (to be minimized and eliminated). What is the group's attitude toward members?

BACK TO COSMIC HOUSE

Each of these factors operates in the culture or environment of the organization, and each affects commitment in the mind of the individual. An analysis of Yun's Cosmic Synthesis, exemplifying total organizations, can serve as the magnifying glass for viewing close up the dynamics involved in constructing or destroying the firm bond.

Many of our personal histories embed a number of variables. Don Stevens, the current case, finds himself in an organization with the whole cast of characteristics (see Table 3.1):

TABLE 3.1 THE MAGNIFYING GLASS

Organizational Factor	Yun's Cosmic Synthesis
Goal Structure	Universal; visionary
Permeability	One-directional; controlled
Leadership	Charismic, with mystery
Progressiveness	High forward momentum
Cohesiveness	Cosmic House, tightly knit
Esteem	Extremely high
People Valuing	People viewed as assets

- Goal structure with mission and purpose to blow away the stars.
- One-direction permeability allowing proselytes in with ease but devotees out with difficulty.
- Charismatic leadership alive with vision and pulsing with mystery.
- Progressive growth seemingly unstoppable.
- Strong cohesiveness in their local Cosmic Houses.
- Highest organizational esteem in the universe (at least as viewed by internals).
- A view of people as assets (although little is known how people are treated when "push comes to shove").

Furthermore, there is high innovation — especially when compared to Boston's normal world — and the culture is well tailored to the organization's objectives. The issue here, we stress, is not how "good" the organization is in some absolute moral or social sense, but how well the organization is designed to capture and hold member commitment.

MOVEMENT AND PROGRESSION

While few corporate denizens will ever experience Stevens's flush of excitement, employees genuinely enjoy the feeling of positive momentum. They are energized by beating inertia, by increasing acceleration, by the rapid achievement of goals. This is almost axiomatic. In all organizations with which we have been associated — whether as member, employee, or analyst — forward progression, its presence or absence, was a vital determinant of commitment.

Even when well short of Yun's sense of stellar purpose, corporate progression is compelling. It is more process than content, more *how* you are doing than *what* you are doing. Once the growth slows at

Cosmic House, as slow it must, the enthusiasm of the Called Ones will undoubtedly diminish, though their mission may remain universal. Conversely, though the new group down the street is just selling some diet food, if their momentum is strong so will be their zeal.

When asked what is most important in keeping him attached and committed to his firm, one employee of a major electronics distributor said: "Our firm is moving. We're on a roll and I like the feeling. I can't be successful unless my company is successful. It's like a good marriage. Once you've got something upbeat, you have reasons to stay with it and keep it going."

A middle manager of a hot company in the executive-placement business put it this way:

> This is a crazy place to work. We're so unorganized that if we get any more business we'll be like a submarine with bolts starting to snap. But I love the tension. It's a constant high being part of a mover. We're getting a reputation for being the best in the business, so I don't mind if at times when I leave the office, tomorrow's *Wall Street Journal* has already been delivered."

Momentum: when present it creates an excitement that feeds on itself and provides positive reinforcement. When going it seems upstoppable. But when stopped, it triggers backlash.

There is danger, of course, in artificial momentum. In the bull market of 1982-83, many corporations saw their stock skyrocket, with virtual daily surges upward. Many employees, even if owning little stock personally, took to the daily ritual of checking prices. When the numbers were rising, it was like a constant charge of energy. After all, this was *their* company, their team. The emotion is hardly different from watching your favorite baseball club climb in the standings. The problem, of course, is what happens when the club loses a few games, when stock prices no longer surge, when they even begin to decline. No matter that the absolute level of the price is still two to three times what it was two years ago — the issue is *relative* movement and *relative* price. If the stock is higher today than it was yesterday, you feel good; if it's lower, you feel bad.[1]

Momentum can have side effects. It often gives employees heady expectations of personal opportunity, which are usually unrealistic. Furthermore, if company leadership is overly optimistic in its forecasts of future growth (believing, as it were, their own press clippings), the seeds of 'reality incongruence" are planted. (Reality incongruence grows with virulence along the corporate underground grapevine. We consider it in Chapter 4.)

WHEN IS A STRANGER NOT A STRANGER?

Allie Burke was about to complete her MBA. Her school of business was nationally recognized, but her self-confidence was somewhat shaky. Graduation would mark the culmination of a major life shift begun five years before.

Until she was 28, Allie had never considered commitment to a profession. Her thinking matched that of generations of women: home and husband would come first. Although Allie had never married, the possibility of marriage always had priority over career, so that work always meant only a job.

Her jolt was a jilt. Allie had been waiting — waiting seven years for one indecisive man. Nobody else came close, so for her it was this one or no one. Although the years of uncertainty were painful, she held hope. Why? What extraordinary feelings she had whenever he paid her the slightest attention! Was this rational? Maybe not; but it was real.

It took Allie six months to adjust to the sight of a wedding announcement containing his name but not hers. The bride was a dancer, and he knew her six weeks. One year later, determined to take charge of her life, Allie Burke found herself sitting in management classes, doing accounting problems, making marketing analyses, playing management games. Her pursuit was a three-year, part-time program to obtain a master's in business administration.

Now was payoff time. Here she was, waiting for an elevator in an ultramodern office building in that complex of new structures adjacent to Beverly Hills called Century City. Placing near the top of her class made her a leading job candidate. Her graduate thesis on "Marketing Strategies for Large Accounting Firms" was well researched and presented, if not creative or insightful.

The Big Eight CPA firm had the whole twenty-first floor, and three more like it. There waiting to meet her would be the tax department. The company had enormous prestige and Allie was nervous. She had been flown out at their expense. It was to be her first interview in the real world, to be followed the next day by another interview with a consulting firm downtown. Allie felt intimidated by Los Angeles, by this building, by the offices, by the carpeting, by the inhabitants, by the pressure, and by the parking rates. This spring ritual, she mused, was more like courtship than placement.

Her first interviews did not go well; she got out with her dignity, and little else. Right from the start she struggled to find common ground with tax partners, tax managers, and tax staff — all the while trying to decide that if they wanted her, did she want them? Vacillation doesn't help concentration any.

Public accounting is a demanding profession, and these boys wanted to know how she would stand up to the time pressure and absurd hours. The hiring partners must see intensity even compulsion, but all they were observing in Allie was uncertainty, even doubt. Only her academic training provided common communication; there was no business base in past employment. To get started on a professional career path would not be easy. She would not be getting an offer here.

Allie had maintained church linkages during this life transition. Her church, whose body of doctrines supported a strong moral posture, was known for its outspoken teachings and public policies. She had never visited the Los Angeles congregation before; indeed, this was her first trip to southern California. But after the disastrous interview, self-esteem was scratching bottom and she needed some encouragement.

As soon as she walked into the informal services that evening she felt at home. It was the same closeness she remembered as a girl back home. Everyone had so much in common, sharing similar traditions, beliefs, and values. Standards of conduct were defined precisely and often in sharp contrast to the competitive whirlwind of outside society.

She was invited to dinner by a church family. Although she had never met these people before, they seemed like relatives. Topics of conversation were readily provided by the church's stand against nuclear weapons and the recent election of a member as a United States senator. Although Burke did not agree with all their political views, the safety, companionship, and sharing she felt overshadowed everything else. In this fragmented, centrifugal world spinning her out, here she was experiencing a centripetal force drawing her in. Group cohesion was comforting. Tomorrow would be a better day.

COMPANY COHESION

Cohesiveness among members has a powerful influence on commitment in the group. Some pioneering business organizations have recognized and capitalized on the potency of "wholistic union." When individuals share experiences beyond their jobs, there is a commonality that binds them together.

Something simple works wonders. Seeing the president of your company enjoy a picnic with the staff or playing ball with the boys is the stuff of which legends are made (especially if he spills the beer or steals a base). Giving employees collective benefit if certain goals are achieved can mold a tight team out of loose players. (One company gives Friday afternoons off during summers if key productivity levels are exceeded.)

Wholism and the group cohesion it builds is not, of course, just a hit-or-miss picnic. Wholism is a relationship intense and inclusive, extending to almost every area of living. It's not for every company — but it works well for some.

The remarkable growth of multilevel sales organizations — Avon, Amway, Shaklee — is in large part derived from building group cohesion. In such door-to-door selling, personal attitudes are more important than product quality. Members are on the same team, working for the same goal, applauding each other's success — the zeal is virtually religious and puts many churches to shame.

"I have built a team," beamed a sales manager of a large life insurance company,

> and my team members have personal relationships off the job which transcend professional relationships on the job. I spend a lot of energy structuring outside-the-office settings to bond together my field salespeople. That, if you ask me, is the foundation of our success. On every possible occasion we include spouses. We are out to build commonality, teamwork, togetherness — and it has paid off. I've found settings where even the most private of our people have been brought into the group.

These overwhelming feelings of "We-ness" that some experience only on a school athletic team or in a crack military unit, others find later in adult work life. The commitment engendered by group cohesion can even overcome deficits in other aspects of organizational life. Such cohesion can counteract the negative impact of economic loss or momentum slippage. Though sales growth may falter, employee confidence can sustain strength. One computer company, said to be in financial trouble and threatened with customer cancellations, took out major ads in major papers — ads paid for by its employees!

There is, as always, a flip side. The stronger the cohesion the greater the impact should anything happen to dissolve the group. A merger requiring relocation, for example, can be catastrophic — worse, in fact, than if the group had not been as close originally. As with progressiveness and momentum, group cohesiveness can have negative effects, one of which becomes evident in the next section.

WHICH WAY GOES THE FLOW?

"Boundary permeability" is the degree to which members of an organization are able to interact with the world outside the organization.[3] It can also include the ease with which people outside can enter inside. Most of our examples are of semipermeable groups, where inward flow of new members is encouraged but outward flow of old members is discouraged. (There are, of course, groups that restrict the flow in both directions — they don't want old members out and they also don't want new members in. Such groups are surely fewer, usually sicker, and not as relevant for corporate analogy.)

In extreme cases, almost all interaction with the outside is forbiddden; the organizational boundaries are closed, shut and sealed. Why do groups erect walls so hard and high? Contact and exposure are what they fear. They worry that members can be swayed, that the taint or pulls of world will break down convictions carefully constructed and tirelessly nurtured. "Contamination," as if by infectious disease, is the word often heard. Commitment to organizational purposes must be maintained — it is their only reason for being — and the task becomes progressively more difficult in direct proportion to contact outside.

Closed or total organizations are fertile substrate for studying commitment; the component variables undergo vigorous interplay in this exaggerated environment. Low boundary permeability generates a pressure-cooker effect, boiling internal elements quickly. Circular reasoning abounds. The logic, or lack of it, is "disproof-proof"; it is impossible to contradict the group since contradicting evidence is not admitted inside the system. Constructing unbridgeable barriers around the organization — sealing it off as if by medieval moat — corroborates claims of uniqueness, which in turn validates continuance of existence.

IN OR OUT BUT NOT IN THE MIDDLE

Bill Handler was something of a secret weapon, a voice teacher's voice teacher with an unusual talent for motivating people. Understanding complex personality was a breeze for Bill. He cared not for ego or status — his hand was out to anyone who needed it. Long recognized among seious professionals, Handler was suddenly being "discovered." Radio and television announcers, network anchorpeople, motion picture stars, and media celebrities from all over the country were flocking to him. He had, went the word, the touch. A week with Bill was worth several national rating points.

Something about his style, they said, just brought out your best. "Lyric," "golden," "throbbing," "enriching" were how clients described his coaching. New techniques were what he taught; new meaning was what he gave. Handler was casual yet intense, comprehensive yet focused. His approach for developing the entire human being was unique. Speaking improved, sure; but more important, so did everything else. "A better person," Handler said, "makes a better speaker." Working with him was fun and he never let up until real progress was made. His admirers claimed that Handler was to the training of professional speakers what Yoda was to the training of Jedi Knights.

There was one problem, however. The southern college at which Handler worked was a closed system, sponsored by an esoteric church that viewed the outside world as essentially evil and the inside world as the only matter of importance. College faculty, all dedicated members of the church, thought the campus to be an oasis of sanity in a society of sickness. Perhaps it was some of the retreat-like qualities surrounding the campus — with its wooded isolation and difficult access — that magnified the mystique of The Coach. Finding a guru in the Himalayas wouldn't be any more difficult than finding Handler in his heaven.

The faculty, rather insular in their ways, were just bewildered. How could Handler get such notice? Anyone without a formal degree was shunned. The big guy seemed little more than mild amusement, a perennial teaching assistant, barely better than a gym jock. Quite a tidy group, these stuffy elitists. Pinball machines in "Tilt" had more spark.

At first the college administration liked all the attention. It was a nice novelty, some excitement amidst humdrum routine. It was also "interpreted" by resident seers. Having famous media personalities strolling on campus confirmed the distinction of the college. It was, some suggested, a spotlight focused from Above.

However, the novelty began to wear thin as that spotlight waxed brighter. Students began to attribute more and more value to the work Handler was doing. Church members started asking for regular reports in their member magazines. "The more successful you are, Bill," whispered a wise old head, "the more trouble you'll have." Jealousy, even in utopia, was making its mark.

The obvious contradiction was not long overlooked. College values dictated that nothing of permanent value could be happening outside its boundaries. The closely guarded compound, they were taught, was more a focal point of Divine concern than Washington, London or even Jerusalem. If Handler's celebrities were deemed important, then the whole house of college cards could collapse. Anything that might diminish the relative worth of campus activity, in this kind of closed system, could not be tolerated. Commitment to vital goals had to be maintained, and Handler had become a definite threat. He was innocent and popular and more than a nuisance — he had to be stopped.

Warnings were followed by reprimands. "You'll have to remember what God says," began the headmaster sternly behind his massive mahogony desk. "*Any one* of our freshmen preaching in a pulpit is more important than *every one* of your friends speaking on television."

Handler was demoted and told he could no longer enjoy the privileges afforded faculty, including parking, dining and master keys.

Any of Handler's stars appearing on campus were snubbed by faculty and scrutinized and sniffed by ever-present security guards and dogs. Handler was informed that what he was doing had absolutely no worth. He was urged to conform to the college image and not have intercourse with worldly society.

Why didn't Handler just quit? His other opportunities were enormous. Conversely, why didn't the college just fire him? The renegade was an irritant. Handler and college, it seems, would each have benefitted by the same separating action. Yet, neither did the obvious, and the reasons are both parallel and paradoxical.

Handler was a believer, a loyal member of a loyal church family. His children were raised in the church; his friends were all members. It was unthinkable for Bill, no matter the outside opportunity, no matter the inside abuse, to leave. Group membership was vitally important and the pressure to toe the line was enormous. Loyalty and structure, as well as transcendence and affiliation, never ceased working their subtle ways. Autonomy and materialism, hopelessly outgunned, never had a chance.

The college, for its part, also had a problem. For what possible reason could they sack him? Official pronouncements had openly authorized his work. The past president had often greeted the visiting celebrities. Many faculty gave him quiet support. What's more, everyone liked Bill, including many administrators. Handler was a model church member. He never played favorites: he'd help a janitor before treating a star; with no pretense or posture, he was a common folk hero. Those who called for his head in private would have a tough nut to crack in public.

Yet there is something deeper at work here — the self-confidence of the church. Eliminating Handler would have been admitting defeat, stating implicitly that someone of impeccable moral standing thought that there was more to life outside than inside. The usual vilification of deserters just wouldn't have worked. Everyone knew Bill Handler, and the packaged propaganda would have been hard for anyone to swallow. It was critical for the collective psyche of the church that Handler himself back down, that he admit the error of his ways. Firing him would only make him a martyr. But Bill stayed on — he wouldn't be fired and he wouldn't quit — and his continued presence helped the church grow.

BOUNDARIES AROUND COMPANIES

Principles pertaining to boundaries, seen in garish extract in total organizations, are common to all organizations. Specific applications may vary but general rules remain the same. Items defining the interface between "in" and "out" can range from beards to button-down shirts, motorcycles to right-wing politics. Company standards, whether recommendation or restriction, mark the boundary, distinguishing the group from the nongroup, differentiating inside from outside. (Imagine two circles, one defining the group, the other defining the nongroup. The closer the intersection of the two circles to null, the easier to maintain commitment focus.)

Business firms, as a rule, do not draw lines in the dirt and dare employees to cross them. Nevertheless, attention to the design of boundary conditions is important. Whether planned or unplanned, boundaries always exist, and whether fuzzy or clear, they define organizational essence. Just as group cohesiveness focuses on we-ness, boundary conditions stress we versus they.

Consider the most profitable sales division of an established furniture producer. They had evolved a we versus they approach toward the rest of the company. This division's manager considered himself bigger and better, and didn't like any sharing of bonuses. When scarcity hit and product had to be allocated, the manager had to be clever. His compensation — his god — was based on a strict ranking of each division's profitabilty. Subterfuge would be his strategy; product he would have to hide.

It wasn't long before this ever-tense braggart was possessed by a seige-like attitude of we (our division) versus they (all other divisions). We had become a closed system. The sophisticated inventory-management system, designed to control allocation, threw the company headquarters into they. Now the division manager had to be more cunning, even dishonest, in hoarding products desired by other divisions.

When three truckloads were sold, he recorded the sale as "four." The total price, of course, had to be real; thus it appeared, at first, that he was underselling merchandise and losing money. When it came to the end of the season, he would sell off his hidden inventory and wind up on top of the pile.

The ardor with which this division manager erected boundaries around his sales group rivaled the most fanatic zealot. His successful strategy fed on itself until top management, fascinated by his sudden rise from bottom to top three seasons in a row, discovered his methods and fired him fast.

Do not think boundary building always yields harmful results. There are desirable aspects, one of which relates to the sharpness of organizational goals, the clarity of company mission.

PEOPLE VALUING: WE LOVE YOU

David Stern was in trouble. He had committed a cardinal sin: associating with the excommunicated. The restaurant was Kosher, but his luncheon companion was not. Shlomo Schwartz had recently become persona non grata with their ultra-orthodox sect, and some gossipy members had spotted them together.

As adherents to a total organization, these followers took their lead from the descendants of a pious Polish rabbi whose lengendary talmudic powers were held as the pinnacle of human achievement. So strict was this group that they would throw stones at any Jews driving a car on the Sabbath, and many even denied the legitimacy of a Jewish state in Israel prior to the coming of the Messiah.

A basic tenet of the sect's teachings forbade meeting with anyone who had been expelled from their midst. Stern and Schwartz had known each other for 20 years — they studied talmud torah together — and both placed high value on their friendship. Stern knew that Schwartz was not hostile to the ways of their fathers; his excommunication had been largely the result of a power struggle between ardent traditionalists and spunky reformers following the death of the old rabbi. Schwartz, a dedicated believer, had been used as a scapegoat.

Stern was saddened to hear that when Schwartz had telephoned a mutual friend in the congregation, the friend had hung up as soon as he heard Schwartz's voice. How could someone so quickly disown a lifelong companion who was best man at his wedding, who had stayed up with him all night at the hospital when his daughter's appendix burst?

Stern could not be too judgmental, however. He himself wasn't that different, he realized. He had been nervous in that restaurant; and now, waiting to face the inquisition, he was almost shaking with anxiety. He had violated the scared "shunning rules" regarding expelled members, and he was going to have to explain why. The congregation meant much to Stern, and it was entirely possible that his contact with Schwartz could mean his own ruin.

Stern was not optimistic about the outcome of his meeting with Rabbi Zvi Guttenberg. The hearing was set for 10:00 A.M. but it didn't begin until almost 11:30. Every minute tension mounted. The uncertainty and imminent expectation were disrupting; Stern was having difficulty thinking straight. Finally, as though right on time, Rabbi Guttenberg came out of his office. When he announced that Stern could now come in, his manner was formal, his voice curt.

The rabbi began by establishing the factual basis of the charge. Did Stern have contact with Schwartz? Stern acknowledged that it was true that he had been with Schwartz in the restaurant. The rabbi's face darkened; he had hoped that the accusation was an error and that Stern had not given comfort to the enemy. The truth was going to be more difficult to deal with, especially since Stern was highly respected for his scholarship and much liked as a person.

Stern and Guttenberg were not exactly strangers. Though the rabbi was a few years older, the men had shared experiences together:

defense patrols in their rough neighborhood, scholarly arguments against other congregations, a trip to Israel to establish a school. None of that mattered much now, thought Stern — the rules are the rules.

The rabbi seemed to be struggling. What would be his next question? Would there even be one? After interminable silence, he said slowly: "*Why* did you meet with Schwartz?"

A "why" question? Could it be that rabbi was going to consider more than a simple "Did you?" Would motivation be balanced against behavior? Would the heart be weighed with the hand?

Stern explained the importance he attached to his friendship with Schwartz, emphasizing that Schwartz was in no way trying to undermine the congregation. What's more, Stern affirmed Schwartz' still strong belief in the movement.

The rabbi paused, taking time to process and try the contending principles. It was a typical talmudic problem. The shunning principle must be upheld. On the other hand, should deep friendship be forsaken in a situation where political and personality factors had triggered the excommunication?

Rabbi Guttenberg finally spoke with profound simplicity: "David, we love you. Do your best to help Schwartz."

It had not been easy for Stern to see Schwartz misjudged and mistreated. The lack of people valuing among leaders, the insensitivity to feelings, had disturbed him deeply. His personal commitment to the congregation and its philosophy had been severely eroded. The compassionate treatment by Guttenberg was one step toward rebuilding his commitment.

PEOPLE EATERS

The power of people valuing is acutely exposed in examining closed organizations. In these groups boundaries are defined by rules and regulations. Total organizations can be "people eaters" par excellence and often cannot accommodate individual needs. Maintaining ultradistinct identity is all that counts. Any compassion might break their spell.

What we observe in the David Stern case is important, and no organizational setting is immune. Managers who are concerned about people produce powerful binding between employees and companies. Executives sensitive to individual subtleties gain efficiency in their leadership. In organizational interviews, we have found people valuing to be a key factor for explaining commitment strength of corporate employees.

One senior executive attributed his remarkable rise in the company to an event early in his career:

I had been given responsibility for introducing a new machine tool. We were small then and I reported directly to the president, who was the son of the founder. Well, the results were horrible — not 25 percent of what had to be sold was sold. I really screwed up, using a discredited system of independent reps instead of company salesmen (which the president had recommended). I was trying to save money, assert my independence, show my stuff — and lost everything. I should have been canned, but all the president said was, "I'm glad you have the guts to fail." Those words changed my life.

The old adage that "soft is hard" is thus reaffirmed. Managers who understand people best run their business best; the nicest, believe it or not, can also be the toughest.

OF CHARISMA AND COMMITMENT

Strong leadership is the essence of dynamic direction. This is especially true when organizations are closed and total. In such situations a charismatic leader exerts enormous influence on member commitment, a power that can twist the organization away from primary purpose if not controlled.

A leader's impact is greatly magnified if he or she founded the organization or has provided transcendent mission for it. In the case that follows, we focus on leadership, although both organization goal structure and esteem are intimately intertwined.

In 1955 William Spears was 38 years old, a rising star in the marketing division of a major retailer. His father had been a minister, and Spears explained his immunity to religion by early exposure to the hypocrisy and politics associated with Christianity. His father's church, apparently, had been a maelstrom of splits and schisms. For every doctrine there were at least two opinions; in every congregation, at least two factions.

Spears had his own way of explaining it: "Twice as a child I was inoculated against illness: once by getting a mild case of chicken pox, and once by watching my daddy fight about the bible."

His change came, as often happens, by accident. One of his friends was becoming obsessed with a group claiming special knowledge about the human soul. These modern-day gnostics had discovered some ancient mechanism, or so they said, to give earthly peace and heavenly vision. They called the process "The Way of Opening," and they said it purged your brain and cleared your mind. Once "Open," believers asserted, you could "See It All."

Spears himself had been asking questions about the purpose of life, but wouldn't look to a church to give him any answers. For two years Spears struggled with the strange ideas his friend was embracing. The experiences of youth certainly confirmed that traditional Christianity had been derailed, if it ever were on the right track.

When his wife died, suddenly and tragically, William Spears became engulfed by blackness. He lost all personal meaning, and this new religion was ready to fill the physical emptiness and spiritual void. For eight months Spears studied the group's writings and then much to the surprise of everyone (including the friend who introduced him), he quit his job in order to pursue his newfound passion on a full-time basis.

The business of seeking souls was not much different from the business of selling retail, and Spears rose quickly in the religious hierarchy. Members commented on his natural gift of "seeing with a third eye and speaking with a silver tongue," and many started to look to him for guidance.

The established hierarchy, heretofore happy to have Spears' energetic support, grew concerned lest his influence exceed theirs. Soon it was *Church Wars, Part II*, as Spears found himself recapitulating the religious power struggles he so despised as a youth. But this was now different; here it was Spears with a vision in his mind and a fire in his eye, and he knew as he knew nothing else, that this *one* time church politics was Divine Purpose.

Breaking away, inevitably, became the only solution, and so at age 43 Spears organized and founded his own church. He was the leader, the boss, the one who made the rules and authorized the doctrines. He started fast. He deemphasized the soul, bringing in some pop psychology from the West and some Zen from the East. He set up a public series of wild seminars, mixing group therapy and mystical Buddhism as if in a blender. The timing must have been perfect because these spectacles were a howling success. Within two years, one could attend a "Spear-Seminar" in 150 cities around the world.

Spears' persuasive personality, enormous energy level, and unique product positioning brought exponential growth to the Movement. By setting himself in direct opposition to all organized religion, he delineated organizational boundaries that were clear and distinct. By using his natural talent, and by pounding the problems with traditional theology, Spears convinced thousands to join with him and discover "Real Purpose" in human life. He hammered away at his message of hope and clung tenaciously to his formula of magic.

As time went on Spears became the father figure of the Movement. He wrote frequently to his faithful. He was the Founder; he had been there from the beginning and his perspective could not be challenged. The infantile theory and numerous imitations didn't matter. Spears' riveting personality, focused doctrine, and resolute convictions earned fierce fidelity among followers. His minions supported the Cause, spread the Word, and brought "Real Purpose" to all who had ears to hear. Spears's own public appearances became less regular, and although there were disquieting rumors of his financial affairs and personal life, his absence only served to build his mystique and reinforce member commitment.

THE DOUBLE STANDARD

Class distinction between clergy and laymen is a prime characteristic of religious organizations. Such social disparity often generates a "double standard" in behavior, privilege, power, license, honor, and reward. What the professional can do, the amateur cannot. One reads with regularity reports of religious leaders involved in personal activities hardly religious. This morality gap is severely criticized by outsiders, yet the faithful usually do not complain. Such support of congregants for their leaders, even when discovered in sin, mystifies observers and bewilders cynics. Yet there is logic here, a form of social contract.

The double standard, interestingly enough, is a two-edged sword. Cutting one way, it affirms the superior rights of religious rank. Cutting the other way, it legitimizes the social position of the laity.[4] Not everyone can be a member of the ruling hierarchy, and the double standard justifies each end of the axis.

A similar distinction exists, if one gazes with broad social sweep, between managers and workers in business organizations. Differentiation in personal behavior, privilege of position, power to control subordinates, license to supercede rules, organizational honor, and degree of reward are all present. What executives are permitted, workers are not. Closeness to senior management, if one pardons the analogy, is akin to closeness to God.

ARE LEADERS ARCHAIC?

Leaders today have a tougher task; employees are more informed and competition for time and attention is brutal. But even in an age of sophisticated technology it would be a mistake to underestimate the impact of strong leadership, in all kinds of companies, for developing employee commitment.

Todd Dragt was a talented member of the new venture division of a major aerospace firm. He was well equipped for skipping up the corporate ladder. Putting together successful business plans was his specialty; he was skillful in preparing the necessary market research and financial analysis. What's more, he was creative and ambitious and loaded with energy.

But was he political and shrewd? No. And so he was shocked when he was passed up for promotion by a pleasant but mediocre fellow who socialized with the divisional vice-president.

The following Monday Todd started looking for other employment. He was offered two fine positions, one with 15 percent better pay, the other with fast track potential. But he decided to decline, and his frustrated job counselor — herself out the placement fee — wanted to know why. "What," she asked, "is holding you to the company?" Todd replied:

> My admiration for the president, nothing more. He's an entrepreneur. Although obviously very successful, he hasn't lost the common touch. I can walk up to him and chat at a company party. He knows me. That means a lot. He's the type of guy I want to work for — and the type of guy I want to become.

Paul Chandler was founder and president of a fast-growing insurance company specializing in group plans for large corporations. Chandler was recognized as having great technical expertise in product design. Financial prowess combined with marketing awareness was an unbeatable combination. Paul was always on the road, "at the front" he said.

Chandler's company was flying high, but bounding success was masking serious problems. Management systems were essentially nonexistent. There were few controls and less continuity. There were no formal lines of authority whatsoever; everyone either reported to the president directly or to whomever they wanted. Most planning and coordination were done by Chandler on the fly, literally between flights. He was famous for his ten-minute calls, with airport sounds on one end of the phone and half the company trying to get his attention on the other end. He was dubbed the "Telephone King."

Employees were inefficient and frustrated and complained constantly. Yet there was little turnover of key personnel, and at first glance that seemed surprising. In comparable circumstances in other firms, executive suites would need revolving doors to keep pace with the changing guards. What was different here? Interviews revealed that the remarkably high commitment to the company was largely explained as appreciation for the president, for the genius and charisma of Paul Chandler.

Identification with leadership, however, does not always benefit the company. Our research with sales-oriented businesses has found that loss of key people can often be traced to the compelling grip that a charismatic manager has on them. When he leaves for greener pastures, so do they.

In assessing the impact of leadership on commitment, we must stress the link between leadership and mission. Indeed, it is often a leader's personal ideal that is translated into the company's grand purpose. Call it ego if you like, but the goal structure of an organization is most often the magnification of one person's dream.[5]

GOALS AND WHAT MAKES THEM

Goals are what every company needs but few understand. When senior managers take advanced business courses, goals are often overlooked as obvious and simple and not worth worrying about. Strategy and tactics are studied, but strategy and tactics to accomplish what? The setting of company goals, not so obvious and not so simple, deserves a good look.

Company goals and company mission are close but not identical concepts. If mission defines the overriding vision of the firm, its grand design, then goals are the specific constituent elements adding substance and flesh to the skeletal form. An analysis of mission, to be complete, must consider its component goals.

Goals can be defined as a "planned position" or "anticipated results to be achieved." Goals can be contrasted with objectives in that most consider the former to be longterm and the latter to be shortterm.

Why should a company set goals? For guidance, planning, motivation, evaluating, and controlling. What do goals accomplish? We enumerate five categories:

- Goals are frameworks for strategic planning and guidelines for operating decisions.
- Goals give internal departments specific orientation and direction, focusing systems on compliance and coordination.
- Goals determine proper structure and staffing.
- Goals motivate and guide the behavior of subordinates.
- Goals provide a basis for organizational control, when actual results are compared to planned positions.

If an organization does not set goals, they are set nonetheless — by default. Every organization has goals, whether defined or not, clear or not, attainable or not. The smart company will define goals, making them both clear and attainable.

Of what is a goal composed? What are its components? We give five factors that characterize every goal:

- *Position:* Where in the hierarchy does the goal fit?
- *Content:* What is the nature of the goal?
- *Measure:* What is the indicator of the goal?
- *Level:* What is the number in the goal?
- *Period:* What are the time parameters of the goal?

(Some examples are diagrammed in Figure 3.2):

Category	1	2	3	4	5
Position	Corporate	Divisional	Marketing	Manufacturing	R & D
Content	Financial Return	Absolute Dollars	Product Scope	High Quality	Innovation
Measure	Return on Investment	Contributional Income	Increase in Market Share	Rejection Rate	New Products
Level	19%	15%	3%	.0007	3
Period	Year	Year	Season	Monthly Average	24 Months

FIGURE 3-2 COMPANY GOALS: CATEGORIES AND COMPONENTS

- A corporate goal might be a 19 percent return on investment every year.
- A divisional goal might be a 15 percent increase in contributional income this year.
- A product goal might be a 3 percent increase in market share in the next season.
- A manufacturing goal might be a rejection rate of no more than .0007 (averaged monthly).
- An R & D goal might be the development of three new products in the next 24 months.

What constitutes an ideal goal (see Figure 3.3)? It should be defined operationally: clear not vague; specific not general; consistent not discordant; measurable not boundless; difficult not easy; achievable not impossible. When the goal-formulation process is working well, there are usually four elements present:

Proper	↔	Improper
Clear	↔	Vague
Specific	↔	General
Consistent	↔	Discordant
Measurable	↔	Boundless
Difficult	↔	Easy
Achievable	↔	Impossible

FIGURE 3-3 GOALS: IDEAL CONTENT

- There is commitment from everyone, especially the group's most senior person.
- There is free communication up and down the corporate hierarchy.
- There is rapid and regular feedback of results.
- There is healthy competition among subordinates.

In recent years, new concepts have changed the way we look at corporate goals. Gone is the fiction that goals are set rationally and logically. The idea of "bounded rationality," developed by Herbert Simon and James March, is the keystone here.[6] No executive can know everything. If executives want to do anything, they must replace "optimizing" — the effort to get the very best result possible — with "satisficing" — the realization that problems need only be solved satisfactorily, not perfectly.

Next, the goal-formulation process was studied within real world organizations. A primary result has been that rationality rarely dominates; often it's hard to find at all. Goals are set in companies, like almost everything else that happens, on the basis of power and position. Corporate politics has been pulled out of the closet and put under the microscope.

In a classic study on power, John French and Bertram Raven distinguished five categories with which a person (P) can be controlled by a social agent (O), whether the latter be a person, group, or part of a group.[7] The relevance here is direct. How are those who formulate goals in companies, the Ps, influenced by the various corporate Os?

Reward Power: P's perception that O can mediate positive value (whether financial, promotional, personal, social or psychological). Example: The executive vice-president gets his division to subscribe to his goals since he has discretionary authority over upcoming bonuses.

Coercive Power: P's perception that O can mediate negative value (whether financial, promotional, personal, social, or psychological). Example: A marketing vice-president influences the president to increase advertising since his sister is the president's wife.

Legitimate Power: P's perception that O has a proper and appropriate right to prescribe behavior for him. Example: The president listens to his financial vice-president in setting return-on-investment goals.

Referent Power: P's personal identification with O. Example: A president who never graduated college respects his young assistant who has attained several advanced degrees.

Expert Power: P's perception that O has some special knowledge or expertise. Example: The vice-president for research follows the recommendation of his chief scientist.

Politics is king in organizational kingdoms. Whoever has the boss's ear has a good grip on the company's soul. Jockeying for position and maneuvering people is the corporate bargaining game, and it's played hard and often in the goal-formulation process.

Studies have uncovered characteristics of the well-known organizational politician. At the top of the list, this fellow has consummate knowledge of company systems and people — not how they work on paper but how they work in reality, the *informal* relationships. He always knows who likes whom, the probable managerial successors, even the current sleeping arrangements. He maneuvers himself into a position controlling the flow of information. He's not too big on line authority — responsibility too soon can knock you out of the box. He is always seen with the right people. Luncheons are important. Finally, he chooses tasks carefully; he only takes those that will win.

Divisions and departments, too, are creatures of politics. They act as if animate. Mere boxes on organizational charts, they have an uncanny sense of their own existence. It does not matter who is operating the shop, there is constant pressure to sustain power and position, to do things according to standard operating procedures, to maintain the established routine, to perform the accustomed repertoire. Departments and divisions will do anything to maintain their mystical being.[8]

GOALS AND METAGOALS

The relationship between goal structure and commitment brings us back to William Spears. Recall that it was by setting himself up in violent opposition to organized religion that Spears overcame his own early abhorrence of religion with its hypocrisy and politics. When he translated this ego experience into the form of a new religion, an "antireligion," and made it the focal point of his life, he simultaneously created a metagoal — a distinctive purpose for his organization. The desire to be part of something that was different, that was not like other organizations, attracted thousands of followers who themselves became committed to this grand design. One man's compulsion had become other men's mission.

The word "transcendence" may sound out of place when talking about machine-tool manufacturing or electronic-parts distribution. It is not. Though "transcendence" has connotations of lofty visions and mystical fantasy, it is relevant, applicable, and necessary for corporate success. (Transcendence overcomes many organizational problems, including internal conflict; recall Harry Roberts, Chapter 2.)

To go beyond simple survival or modest growth, companies must develop a goal structure driven by an overarching, visionary image. By holding out larger meaning that employees can engage, executives will motivate hearts and minds as well as wallets and pocketbooks. Managers of profit-making companies should learn the lessons of total/religious organizations; though all aspects of closed systems may not be desirable, their ability to win commitment is worth watching. Energizing transcendence, generating visceral support for policies and programs, is what it's all about.

How can it be done? Some examples:

- Transcendence for American automobile companies means turning back the Japanese invasion.
- Transcendence for the big semiconductor manufacturers means being the first to put a million bits on a chip.
- Transcendence for a struggling specialty retailer means cutting back to regain profitability and save the ship.
- Transcendence for a medium-sized chemical company means producing new products to sweep the market.
- Transcendence for a textile company means being the lowest-cost producer.
- Transcendence for a package-good producer means getting high shelf space and leading market share.
- Transcendence for a small computer company is signing an exclusive contract for the IBM PC.
- Transcendence for a medical center is a research breakthrough on a rare disease.
- Transcendence for a museum is teaching more children with the same subsidy.
- Transcendence for the government is reducing that damn deficit.

Presidents, give an ear: Go for transcendence!

CHAPTER FOUR

MEANING AND MISSION:
WHY COMMITMENT WORKS

"What about me?" muttered Roger Alberts, forgetting for a moment that personal pique was off-limits for a man of the cloth. "Why wasn't I advanced?"

"It's God moving," answered his wife, quietly wondering, if God was moving, why He was moving through Herb Edwards, a fat minister with a fatter grudge?

Their church looked to the nineteenth-century writings of a woman who communed, so she said, with the archangel Gabriel. The bible, she wrote, had to be "renewed" before the "Advent of the Spiritual Wanderer." Her writings, quite conveniently, gave off all the airs of just such a "renewal."

Hierarchical authority and rigid reporting characterized the church's structure, just as a mixture of spiritualism and mind science dominated its doctrine. Ministerial rank, not unlike a military system, was the promotional incentive, with each step up the ladder rewarded with higher compensation, status, and authority — especially that Authority, which, the church stressed, "God must give and men must fear."

Albers was totally committed. He held back nothing from the church. Its pronouncements he believed to be Divine. Its leaders he revered as saints. Its doctrines he would preach from the rooftops. Its laws he would die before transgressing.

Albers had experienced two levels of advancement within the church hierarchy, each accompanied by all the exaltation of inner glory and public praise. But now, with his next ordination more than a year overdue, he appeared to be stuck. Even though Albers was recognized as a gifted minister, a defender of the faith, and an evangelist to the world, colleagues who had been his seminary classmates were "ranking" (a verb in church parlance) faster than he.

For Albers, ranking meant everything. Ministerial advancement was the prime confirmation of his spiritual growth, of his acceptance by God, of his self-image and worth. Regular recognition by the only

Body that mattered was being denied. Church teachings, which he firmly believed, stressed that God Himself was the prime decision maker in ministerial promotions, and that He always worked through those senior in authority. "God," went the well-worn phrase, was a "great believer in Authority." Albers was a true believer, and proud of it.

As each ordination season came and went, Albers grew more depressed. Frustration ripened into cynicism. Being passed up for promotion was now an overt affront as each of his former assistants stepped over him on the vaunted "ranking ladder" — which was posted in church headquarters much as "tennis ladders" are listed in athletic clubs.

Herb Edwards, Albers concluded, was his nemesis. How the braggart ever wormed his way into the High Pastor's Chambers he could never guess. Edwards's appointment as the Official Elder of the Chambers was beyond his ken. He was starting to believe the gossipy tales.

Blackball — that was Edwards's trump card, thought Albers, and he's playing it again and again, like a riverboat gambler on a drunken hot streak. The man's thirst for revenge was unquenchable. His jealousy, Ablers imagined, went back a dozen years. They had been constant rivals: on the grade sheets (Albers was number one in the class, Edwards number three); on the athletic field (Albers captained the baseball team, Edwards warmed the bench); even over the same woman (she married Albers, after first dating Edwards). Edwards had struck out three times — Albers enjoyed the remembrance — but the game was just beginning. Losing to me, Albers reasoned, was something the Official Elder was determined never to do again.

Albers's friends became concerned when they heard him jabbering incessantly, with bitterness beginning to darken his tone. Not only was he ranting about Edwards's backstabbing, he was also raving about unfairness in the organization. Such commentary, flouting the face of clear church teaching, was a contradiction in terms. Since God was in charge of the church, and since God was fair, then ipso facto the church must be fair. To deny the church's fairness was to deny God.

Once Albers allowed human factors to become a legitimate explanation for his own "stuckness," his commitment to the church deteriorated rapidly. The extent of his change was astounding. The same church for which he had once been prepared to offer his life, he was now not ready to lift a finger.

Although Albers stayed in the ministry, he began a process of "psychological retirement." His body remained in the pulpit, but his heart wouldn't go near the building. And his mind went altogether elsewhere. He put out a bare minimum of work effort, just sufficient to keep paycheck coming in and family living on. Three years later we find Roger Albers completing a degree in computer programming, having taken the coursework in secret.

STATUS: WHAT'S IN IT FOR ME?

In Chapter 3 we discussed "progessiveness," the sense of forward motion, as an organizational variable that influences member or employee commitment. At least equal importance must be allocated to "personal status," the position or recognition of the member within the group.

An interesting factor here is that personal status is somewhat independent of organizational momentum; the commitment derived from position is not tightly coupled with how well the organization is moving. Just as most little leaguers come home feeling good after hitting two home runs even if their team has lost, so increasing personal status and career advancement within struggling companies can augment commitment. Conversely, personal demotion or lack of advancement will threaten commitment no matter how successful the organization.

A vice-president on the verge of quitting his company was suddenly asked to assume the presidency after a financial scandal blew out the top brass. "I felt a surge of adrenalin," he said reflecting back. "Instantly, what I had thought were 'lousy products' in a 'stagnant industry' were transformed into 'fascinating products' in a 'challenging environment.' Don't ask me to explain it rationally, but it's the way I felt."

Using status as a motivational mechanism can produce dramatic results. "I had a problem with one of my most creative talents," commented a chief executive of a large advertising agency reliving the drama.

> He was a project manager and constantly late with copy. Moreover, he was always irritating people — and seemed to like it. His boss, a traditional executive vice-president, recommended dismissal. But the kid had great ability. I'd been in the business twenty-five years, and I hadn't seen three people with more natural stuff. I didn't want to lose him. What to do?
>
> Transfer or lateral movement was worse than firing him. He'd stew and fester and be more of an irritant. So I took my life in my hands, and made everyone question my sanity. I *promoted* the oddball. I put him in charge of the entire department and made him a senior vice-president. I told

him I had full confidence in him. He was surprised, though he tried not to show it. I'm sure he had thought it was curtains when I called him into my office. At first I had to watch him carefullly, though quietly — he could have had a good run at blowing the company. Well, it worked. It was like flipping a switch. Promotion symbolized confidence and confidence triggered performance. He's Creative Director today — and a hell of an administrator.

In a closed system where status is virtue, we can see most clearly the impact of non-advancement on an individual. Others may respond differently than Roger Albers and fight for promotion, and if they should receive it, God would once again be fair and the church true. Old commitment levels can be regained, and any previously perceived injustices can be seen as only temporary triumphs of the forces of darkness.

Closely related to status, but worthy of separate consideration, are the "rewards" that an organization provides individuals. In developing employee commitment, rewarding personnel is one of the most powerful variables under a manager's control.

The nature of rewards varies across individuals and organizations. For some it is financial compensation — salary, bonuses, stock options, and the like. Often such monetary benefits are symbolic of deeper levels of psychic satisfaction — the feelings of belonging and importance. When employees receive stock options, even at exercise prices above current prices, commitment is often enhanced, often well beyond more direct financial benefits.

For many individuals, rewarding with opportunity may predominate in importance. Giving employees a real shot at growth, whether positional with impressive titles or personal with fulfilling tasks, can make maximum motivation. Managers should examine each subordinate's private reward structure. (The social context is important here and should be factored into the equation. Whatever constitutes status in a given organizational culture must be considered since it will be the ultimate test of comparison.)

VARIABLES OF INTERACTION

In the previous two chapters we examined the impact of various factors on individual commitment: pure personal variables (Chapter 2) and pure organizational variables (Chapter 3). Now we look at the melding of the two: These are the factors arising out of the intricate interaction between individuals and institutions. The thrust, remember, is our working definition of commitment, the firm bond between personal meaning and company mission.

Rewards and status, the concepts of the Albers case, are examples of variables that are generated in the intimate interplay between employee and company. These are factors that do not exist independently, but *emerge* as the product of what is almost a chemical reaction. The elements that go into the test tube of organizational experiences — the pure personal and organizational factors — may be very different from the compounds that come out.

Those variables emerging out of the interaction between individual and institution we label "organizational experience." We set two classes: meaning/mission-related variables, and other organizational experience variables important in the determination of commitment.

Some of these interactional factors are listed if Figure 4.1. We stress, as is our custom, that these variables just *represent* the class; they do not exhaust it. Each will be used in case examples to illustrate what the interaction between member and group can mean for commitment, the organic link between mission and meaning.

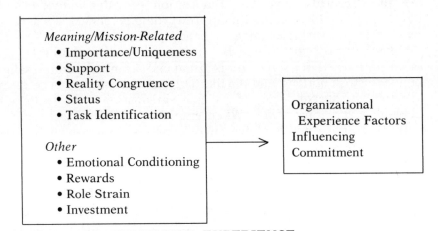

Meaning/Mission-Related
- Importance/Uniqueness
- Support
- Reality Congruence
- Status
- Task Identification

Other
- Emotional Conditioning
- Rewards
- Role Strain
- Investment

Organizational Experience Factors Influencing Commitment

FIGURE 4-1 ORGANIZATIONAL EXPERIENCE FACTORS INFLUENCING COMMITMENT

MEANING/MISSION-RELATED FACTORS

Meaning/mission-related factors result primarily from the direct interaction between meaning-related factors (individual variables, see Figure 2.1) and mission-related factors (organizational factors, see Figure 3.1).

Importance/Uniqueness (Perceived): The relative importance of the organization, whether real or perceived; the differences between this organization and all other organizations in the mind of an individual. How "special" does the member consider the group?

Support: The extent to which the organization provides an individual with freedom and help to do a job; the amount of collective aid in all facets of group membership or company employment. How much can the individual rely on the organization for physical and mental sustenance?

Reality Congruence: The correlation between what the organization professes to be true and what an individual believes to be true (opposite: "credibility gap"). How accurate are organizational pronouncements; more important, how much are they believed?

Status: The personal position of an individual relative to others in the organization; the degree to which a person is recognized in the organizational culture. How prominent is the employee, and what does that prominence connote in the company?

Task Identification: The degree to which an individual enjoys a specific job or responsibility; whether one invests ego as well as effort in fulfilling the position. How much does the person like the job compared to other possibilities?

OTHER ORGANIZATIONAL EXPERIENCE FACTORS

Emotional Conditioning: The affective, nonrational aspect of an individual's commitment to an organization. The general feelings of a person toward the organization, independent of specific factors. How strong is the tie between member and group, and how difficult would it be to break?

Rewards: The psychic and/or financial improvement of an individual's condition as a direct result of specific organizational action. What does the individual get, how meaningful is it, and how important compared to other possibilites?

Role Strain: The amount of stress experienced by an individual when having difficulty complying with role expectation.[1] The tensions of playing parts cast by others; the conflicts between competing aspects of life (as between job and family). How does one cope with uncertainty in an organizational position?

Investment: The degree and quality of ego and effort sunk by the individual into the organization (prime examples are time, money, and reputation).[2] How much of yourself has been invested in your company, and what would it take to walk away from it?

PARADISE LOST

Richard Wardsworth Yiramoto was not your typical member of the Honshu Circle, a new religious movement. Its leaders claimed "ancient

Oriental heritage," but it had been born in San Francisco and raised in Los Angeles. Oriental in name if not in members, the Circle boasted a curious ecumenical sampling of Protestants from the Midwest, Catholics from New England, and Jews from New York — though in proportion to the general population, Jews exceeded their fair share.

Yiramoto's Japanese background was simultaneously admired and feared by Circle officials. Admiration was based on the group's Oriental bias, since its philosophy was derived from the writings and wisdom of holy men from the East. Fear was based on the newcomer's rapidly growing influence over Circle policy.

Yiramoto was entirely American by culture, though half American by background. His father was a computer scientist working in Silicon Valley; he had come from Japan to head his company's American research facility. His mother taught mathematics at a nearby high school. Richard had grown up in a thoroughly rational environment, winding up with a degree in engineering and a good job in industry — but there was more to life, he sensed, than equations and number crunching.

Richard was first attracted to the Circle by their strong adherence to the "Ancient Way," a composite picture of "earthly peace and heavenly vision" unsullied by the "corruption of competition" and the "pollution of hatred." He had been particularly impressed that their teachings were an accurate reflection of what the ancient masters had written, as opposed to some recent ripoffs of the sacred writings. Often he mused how beautiful it would be if everyone put personal peace ahead of combative striving, and how there must be something more to life than muons making tracks in bubble chambers. And so when Richard found a religious order claiming to reintroduce the "Ancient Way," he forsook all to take up the banner.

The Circle asserted that there was no place else on earth where the Ancient Way was being taught so faithfully, where such peace and harmony were present, where calm contemplation was so virtuous, and where the serenity of truth was the golden rule. Most important, however, was scriptural fidelity. Yiramoto had found his paradise.

Trouble in paradise began when Richard started to see interpretive problems in Circle teachings. Most were caused by ignorance of the original languages — ancient Japanese and several dialects of Chinese. Though knowing only a smattering of Japanese, and never much of a scholar, Richard desired to read the original words of the masters. He began vigorous study, six hours a day for months. He sought Circle doctrine at the deepest level.

What he found he did not expect. There were mistakes, out-and-out errors of reading caused by simple misunderstandings of complex characters expressing profound thoughts. The mistakes did not upset him — everyone makes mistakes — but the reactions to them did.

When, in the best of attitudes, Yiramoto presented Circle leaders with their erroneous interpretations, he was told not to rock the boat and to remember who was paying his check.

The earnest seeker of the Ancient Way was mortified. He had given up outside life to study with the Circle. He had come to help quietly in the more perfect study of the wisdom writings, according to their well-advertised credo: "Show us the Word and we Kneel, show us the Truth and we Bow."

But when Yiramoto brought the "Word" and the "Truth," all he got was a "knee" and an "arrow" — the former in the stomach, the latter in the back. Rumors were set ablaze: "The Jap," the leaders whispered, "is planning a sneak attack."

A friend among the threatened hierarchy confided to Richard:

> You have to understand. If we change our teachings, our members will begin to doubt. They will wonder whether we are really in touch with the infinite resonance of the universe. We will lose face. The Circle must expand, and causing member uncertainty is not the way to do it. Our members must be resolute. Stalwart. Uncompromising. We are calling on them for sacrifice. They must support our mission with their time and resources. We must never shake their confidence. Doubt, you know, is very bad.

"But what about truth?" Richard asked, but only to himself. He was stunned but stayed. After all, no other group was teaching the way of "earthly peace and heavenly vision," and therefore no other place had such moral beauty. There is no place else to go, thought Richard.

As time passed, the "clean" areas of the church, those that gave it its uniqueness, contracted in Richard's mind. Of necessity, the "dirty and muddy" areas expanded. Equally disconcerting, he began noticing other groups, religious and non-religious, that promoted "earthly peace and heavenly vision." Maybe not in those words; maybe not with the same wriitngs; maybe not with the same masters — but they were honest and intelligent people seeking meaning and hope, people putting into practice what they had put into words.

Richard not only saw more errors in the teachings of the Circle, he also had to face gaps between teaching and living among Circle leadership. He was not demanding spiritual perfection, but he was at least expecting moral effort. Unfortunately, even this minimal standard was all too often absent. His moral heaven had become an immoral hell. Paradise was lost.

UNIQUENESS AS GLUE

As long as Richard Yiramoto perceived and attributed uniqueness to the Circle, some special quality unavailable elsewhere, his organizational commitment was safe — even against the attack of other elements, such as moral inconsistency. The realization that other places may be as visionary, or more visionary, was the scalpel that began cutting away his commitment.

Organizational uniqueness is not restricted to closed systems and total organizations. Said one employee having just left a large computer manufacturer:

> We were told continually that all other firms were disorganized tangles of confusion. We were, according to the party line, the epitome of precision, untouchable in the industry. I've come to find out that all companies have weeds. I'm trying to find the one that gives me the least problems. It's a hard search.

The lesson of uniqueness is a positive one. Yes, it can misrepresent and distort. But, when used properly, it is a powerful tool for building organizational strength and securing personnel commitment. The exaggerated examples of total organizations, remember, are not presented to show the errors of uniqueness — these are obvious enough — but rather to evidence the *power* of it. If feelings of special distinction can hold people in strange organizations when all other factors would pull them out, then, indeed, the sense of organizational uniqueness is a potent force.

Corporations should build on their strengths, those elements of the company where they have comparative advantage, if not outright dominance. Commitment correlates directly with an employee's perception of company importance and exclusivity. Many firms that do not have unions — such as IBM and Eastman Kodak — give employees the confidence that nobody could treat them better. True or not, it's the way they feel. Many key personnel in successful entrepreneurial ventures have that special exhilaration of the explorer and pioneer. Managers in all firms, understanding this principle, can build a sense of corporate uniqueness, an expression of individuality with which employees can identify.

Some mechanisms for generating perceptions of uniqueness might include the following: specific companywide profit-sharing plans; special social occasions if certain performance figures are met; some flexibility in choosing work hours or styles; exclusive arrangements for employees tied into the local geographic area (such as reduced rates for health clubs, amusement parks, shows, restaurants, and so forth).

There is, as always, the other side. When claims of uniqueness are exaggerated and then proved to be false (as must happen in time), then the seeds of "reality incongruence" are sown. Its impact on commitment is not small and not good.

THE MYTH UNVEILED

Alice Ritter was scared. She had always been curious about her best friend's religion, and one day just decided to accompany her to church. The meeting was conducted in secret, and all doors were guarded by imposing men. The sermon, longer than any she had heard before, dealt with the "end-time" cataclysm coming on earth. The preacher spoke with firmness and force, and she was impressed by the step-by-step detailing of world events that would signal the "end of days." The man was so strong, so sure.

The preacher, it seems, had had a vision. He was taken, as he reported events, into the "electric chambers" of a vast "Wheel within Wheels" (taking ample literary license from the prophet Ezekiel, though not giving him a footnote of credit). There he met a huge creature with many wings and mouths. Each wing was singing a different song and each mouth was uttering a different prophecy. Such, he was told by an overarching voice, represents the cacophony of confusion on earth. Then there appeared a new creature with one wing and one mouth, and this was the Being who explained it all to him.

The preacher burned with fire. Only those in his congregation, he shouted, could be saved. This same Wheel would come back again to take them to safety, to save them from devastation. Time was short. Maybe a few years; more likely a few months. Obedience was essential. Only the preacher knew the "Way of the Wheel." To be saved, one must follow him.

That evening Alice looked at her small daughter clinging to a stuffed monkey as she fell asleep. Alice wept as she remembered the lurid description of what would happen to little children in the final catastrophes. She decided right then to save her family. Alice joined the church and began to follow its behavioral commands and complex rituals.

Her life became dominated by the church. She had violent arguments with her husband over its obedience requirements. Sex was a "special sacrament" and could be "partaken of" only at certain times of the year — or so said, according to the preacher, one of the Wheeled Creatures. Within a year Alice and her husband were divorced. He could not live with her religion, but she had found her true family in the church.

Alice watched for floods and droughts, pestilence and disease. She felt vindicated every time a war broke out or a natural catastrophe occured; she was reassured every time somebody got bit by a rat or crushed by an earthquake. Her preacher used such events to confirm that God's timetable would not fail. The small church awaited eagerly the date that the preacher had concocted through a convoluted set of calculations and magic numbers. (What Jesus told his disciples never bothers date-setting preachers: "In such an hour as ye think *not* the Son of man cometh," Matthew 24:44; "It is not for you to know the times or the seasons," Acts 1:7).

When the established date passed and a different history was written, Alice was concerned but not destroyed. The preacher revealed to his stunned audience:

> The Wheel has returned, but the Winged One has been merciful. He spares us special time to prepare ourselves. We are not yet worthy to escape His Terrible Wrath. We must go into the world and bring out the unconverted. Only by saving others will we save ourselves.

A delay might occur, Alice reasoned, but the events were still certain. Many in church went wild with evangelistic fevor. Alice helped, but she was not the proselytizing kind. The church went through paroxysms of change, change of doctrine, change in mission. The preacher took to television. The church grew, and even gained some respectability. Alice's small daughter was now a teenager, and she wanted nothing to do with mom's religion.

Time marched on and, inexplicably, events continued to defy the preacher's prophecies. (He made so many you'd think he'd hit a few by chance.) Alice still attended church for social reasons, but started compromising the rules of obedience. If she had no social attachment to church members, she would have probably stopped attending. Although she didn't feel it was impossible for the prophecies to be fulfilled, it was becoming more of a myth, useful only to give the church distinction and definition and, by extension, self-importance.

Alice's commitment to this total organization was characterized by a structured explanation of reality, however unreal. The belief system was internally consistent — all possible challenges to its veractiy were not allowed to be considered, and therefore it was impossible to refute what was being taught. (All world events, for example, seemingly opposite to what was predicted were labeled "Satan's Deception" — and members were adjured "not to be deceived.") Only that which confirmed belief was considered true and admissible. The reasoning was circular, the system closed.

When the group's prophecies did not materialize, Alice's nature of commitment shifted. Adherence to church regulations for personal conduct became less important. The social benefits became the totality of her involvement.

CORPORATE CREDIBILITY

Strong commitment is important for corporate success. But commitment in the short term should never be bought by sacrificing credibility in the long term.

Credibility is an odd animal. You start out with it free; people generally believe what organizations say. Credibility is hard to lose; people are generally forgiving and allow companies margin for error.

Why then the frequency of credibility gaps? Bureaucratic organizations seem bent on self-destruction, giving mixed signals and confusing employees. And once credibility is destroyed, it is difficult to rebuild; taken in once, people are wary of being taken in again. ("You fool me once," goes the adage, "shame on you. You fool me twice, shame on *me*.")

Organizational planning and goal-setting is an integral part of every professionally managed firm. In establishing objectives, inflated performance projections may give a quick fix — but the price is high and the penalty long. Overstatement and hyperbole may whip up enthusiasm among the troops and artificially strengthen the bond between employees and company — but only temporarily. In forecasting the future, wild optimism may lead to peak levels of commitment — but only for a limited period of time. In the long run, only *positive realism* can provide lasting commitment. When current projections and forecasts match future performance and results, the firm bond is permanently strengthened.

Exaggerated claims to the company are like narcotic drugs to people. They are habit forming and addicting; the more you use them, the more you need them. With every unfulfilled expectation, the dosage required for the next round jumps up, so that soon no claims can be large enough since the discount rate in employee's minds reaches 100 percent.

Unrealistic projections may feverishly excite the uninitiated, but they carry the seeds of future destruction. The withdrawal symptoms for employees overdosed on "hype" are protracted and painful. Even the truth, when it follows hype, is not believed. Executives find their power drained. A corporate credibility gap is most irksome to close.

"I was burned once," lamented a vice-president in a small growth company:

> I was the original True Believer when told that we would double in size next year, go public, and I could expect a 50 percent increase in pay plus cash for my options. "Bank on it, Bob," our CEO said with a knowing smile. Well, that's exactly what I did, I "mortgaged" on it, buying a house we could ill afford. You can guess what happened; the market flattened, the industry became highly competitive, we didn't grow at all much less double, and I was lucky my salary wasn't cut. We're still struggling with personal finances.

The executive, when pushed, admitted that his work performance had suffered as a result.

Commitment and cynicism, like love and hate, find close proximity around the circle of human emotions. The higher the commitment, the more potential energy available to generate cynicism. High commitment means high investment of ego, and high investment of ego turns sour quickly when insulted or ridiculed. Ease of movement around the circle depends on direction. Flowing from commitment to cynicism, from love to hate, is sadly simpler than trying to go in reverse. The trek back from cyncism to commitment is all uphill.

Growth projections are the easiest trigger for knocking out reality congruence. Everyone loves to hear that the company is moving forward, that sales are skyrocketing and profits soaring, and that promotions and raises will be handed out wholesale. Senior executives must avoid the temptation to tell employees what they want to hear. Stretching the truth is treacherous. Avoid the trap. The short-term fix is not worth the long-term sickness.

DISSONANCE AND THE NOISE IT MAKES

"Cognitive dissonance" is a powerful predictor of human behavior. Developed by Leon Festinger, the theory states that when a person's behavior does not reflect his beliefs, then "dissonance" must develop; and the only way the person can reduce this dissonance is to change his behavior or his beliefs.[3]

Recall the Alice Ritter case. It may have seemed odd that when the prophecies did not materialize on the date specified, her church, rather than admitting their mistake and disbanding with depression, did exactly the opposite. They went out proselytizing with elation! Their quest for new members, previously limited, became voracious. The behavior can be explained by the theory of cognitive dissonance (the example is similar to one in Festinger's book *When Prophecy Fails*[4]). Church members had made heavy psychic investment in those prophecies, and perhaps some financial ones as well. The unfulfilled predictions were dissonant with previous behavior. How to reduce this dissonance? One way was to *convince others* that the end-time was approaching. This restored confidence in their construction of reality.

The following example further illustrates cognitive dissonance (based on actual experiments). Suppose we divide some volunteer college students into two groups. Both groups watch the same very boring lecture on poor quality film. Each group was paid for participating in the experiment, one group 25¢, the other $25. The lecture drags on endlessly, the two hours seem like twenty. At its conclusion, a questionnaire checks the students' opinions of the lecture. Which group liked the lecture more; the group paid 25¢ or the group paid $25?

The theory of cognitive dissonance predicts the right answer. It says that the students being paid $25 are being compensated well for their suffering and therefore can express their true feelings that the lecture was horrendously boring. Those paid only 25¢, on the other hand, have just wasted half the evening for a miserable quarter — not even enough, having missed the school bus, to pay carfare home. Those facts create dissonance, and the only way to reduce this dissonance, since they cannot change their behavior, is to change their belief. Though the film was wretched and the lecture was worse, the poorly paid subjects begin to believe that it was not all that bad, that it had some interesting features, that one could learn something from it. Beliefs changed to match behavior. To seek reduction in dissonance is a very human desire.

Roger Albers was confronting classic cognitive dissonance caused by his not being promoted. He decided to take psychological retirement from his church. Whatever his reason, whether human frustration or reality realization, he started going outside, building an independent career, and diminishing his commitment to the ministry. Considering his firm and fierce beliefs, such behavior caused dissonance. The only way to reduce the dissonance was to change his beliefs. However subconsciously and however slowly, Roger Albers no longer saw God involved in the church.

Cognitive dissonance is equally effective in explaining behavior in the other direction — in staying with an organization when you know it is wrong.

REWARDS AND BELIEFS

Patrick Harris was the missionary leader in Australia of an American conservative church. He was Australian by birth but had been educated in the United States. He had been in his middle twenties when he became impressed by the church's unequivocal stand that the bible is the absolute Word of God, inspired in meaning and inerrant in text. No compromise here. No waffling. The logic was clean. If the bible was inspired by God, it could not include error. Harris had been searching for certainty, and nothing was better than this.

After joining the church, he studied for the ministry on a part-time basis, all the while working as a middle manager for a trading company. Upon ordination, Harris went full time to his calling. A handsome man with fine leadership qualities, he was the natural choice to lead the ministerial campaign in Australia, a country where American churches are not held in the highest esteem.

Harris was intelligent and honest, wholly dedicated to the Word of God. Braving the bricks of his fellow countrymen, surmounting difficulties too numerous to repeat, he built the church in Australia. From small struggling enclaves of believers, mostly poorly educated and improverished, Harris molded a strong organization, one with financial strength and community influence. Harris' own circumstances mirrored his church's. From living hand-to-mouth in those early years, relying on the food-offerings of parishoners for survival, Harris, now in his middle forties, was ensconced in a fine estate and driving a Jaguar.

Suddenly, the church's politics began to swing left and its doctrinal commitment began to fall down. The aging president of the church, always admiring educational excellence, had gathered around him a group of older men with distinctly liberal leanings. They had been trained in the leading seminaries of their day, when "higher biblical criticism" was the rage. To demythologize the bible, they were taught, is the highest good.

Success sometimes plants the seeds of its own destruction. Though founded on biblical inerrancy, the social success of the church made it more susceptible to mainline pressures. The younger, more conservative scholars, seeking to keep the president hewed to the biblical fidelity he once espoused, were viewed as threats to the emerging leadership.

The liberals baited their trap. The doctrinal test case was carefully chosen. The president, they knew, was under considerable personal pressure to relax a certain stricture. Once the conservatives were lined up against the change, the spring would be sprung.

The conspirators worked their mischievous plot. The young conservatives, blinded by resolute belief in the bible, found themselves lined up against the president. The liberals, having the president's ear and using the pretext of rebellion, expelled them en masse. It was, the older men boasted, a "surgical excision of cancer." The conservatives fought back, and thus justified the reason for expelling them in the first place.

It was a time of confusion in the church. Charges were trumped up and scapegoats created. Organizational control, more than doctrinal conviction, had taken charge of the church.

Those who believed the bible and taught true doctrine were labeled "unconverted infidels," "confusers of the brethren," and "agents of Satan." Various side groups broke off, vowing to maintain the "faith once delivered." But the splintering groups splintered and splintered again. None of them prospered. Many members faded away, not willing to associate with a church gone mad. No social club here; if biblical doctrines were going to be overturned, conscience demanded their leaving. It was traumatic, but there was no choice. One couldn't, they reasoned, remain in the church and give the veneer of support. Even the bible admonished believers to "abstain from all appearance of evil."

Pat Harris knew the game — the young conservatives were right, the bible was inerrant. But he also knew the score — the older liberals controlled the boss and they would soon control the church. Australia was a long way off, but in an electronic age, when the church grapevine is the overseas telephone, gossip travels with the speed of light.

Harris kept his profile low; he remained a good pastor and obeyed all directives from church headquarters. He did not stress the "new doctrines," but he did not oppose them either. He had many friends who had been forced out of the church. He knew it was a power struggle and the ones in were the ones wrong — wrong about doctrine and wrong about politics. He was sickened, but he remained. He was closing in on 50, with no other profession and no possible fallback. What else could he do?

The months passed and the intensity of propaganda increased. The old "enemies," though long gone, made convenient whipping boys. The new leadership pursued them, discovering plots, telling tales. The more dangers that could be invented, the more the need for martial law. The more the conservatives could be beaten, the easier to establish liberal control. So words of violence poured forth from church headquarters, the older scholars goading the fading president. It was the ultimate power play. Once he was gone, they had it all. All the political power, for sure; and, without the bible in their way, the really big prize: all the doctrinal power.

Pat continued in the same vein: reading the propaganda, distributing the new literature, preaching the new way, supporting the church. The new church leaders lauded Harris for his loyalty, the new touchstone of the new truth. He received additional benefits from public praise to personal salary. He was asked to travel widely, representing the collective leadership.

Church pronouncements kept vilifying the "apostates," and Pat kept reading the absurd attacks. He was a bulwark and the members stayed. But what Pat Harris was doing Pat Harris didn't believe.

Yet the more he did it, the more he believed it.

After a time, Harris began to "see" that the bible did have some error — God didn't dictate every word to angels, did He? Men are fallible, aren't they? Things written in the first century could hardly be required to be relevant in the twentieth! It was a blessing from God, Green concluded, to "rewash" the church!

And the new leaders of the church? Well, the doctrinal changes they were making were very scholarly, very erudite. Harris could feel more intellectual. And the new code of conduct was more flexible, more humane, more to the liking of the people. New freedoms of behavior were permitted. The church, he mused, should be able to attract more members now. Furthermore, there was peace in the church — no one dared oppose oligarchical rule — and than meant financial stability for the ministry in general and for himself in particular. Funny thing, a person's belief system.

Cognitive dissonance was well at work. Harris' behavior — supporting the church in its doctrinal shift and human callousness — was dissonant with his belief. Yet he couldn't change his behavior. His life-style was set; his kids were in private school; his elderly parents were sick — he was trapped. He made excuses for himself in those early months of turmoil. Soon he would quit. Soon he would learn some outside trade. Soon he would tell the truth. But he lived in the same house, drove the same car, sent his kids to the same school — and "soon" never came.

But what did come, and admittedly it took some time, was change in belief. Harris was just human, no better and no worse than most of us, and he could not withstand the relentless pressures of dissonance, so unforgiving, so subtle.

EMOTIONAL CONDITIONING

In Fred Wagner's church, "Moral Wholeness" was the highest good; the central doctrine of the insular church involved "coming out of the world and being separate." Members were told regularly that if they were a success in this world, they were in jeopardy of losing out in the next. All the riches of the earth, they were taught, are not worth a small corner of heaven. "Don't trade in a jewel for a jalopy," went the admonishment. "A bird in the hand is *not* worth a billion in the bush" was a common church proverb.

Fred, however, had reached a crossroads in his life. He felt a strong need to build something on his own. For the past 15 years he had been a dutiful, though not outstanding, manager in a medical supply company. Now Fred was ready to make his big move. It had been in serious planning for almost a year. He along with two associates were about to start a new company.

Conversations about striking out on their own had been going on for over two years, but Fred had always reneged when it came time to take the plunge. What his friends did not understand was that Fred was trying to reconcile being a success in the world with being a success in the world to come.

Encouraged by his friends, though with continuing ambivalence, Fred agreed to form a corporation, and the three partners each contributed equally to its initial capitalization. Fred's $7,000 represented a good chunk of his life savings. After signing the documents, Fred left for his church's annual religious rejuvenation.

Every spring the church conducted a three-day retreat during which members were to recommit themselves to God and to church. Fred usually attended in the Colorado Rockies, and had been doing so for the better part of a decade. The retreat involved attending services and seminars as well as participating in small-group prayer meetings. The three days were packed full: singing religious hymns around great outdoor bonfires; listening to powerful sermons on the curses of wickedness and the blessings of obedience; sharing trials and troubles, hopes and dreams, with members from far-off places.

When Fred returned from Colorado, he immediately went to his business associates and informed them that he could not go through with their plan. They were astounded. How could Fred have been flipped over like a flapjack? Fred stated that he understood expenses had been incurred and that he would bear his fair share. He apologized but said there was no other way.

Fred underwent a fervent experience in the Rockies that renewed emotional ties with his religious group. Seeing old friends, visiting old places, singing old songs, and talking about old ideals elicited responses in him that were as predictable as saliva drooling from the mouths of Pavlov's dogs. From the perspective of the church, Fred had been renewed; from the perspective of his friends, Fred had been had.

CORPORATE EMOTIONS

We accept the emotional connection between churches and believers. But between corporations and employees? Does it make sense for profit-making companies to play with "feelings"?

"When I left the firm, I never thought I'd ever look back with nostalgia. I was wrong. You can't work some place for five years and not leave some piece of your heart there." So said an executive who had upgraded himself with a bigger position at a rival company — and his attitude echoes the feelings of many employees toward their former firms.

Emotions, almost by definition, are not logical; as such their power to build commitment is enormous. The affective ties between members and groups, employees and companies, should not be underestimated — irrespective of the nature of the organization. Some of the deepest links that bind individuals to institutions are not subject to rational analysis, but are born and bred in the subconscious passions of the human mind.

While closed systems and total organizations can be particularly effective in engendering and rekindling emotive feelings, commitment to all forms of organizations have an affective component. Many companies have constructed, often inadvertently, some of the essence of total organizations. "When someone left the firm," observed a middle manager in a major oil company, "we felt as though he or she had died. This was the only place to be. How could anyone leave?"

Group experiences are especially conducive for building emotional linkage. Weekend retreats for planning strategies, joint social activities, company-sponsored athletic events are the kinds of experiences that generate warm feelings among personnel.

A firm that wants to keep key people committed is wise to build a reservoir of intense, positive organizational experiences. The role that emotional conditioning plays in firm bonding should be an integral part of any human resource strategy.

ROLE STRAIN: ENOUGH IS ENOUGH

Daniel Hardy, the person, was being invaded; he was fighting an all-out, three-front war. Everything that was important to him was under assault. His life was coming apart.

For 18 years Hardy personified the ideal minister in his closed-system church. He was well educated and gave intellectually sound and emotionally inspiring sermons. He was a family man whose beautiful wife, Angie, was wholly supportive of his work. He was a man of high value and clear purpose.

It all began with a transfer of assignment. For whatever reason, his church's mission department transferred Hardy to the Appalachians, an area that did not appreciate his polished, professional style. For the first time in his ministry, Hardy found himself being compared unfavorably with other ministers who had been in the same area previously.

Soon some negative feedback began working its way back from the congregation to church headquarters, through the normal channels of "official inspection visits" and the more effective channels of gossip and grapevine. Church member dissatisfaction was the kiss of death. The church prided itself on pastoral service and Dan Hardy was doing a nosedive. After six months of struggle, Hardy concluded that he was experiencing something new: failure.

"The boy is just not one of us folks," mused one oldtime member, a widow in her late fifties. "He cares for those books of his more than he cares for the flock. Always studying something. Now our Mr. Fuller, he was a real pastor. No fancy speaking, mind you. Just a lot of caring. Why he'd love to come by and spend the afternoon with me."

Hardy's wife was soon affected. Angie tried to be a good pastor's wife, but these people didn't relate to her either, and the feeling, she had to admit, was mutual. "Uppity Angie" was what they called her, and the day she heard the nickname being whispered, she knew it was over.

Angie no longer had an identity. Previously she had seen herself largely as a support for her husband's ministry; but given its current state, there was little to uphold. His failure meant her failure, if only by default. But fail was something she had never done, and success was not something she could live without.

Reentering the job market was easy. Angie's buoyant personality, administrative skills, and, yes, her coquettish attractiveness, quickly landed her a position as an executive assistant. Her boss was the regional manager of a Fortune 500 company; he ran a division with 3,500 employees and exuded confidence and power. Angie was a fast study and soon had wide latitude. Though she was "staff" on the formal organization chart, everybody knew that if you wanted something done, "Angie's the One." The transition was almost instant. This "minister's wife" no longer lived for her husband; she now lived for her work.

Hardy's marriage deteriorated in stages. Angie's long hours at the office was the start. Dinner away from home became the rule, not the exception. Hardy, troubled by his own career crackup, grew jealous of his wife's progress. The words he used on occasion, once when she didn't return until 3:00 A.M., were inflammatory and exacerbated the growing problem in their relationship. The end of their marriage occurred almost a year to the day after Angie had begun her new career and new life.

First the career went — then the marriage — now the values. The granite-like commitment Hardy had to his church and its doctrines began crumbling. Although he gave the pretense of remaining loyal to his organization and true to his beliefs — he was not as marketable as his wife — his personal life skidded in virtually every area of church teaching.

Hardy's disintegration is easy to follow. First, "role strain" was the product of his insurmountable difficulty in fulfilling the set of expectations his Appalachian ministry demanded. Next, increasing stress catalyzed the break with Angie. Finally, both the role strain and the divorce eroded commitment. His goals were now simple: a regular paycheck and not getting caught in the sack.

The variable "support" also figures in Hardy's change. Enjoying organizational, congregational, and spousal support in performance of his responsibilities, his commitment thrived. When support faltered, so did commitment. A lower level of "task identification" with the Applachian ministry also undermined his church attachment.

For most people, Hardy's commitment disintegration would lead to one of two paths. Either he would try to maintain his current mode of living (continuing to conceal his vast variance from church canon), or he would resign and start life anew. Another track, however, was chosen by Dan Hardy.

What triggered the reaction we cannot know. Some would say unbearable guilt; others would see God's intervention. Proponents of cognitive dissonance would see its subconscious imprint. But whatever the cause, it unleashed a whirlwind.

Hardy embarked on a violent campaign denouncing the evils in society. He became especially vitriolic about equal rights for women and what he claimed was the resultant destruction of the family. Hardy even attacked other ministers in his own church. A self-styled vigilante, he took to exposing those not absolutely adhering to all tenets of church teaching. He appointed himself doctrinal detective, ferreting out heresy or compromise; and then as jury and judge, he pressured the church hierarchy to mete out punishment swift and sure. Human weakness meant nothing to Hardy; strict obedience and "moral purity" were all that counted. Joe McCarthy never got a communist as well as Dan Hardy got a heretic. Admired by zealots and feared by everyone, Dan Hardy was loved, sadly, by no one.

What is it about organizations that gives the nod to witch hunters and reactionaries? "Crusading conservatives" generally have an easier time than "flaming liberals," even though both are usually just as wrong intellectually and equally as harmful morally. The answer lies in the assumption of independent existence that organizations assume, and in the natural tendency for hierarchies to secure their own continuance. Absolute truth or moral rectitude is completely irrelevant here. What counts is sustenance and support for the existing order.

CORPORATE CONFLICT

Role strain in companies arrives in different guises. There is the difficulty an individual has in living up to the organization's expectations. There is the classic balancing act between work and family. There is also the tradeoff between vocation and avocation, between how a person makes a living and how a person wants to live.

"The best law firms in town had no provisions for maternity," complained a brilliant beginning female attorney who wanted to have a child in a few years.

> If I started with them and became pregnant, I'd have to leave. I want to build a solid career, not skip around. But I also want to be a mother. I decided to go second class for the law firm, but it has always bugged me.

"They light you up at both ends around here," explained a Ph. D. in molecular biology who was a five-year veteran of the R & D wars in a major pharmaceutical company.

They burn you up and throw you away. The "business of science," I've come to learn, is very different from "science." We're subjected to intense and contradictory demands. On the one hand, we must be super efficient. Not a penny wasted. On the other hand, God help us if a competitor beats us to a breakthrough.

"Studying philosophy is where I'm at," explained a scholarly thirtyish man who was content to remain a file clerk.

I cannot divide my psychic energy. Either I move up in the business world and make my career my life, or I keep a simple job to pay the bills and devote myself wholeheartedly to my studies. I chose the latter. Perhaps I'll write a book some day. It doesn't matter. I'm doing what I want.

"They wanted me out, but they couldn't fire me," lamented a recently retired executive from a large package goods company.

The president and I came out of marketing together — and he wouldn't stand for it. The only way to shake me off was to get me to request "early retirement." So they programmed me to fail. Every task I was given was the tough one. They overloaded me. It was when they dumped on me the low-market share lemon that I knew what their game was.

"Why are they forcing me to learn these damn computers?" asked an executive who kept requesting anonymity several times after we assured him that no real names would be used and all companies would be disguised.

I'm no damn good with numbers. I'm a field man. I'm a troubleshooter. Action's my game. I can make things happen, but I can't write reports. Why don't they see that? I don't care what the computer can do, it can't make things happen.

For most there is an optimum level of role strain. At very high and very low levels, the tension is inappropriate and commitment is sabotaged. Most employees want to be challenged. Growth comes from some pain.

BETTING ON THE FIRM TO WIN, PLACE, AND SHOW

Investments come in various forms — time, effort and ego are each as important as money, perhaps more so.

Richard Roland had two ambitions: he sought to control the crusade against nuclear power and he craved the finest material possessions.

Of these aspirations, he had made substantial progress in fulfilling the first — he was a long-time leader in the antinuclear movement. But the second was totally unfulfilled — the middle income life-style could never satisfy his gnawing appetite, and frustration was causing a constant boil.

Undoubtedly, Roland's boisterous personality would have served him well in a successful sales career, but he had dedicated his life to radical politics. Trained in the antiwar movement of 1960s, Roland had been pursuing power in left-wing causes for close to two decades. For the past eight of those years he had set himself against the bomb. The organizations he joined he soon wanted to run. He thought he knew what to do and what would work, and he devoted all his time to establishing his position.

Though Roland's external political skills were debatable, his internal ones were not. Three years ago he became managing director of NO-NUKES (there were several celebrities with higher though titular positions). In running the group, Roland used the cosmetics of democracy to enforce his rule of rigidity — but the system was as closed and the organization as total as any of the religious sects he regularly ridiculed.

Throughout the years, Roland had opportunities to develop potentially profitable interests outside the movements, but had not pursued any of them. Perhaps his lack of pursuit could be explained by his singleminded commitment to the antinuclear cause, but a more likely explanation was basic laziness. While Roland wanted material reward, he would not work too hard to get it.

So Roland had invested the entirety of his efforts within the movement. He had not hedged his bets. Everything he had was placed on attaining his goals within this one organization. All his bets were riding on the nose of this one horse. His contacts on the outside were nil. He was betting nothing on the side.

Roland was a zealot but not a fool. What made his strategy particularly vulnerable was that the future success of NO-NUKES was by no means guaranteed. Recent years had brought internal strife and schism, and the antinuclear pie had been already carved up into several pieces. Each time he passed up another outside chance at making money, he in effect placed another side bet on NO-NUKES.

Roland became intensely jealous when he saw his aides build and maintain outside financial interests. Particularly galling was watching the NO-NUKES operations director build a successful business in real estate. (The "Op D" was in fact his chief rival in the organization; there were philosophical differences between the two men on policy and governance, and there was still bitterness regarding Roland's taking the top spot with his tactless power play.) Seeing someone who was succeeding in hedging his bets infuriated Roland, and he took his best shots trying to stop the fellow from "polluting the purity" of the organization's mission.

OUTLAWING SIDE BETS

"Side bets" are the curse of closed systems, an anathema to total organizations, the antithesis of complete commitment.[2] The more one wages *off* the center, the weaker the firm bond *in* the center. The more an employee has tied up in the organization — time, effort, money — the more committed the employee will have to be. Side bets build independence; center bets strengthen dependence.

It is said in the book of Matthew that "where your treasure is, there will your heart be also." This illustrates the principle of "where one bets," and the importance, from the company's viewpoint, of employees placing all their side bets on the firm.

Strengthening the commitment of members is an important goal of organizations. Accomplishing this, however, is no easy task. A common strategy is to be sure that no member hedging takes place. Years of sacrifice and investment, during which all side bets are placed on the company, lock in personnel commitment. In most cases, if the policy can be enforced, it is successful.

"We have a strict code against our employees earning any outside income," explained the vice-president of personnel of a large distribution company.

> We even require annual affidavits from our senior managers. In our business, since we handle several thousand products, it is easy for conflicts of interest to arise if our people begin getting involved with outside interests. We even have restrictions on spouses.

Conflicts of interests are a real (and often complicated) issue. But the policy as stated certainly eliminates any side betting action as well. Commitment to the company is strengthened whenever betting on the side can be eliminated.

ENCOURAGING CENTER BETS

Companies should develop healthy mechanisms to obtain and build employee commitment. Encouraging investment of employee time, energy, and money in the company is critical. The more financial and psychic bets that are placed on the company, the more an individual will concentrate on corporate purposes.

Stock option plans, for example, can be made so attractive that employees are compelled to participate. Some companies will match employee contributions dollar for dollar up to some limit; others will offer substantial discounts below market value. In each case, there may be tax benefits increasing the incentive. The more valuable the employee, the more attractive the package. (To lock up key executives, many companies now use so-called "golden handcuffs". The financial rewards are substantial, but severe penalties are exacted for leaving.)

Personal security is probably the most effective means to smother side betting. If employees feel at all uncertain about their jobs, they are more likely to be receptive to investment opportunities outside. If they are completely confident in their positions, they won't give a second look. A good retirement program is an important company ally.

New technologies bring new issues. The development of a cottage industry in software writing on home computers poses some difficult policy problems for companies employing programmers. Can employees writing at work for the business also write at home for themselves? What happens if they begin to sell their software programs and accrue personal profits? Too fast of an answer in the negative will chase away the best and the brightest.

Again, all things have limits. If pushed too hard to make investments in the firm, many employees will resist. Employee center bets should be earned through organizational responsibility.

CHAPTER FIVE

COMMITMENT CONSTRUCT: MODELING THE BOND

We come to the fulcrum of the book, the pivot of the story. In the first four chapters we used case histories to develop understanding of commitment. The approach was *inductive*. Now we flip over. In the last four chapters we use our understanding of commitment to analyze case histories. The approach will be *deductive*. The key is a commitment model, which will be built in this chapter.

Up to now, we've employed personal examples to illustrate the formation or deterioration of commitment, looking through our "special lens" of total organizations to magnify all organizations. In Chapter 1 we defined commitment as the link between personal meaning and organizational mission. In Chapter 2 we explored personal factors influencing commitment, highlighting some individual meaning variables. In Chapter 3 we probed organizational factors affecting commitment, emphasizing some collective mission variables. In Chapter 4 we developed interactional factors affecting commitment (based on an individual's experience in the organization), stressing some meaning/mission-related variables.

In this chapter we construct a model for commitment. Some parts of the model will be old friends; other parts will be new. We may put you through a bit of a mental workout, but it will be well worth your effort.

MODELS: WHY USE THEM?

Understanding commitment requires recognizing its components. Once we have the essential pieces we can begin building a model. The model is being constructed inductively and applied deductively. First, the component pieces are found and formed from case histories and research literature. Then, the model is used to describe, discern, and predict how commitment works in diverse organizational settings and personal situations.

Models are everywhere. They are used on personal computer spreadsheets and for portraying biochemical molecules. Aeronautical engineers test new aircraft designs with numercial models on super-computers just as automotive engineers test new car designs with clay models in wind tunnels. For all their sophistication, models are just simplified versions of what really exists. Models, is short, *represent* reality; they are *not* reality.

Models are reduction tools. They boil down what would otherwise be an unmanageable and unintelligible mass of data to manageable and in-telligible proportions. Models can capture intuitive understanding by highlighting the essential signal and ignoring the masking noise. Yet models must be kept honest; they must be subjected to verification. Real-world meaning is the touchstone. Just as models are needed to ascertain the relevance of data and events, data and events are needed to maintain the relevance of models. The process is recursive, each pole critical.

An analogy may help. Models may be compared to nets that are dragged through oceans of fish. Only fish of a certain size are caught; the vast majority pass through untouched and unnoticed. The nets, in the analogy, are the models, and the fish are the data. These data are not wholly passive in the process; imagine — and here the analogy strains — the fish modifying the netting as they pass through, so that on subsequent passes the model-net becomes structurally improved and will thereby catch even more relevant data-fish.

The ultimate proof of a model is its applicability, its capacity to describe and predict. How accurately is reality portrayed? How faithfully are future events projected? There is a tradeoff here, and a test. A model must produce more explanatory elegance and predictive power than it gives up in lost detail and ignored data. In this chapter we model commitment; the application is the entirety of the book.

COMMITMENT STRENGTH TYPES

Commitment in total organizations is neither constant nor consistent. In fact, the pure-form magnification reveals more levels and nuances than can be appreciated in normal organizations. Figure 5.1 presents six types of commitment strength. They are arrayed linearly in de-scending order.

Partisans radiate maximum commitment. These are dedicated and persistent, the proselytizers, the backbone of total organizations. Un-shakable in mind and deed, zealous in fervor and intensity, they are ready to sacrifice their lives, figuratively or even literally, for the assumed good of the organization. Wholehearted belief, irrespective of personal benefit, is the key characteristic of a partisan. (There is high correlation between our "partisan" and Eric Hoffer's "true beliver.")

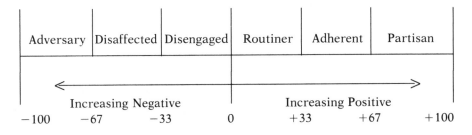

FIGURE 5.1 COMMITMENT STRENGTH TYPES

Adherents are motivated to promote and protect the organization. Their motivation is typically a blend of internal and external elements. They behave proactively to support the system. Positive organizational action is important to them, although the basis of the importance is often enlightened self-interest. Building the organization for personal reward is the essence of an adherent.

Routiners are a shade more positive than neutral, requiring direct external motivation to fulfill organizational expectations. Work is done but action is passive, and consequences are of little personal value. Keeping the status quo is all a routiner wants.

Disengageds are psychologically retired, slightly more negative than neutral. Jobs are done and tasks are accomplished, but barely within the allowable range of organizational acceptability. There is no personal interest. Their passive presence can produce a deleterious effect on other workers, depressing motivation and dedication. Dragging an organization down is the contribution of the disengaged.

Disaffecteds may or may not be connected with the organization. If they departed, it was probably due to some disparity between personal expectations and organizational realities. Whether within or without the organization, they work to hinder or destroy it, especially when doing so will serve their own benefit. Personal profit from hurting an organization is what the disaffected seeks.

Adversaries are energetic foes of the organization, operating actively and maliciously either from inside or outside. They seek, at the least, dramatic change in the organization's goals, policies, structure, or leadership, and often nothing less than the overthrow of the system will suffice. Destroying an organization, irrespective of personal benefit, is the mission of an adversary.

These six types of commitment strengths reflect varying degrees of willingness to exert personal effort to support (or hinder) organizational goals.[1]

Organizational commitment profiles representing the frequency of members/employees in each commitment type can be drawn. Figures 5.2 to 5.7 present sample profiles for vibrant total

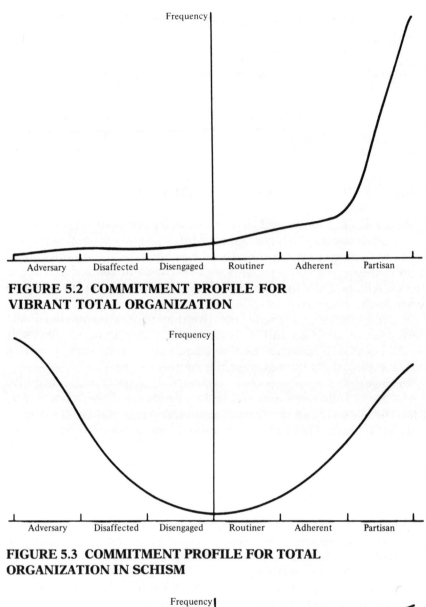

FIGURE 5.2 COMMITMENT PROFILE FOR VIBRANT TOTAL ORGANIZATION

FIGURE 5.3 COMMITMENT PROFILE FOR TOTAL ORGANIZATION IN SCHISM

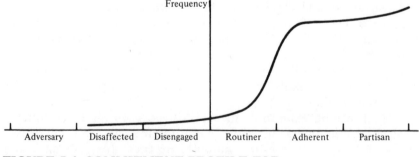

FIGURE 5.4 COMMITMENT PROFILE FOR SAMPLE START-UP COMPANY

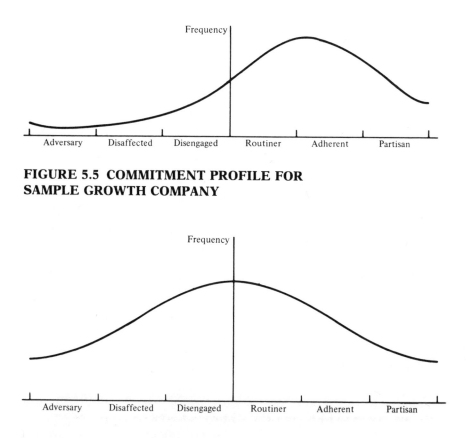

**FIGURE 5.5 COMMITMENT PROFILE FOR
SAMPLE GROWTH COMPANY**

**FIGURE 5.6 COMMITMENT PROFILE FOR
SAMPLE MATURE COMPANY**

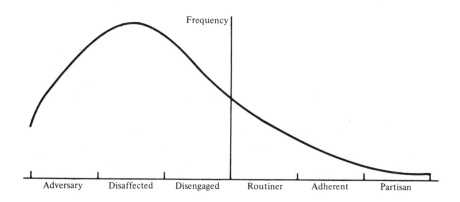

**FIGURE 5.7 COMMITMENT PROFILE FOR
SAMPLE BANKRUPT COMPANY**

organizations; total organizations in schism; start-up companies; growth companies; mature companies; and bankrupt companies.

COMMITMENT STYLE I: CORE

Our commitment model postulates three styles of commitment strength: core, calculative, and cog (Figure 5.8).[2]

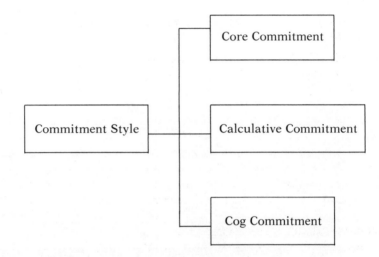

FIGURE 5.8 STYLES OF COMMITMENT STRENGTH

Core Commitment involves profound personal belief in organizational goals and their melding into one's own identity. It means that an individual wholly accepts organizational ideals and values and has internalized them. When the aims and mission of the group have been incorporated into a person's psyche, we call this commitment "core positive" — core(+). Such a person will adopt and reflect the style of the organization, the culture of the company, and the attitude of the group. An individual with core(+) commitment has the organization's welfare at heart; building the institution is the key consideration — perhaps even the starting point — in deciding general behavior and specific action. (Recall the Phillip Walker real estate case, Chapter 1; Walker's desire to help Phiro & Daniels become a premier real estate firm reflects core(+) commitment.)

"Core negative" — core(−) — commitment is present whenever an individual is an active enemy of the organization. The person is staunchly opposed to the group's mission and values, and this adversarial position is the central purpose of life. A true core(−) seeks to destroy the organization irrespective of personal gain. (We concentrate on core(+)s; core(−)s are beyond our scope.)

COMMITMENT STYLE II: CALCULATIVE

Calculative Commitment starts with the individual, not the organization. The prime consideration is personal gain. How effectively are one's total needs being satisfied? How does the individual benefit from the organization, or from a position in the organization? How much is one making — "making" in the broadest sense? What has the company done for me lately? Calculations, measurements, are important here. What is one's total net income — financial and psychic, now and in the future? Comparisons are part of the picture. The total net income one could derive elsewhere is determined and comparisons are made. (Walker's projecting the income he would receive as sales manager versus salesman is illustrative of the analysis involved in calculative commitment.)

"Calculative negative" — calculative(−) — occurs when it is in one's best interests to work against the organization. The motivation is purely personal benefit, meaning or conviction is completely irrelevant. Examples of calculative(−) include selling stocks short, spreading bad rumors about a love-rival, and mercenaries/bounty hunters/hired killers. (Note that we will use "core" and "calculative" without "+" or "−" to mean positive.)

COMMITMENT STYLE III: COG

Cog Commitment is present in an individual when work is seen only as a necessary routine. Little meaning is present, little emotion is felt. In cog(+) commitment, the teeth of the personal-organizational gears are normally engaged, although it is the organization that provides the energy for motion. The job gets done, but externals are necessary for motivation.

"Cog negative" — cog(−) — occurs when the individual hopes that the teeth of the personal-organizational gears are in contact a minimum amount of time. That person will try to limit activities with the group. When engagement is forced, cynical comments about the organization are common. The individual may be present physically but is absent mentally.

THE PARALLEL UNIVERSE

Though we are presenting commitment as one-dimensional and flat, it is more properly portrayed as two-dimensional and folded. The continuum of commitment strength is like a parallel universe. Low, medium, and high levels of commitment in the positive direction all have mirrors in the negative (Figure 5.9). Although emphasis in this book will be on individuals with commitment strength measures of about −30 to +100 (see Figure 5.1), it is instructive to view the complete picture.

	Commitment Style		
	Core	Calculative	Cog
+	Partisan	Adherent	Routiner
−	Adversary	Disaffected	Disengaged

Commitment Valence

FIGURE 5.9 PARALLELISM OF COMMITMENT STYLES

In fact, it is often a quick crawl through a "worm hole" to get to a corresponding commitment style of equal intensity, but opposite force. Thus at the extreme ends of the scale, Sauls become Pauls, and Vaders cross over to the "dark side" (and perhaps even return to "Jedi heaven" in the end). Crossovers at lower levels of commitment strength are also common. A comprehensive diagram — integrating commitment types, styles, and strength measure — is provided in Figure 5.10.

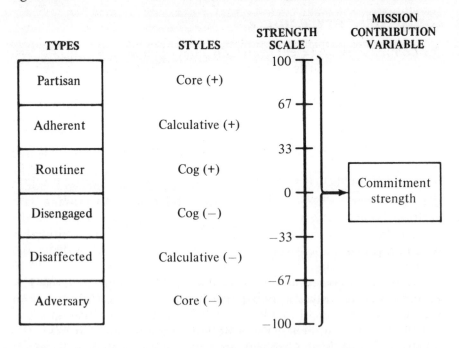

FIGURE 5-10 COMMITMENT TYPES, STYLES AND STRENGTH

Aspects of core, calculative, and cog commitment can be found in most every individual. One style, however, usually dominates. This is especially true with respect to an individual's commitment style in response to organizational mission. At different moments in one's career with an organization, the style of commitment may shift. To cross the boundary into a new predominant style is often not without trauma. Consider the case of William Blanchard.

FROM CORE TO CALCULATIVE

Bill Blanchard was 20 years old when he began attending a church-related college located in the Southeast. The church, an evangelical wing of a major Christian denomination, made major impact on Blanchard's spiritual beliefs and personal values. In recalling this period of his life, Blanchard talks of the profound personal happiness, the deeply satisfying comfort he experienced by being in harmony with the "Great Cosmic Purpose" that the church taught, and with the mission the church personified. The church and college provided a structured, sheltered environment that encompassed all aspects of thought and behavior. Blanchard's life became the church. All his friends were in the church and virtually everyone he knew believed the way he did.

After graduating from college, and following some missionary work in Africa, Blanchard was told he would be joining the faculty. Blanchard was overwhelmed with joy; he was thrilled by the opportunity to work full time in a cause that was shooting at the stars. Enhancing his sense of purpose, he believed that the appointment reflected the Will of God. It was the Almighty intervening actively in his life.

For five years Blanchard's identity was absorbed in the goals and objectives of the church and college. When they sought to raise $2 million in a national telethon, he was up for 48 straight hours organizing the students, answering the telephones, and praying with petitioners. When he was asked to replace the coordinator for the Alaskan revival two days later, he was on the next plane, calling his wife back home only after he landed in Anchorage. She, a dedicated member, was proud.

Blanchard was a partisan, a "true believer." Decision making in all important areas had been surrendered to his organization and its transcendent mission. Blanchard's commitment was exclusively core.[3] Career alternatives were not desired, not considered, not even imagined. He made no calculations. Life was the church, its goals his goals, its values his values. To live was to live for the organization; to be fulfilled was to fulfill organizational expectations. Sure he was expecting his reward at the "rapture of the saints"; but dedication to the group now, even more than personal gain then, was his driving motivation.

One day, however, the calculations began. Blanchard was hard pressed to remember when the change began. It was with some sadness that he recalled first considering the numbers; for in many ways calculating commitment meant departing Eden.

"I woke up to a more objective view of the church," Blanchard said with some nostalgia.

> I felt it legitimate to evaluate its strengths and weaknesses. I never questioned our leadership until they announced that our annual telethon had exceeded expectations and raised over $3 million. Well, I was in charge of tabulations. I *knew* we had promises of only $1 million and much of that shakey — at best well short of the $2 million target. Sure there were "reasons," as I tried to convince myself. But frankly it was doing the "evaluation" much more than discovering the "weakness" that caused my change. Personal appraisal, independent thinking — that was the profound part. In order for this to occur, I had to project some distance and the organization had to lose its halo.

For a number of years after this awakening Blanchard remained with the college. However, his commitment type began a steady shift from partisan to adherent. A transformation was occurring, no less dramatic because it was slow. Apparent to no one, the change was irresistible.

Blanchard still identified with many of the values espoused by the church. The importance of family cohesion, for example, was a prime principle of life and he shook his head at the high percentage of divorces among friends who had quit. The bible, he knew, was wholly inspired, the inerrant word of God. Nonetheless, Blanchard became ever more calculative, ever more evaluative in his interaction with the organization.

For the first time he began to compare financial opportunities that might be available to him on the outside. No quick moves were made but numbers were being crunched. He began to weigh the "psychic income" derived from his present position with other alternatives. What would be wrong with learning about insurance or real estate, just to be safe? Although core commitment had not vanished, calculative commitment was the rising tide.

There is inherent conflict between core and calculative commitment, and William Blanchard personifies it. His case illustrates the shift that often occurs in the organizational careers of many individuals. The fact that his organization was religious and that his allegiance was fervent only magnifies the normal relationship between individual and institution. Anyone familar with the corporate cultures of large companies can appreciate the parallelism.

In Blanchard's case, the commitment transition was one in which calculative became ever stronger in its perennial battle with core. More useful for companies is travel in the opposite direction, from calculative up to core. How such movement is stimulated, as we will see, is an important human resource strategy for organizational development.

THE ANTECEDENTS OF COMMITMENT

The commitment styles relating individuals to institutions were derived from personal histories. Whether core, calculative, or cog, each style is founded on past experience. There is a series of antecedents that lead to the growth and formation of each commitment mode.

In chapters 2, 3, and 4 we introduced three primary classes of antecedent variables (see Figure 5.11):

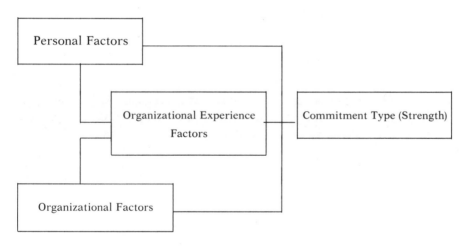

FIGURE 5.11 ANTECEDENTS OF COMMITMENT TYPE (AND STRENGTH)

Personal Factors: Individual needs as well as other personal variables influencing commitment, independent of any organizational association.

Organizational Factors: Key factors of the organization affecting member commitment, independent of any personal association.

Personal-Organization Factors: Those elements that emerge from the interactions between individual and organization, the experiences that develop from group association.

Let's review the variables in each of these classes in preparation for assembling the full model.

PERSONAL FACTORS (Figure 5.12)

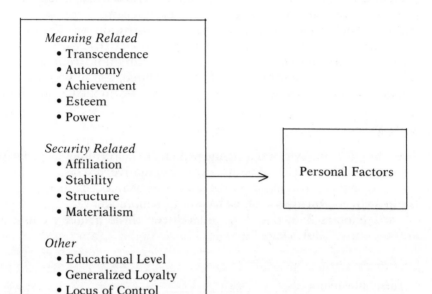

Meaning Related
- Transcendence
- Autonomy
- Achievement
- Esteem
- Power

Security Related
- Affiliation
- Stability
- Structure
- Materialism

Other
- Educational Level
- Generalized Loyalty
- Locus of Control

Personal Factors

FIGURE 5.12 PERSONAL FACTORS INFLUENCING COMMITMENT

Meaning-Related Variables

- *Transcendence:* Beyond self; interest in ultimates.
- *Autonomy:* Independence from authority.
- *Achievement:* Fulfillment in completing tasks.
- *Esteem:* Sense of personal worth.
- *Power:* Capacity to influence.

Security-Related Factors

- *Affiliation:* Sense of belonging and association.
- *Stability:* Comfort of routine and status quo.
- *Structure:* Dependency on others.
- *Materialism:* Money and wealth.

Other Personal Factors

- *Educational Level:* Amount and kind of schooling.
- *Generalized Loyalty:* Desire to belong; sense of duty.
- *Locus of Control:* How life directed — internally or externally.

ORGANIZATIONAL FACTORS (Figure 5.13)

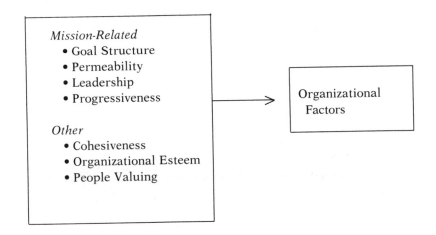

**FIGURE 5.13 ORGANIZATIONAL FACTORS
INFLUENCING COMMITMENT**

Mission-Related Factors

- *Goal Structure:* Group mission, purpose, grand design.
- *Permeability:* Degree of flow between group and society.
- *Leadership:* Nature and character of the boss.
- *Progressiveness:* Degree of forward motion; momentum.

Other Organizational Factors

- *Cohesiveness:* Group coherence; internal attachment.
- *Organizational Esteem:* Sense of group value and worth.
- *People Valuing:* Degree to which employees are treated as assets.

INTERACTIONAL FACTORS (Figure 5.14)

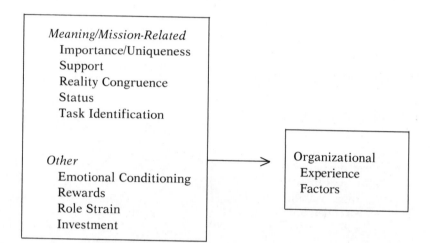

Meaning/Mission-Related
　Importance/Uniqueness
　Support
　Reality Congruence
　Status
　Task Identification

Other
　Emotional Conditioning
　Rewards
　Role Strain
　Investment

Organizational
Experience
Factors

FIGURE 5.14 ORGANIZATIONAL EXPERIENCE FACTORS INFLUENCING COMMITMENT

Meaning/Mission-Related Factors

- *Importance/Uniqueness:* Distinguishing the group from others.
- *Support:* Group sustenance and help.
- *Reality Congruence:* Confidence in group pronouncements.
- *Status:* Personal position in the group.
- *Task Identification:* Enjoyment of job.

Other Interactional Factors

- *Emotional Conditioning:* Affective, nonrational elements.
- *Rewards:* Psychic and financial benefits.
- *Role Strain:* Job-related stress.
- *Investment:* Degree of ego and effort sunk into the group.

THE PICTURE AND THE FRAME

These three classes of variables provide the framework for our examination of commitment. Each has been developed and amplified through the use of actual case histories, real people living in real organizations (with only the requisite masking to protect identities). We ask two questions: How do these factors determine the style and strength of commitment? And how can they be modified for the ultimate good of individuals and organizations?

We tighten our focus. Our primary interest is the nature of personal meaning and company mission — linking individuals to institutions in our definition of commitment. Thus we give certain variables special attention: meaning-related personal variables; mission-related organizational variables; and meaning/mission interactional variables (reflecting organizational experiences). Here we find the breeding ground of core commitment.

MODEL OUTPUT: MISSION CONTRIBUTION

Commitment strength is a central element determining how much an individual contributes to the goals or mission of an organization (See Figure 5.15). It can be assigned numerical weight (strength scale), a function of commitment type. Other things being equal, the more willing employees are to exert effort on behalf of a company, the more extensive their contribution will be.

Other things, however, are rarely equal. In Figure 5.15 we see that, in addition to commitment strength, elements such as individual ability/competence and role performance must also be considered.[4] ("Ability/competence" defines the general capacity and specific ability of people doing their jobs. "Role performance" refers to the vitality of individual responsibility and the extent to which it can be exercised.)

"Mission contribution" is the model's ultimate output. It is what all employees bring to the corporate table, what they deliver to the party. Mission contribution answers the critical question: *How much is an employee doing to help the organization?* The quality and quantity of work output is what the model assesses.

The mission contribution of an individual can be estimated in a quasinumerical manner. Simply multiply measures of the three critical variables: ability, commitment strength, and role performance (see Figure 5.15). The result is a reasonable estimate of employee contribution and worth.

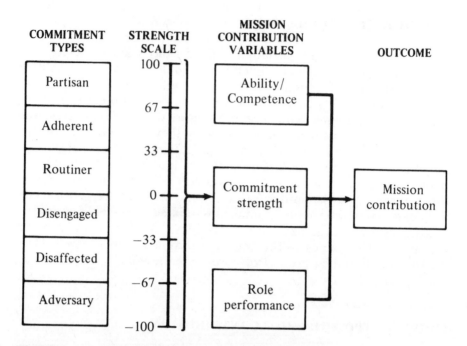

FIGURE 5-15 RELATIONSHIP OF COMMITMENT STRENGTH TO MISSION CONTRIBUTION

The model enables us to go further. We can estimate how well the entire organization is accomplishing its goals, the direction it's going, the energy it has. If we assume that the company is the sum total of all employees (in an atomistic sense), we can assess its total mission-directed strength by summing the mission contributions of all individuals interacting with the organization. Individuals with positive commitment strength will enhance this "mission contribution index"; individuals with negative commitment strength will depress the index.

In affecting performance of an organization as a whole, the commitment strength of senior management weighs most heavily. Nothing is as critical for the achievement of organizational goals than the commitment of the chief executive.

ASSEMBLING THE MODEL

The full commitment model is pieced together in Figure 5.16. The flow is from left to right. The three primary drivers, the energizing inputs to the model, are personal factors, organizational factors, and interactional factors (organizational experiences) — the first two are independent, the latter is the product of the previous two. All activate the model.

FIGURE 5.16 THE COMMITMENT MODEL: ANTECEDENTS, TYPES, STRENGTH, CONTRIBUTION VARIABLES AND OUTPUT

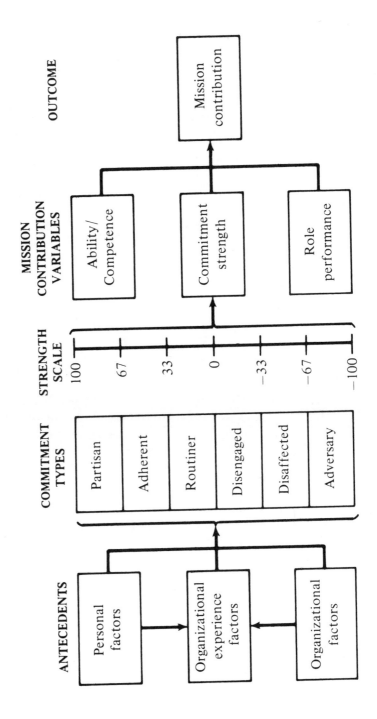

Commitment types form the central structure (or backbone) of the model, which, at its output end, yields "commitment strength." Commitment strength then generates the final output — mission contribution — with modulations by ability/competence and role performance.

The model is designed to represent reality and clarify thinking. We will use it as a template for understanding personal behavior and group events as individuals interact with institutions.

PART II
USING BUILDERS AND BREAKERS

CHAPTER SIX

COMMITMENT BUILDERS:
FORMING THE BOND

People make companies. Developing successful organizations requires forming substantial commitment. In our tightly wired world, where communications are swift and information is dense, people are more eager to learn and commitment is harder to build.

For a decade and a half, our culture has declared "open season" on major institutions, public and private. The media have researched and investigated, then exposed and publicized, numerous cases of government error and corporate scandal. America's trust in its institutions is not high, and building commitment between employees and companies is not easy.

Every manager in every company, regardless of size or industry, is faced with the same fundamental problem: how to motivate employees to work for the goals of the organization. It does little good for superiors to coerce subordinates through external direction. Such management would require constant supervision, which is inefficient and wasteful, and would clog the system in bureaucratic quicksand.

Personnel must be encouraged to accomplish organizational objectives through internal motivation. This is the only way to construct a self-generating system and achieve operating leverage. Internal motivation is a direct derivative of personnel commitment. Employees committed to the organization will fulfill their duties in the most efficient manner, requiring minimum controls and producing maximum results.

ORGANIZATION AND STRUCTURE

In Part I we built the model; in Part II we use the model. In Part I we worked inductively, constructing the model from case histories and personal examples; in Part II we work deductively, using the model to explain cases and understand examples.

In Part I we studied the nature of commitment by describing the concepts it links. We defined *commitment* as "the 'firm bond' between personal meaning and company mission." By understanding the essence of meaning and mission and the interaction between them, we sought understanding of commitment.

In Part II we apply what we learned in Part I. We use the commitment model as a template for exploring case examples in organizations, whether ideological or economic. By matching real-world events with theoretical constructs, we highlight relevant issues.

Out of the elements of personal meaning, organizational mission, and meaning/mission variables, we synthesize "builders" and "breakers," the compounds of commitment. Some compounds are relatively simple blends of inputs; others involve more complex chemical reactions. All, however, become primary prescriptions for building or breaking the firm bond.

Our specific objective is pragmatic: How to learn what strengthens and what weakens the firm bond, and how this knowledge can be applied for the management of companies and the helping of people.

In Chapter 6 we deduce from the model five *builders* of commitment, and show how each strengthens the firm bond in religious and business organizations. In Chapter 7 we deduce from the model five *breakers* of commitment, and show how each weakens the firm bond in religious and business organizations. In Chapter 8 we apply what we've learned about commitment for the welfare and benefit of *individuals*. In Chapter 9 we apply what we've learned about commitment for the productivity and benefit of *organizations*.

Our framework continues using total organizations as the substrate within which we dissect out and isolate commitment. In each chapter, we view through our "special lens," holding total organizations as the magnifying glass to highlight commitment in all organizations. The results, we trust, will be a richer understanding of the nature of commitment. In optimizing both personal fulfillment and organizational effectiveness, we strengthen the firm bond.

THE BUILDERS

We focus on five mechanisms for building commitment, five descriptions of an ideal relationship between organization and employee. There are others, of course, but these are some of the best. Each is powerful in its own right, and although in real organizations many would be working in concert, each will be discussed by itself (Table 6.1).

Antecedent elements from our commitment model (Chapter 5) are suggested in Table 6.2. These are the ingredients from which we distill

TABLE 6-1 Commitment Builders: Forming the Bond

Identification

Confidence

Momentum

Responsibility

Accomplishment

---

the five building compounds. Note that in accord with our definition of commitment (being the link between meaning and mission), most antecedents relate to these elements. (Others included are "catalysts" to the reactions.)

Identification: The melding of interests between person and group; the extension of personal ego to include organizational essence; the expansion of empirical self. Related concepts: meaningfulness, the sense that group membership is important in some larger (perhaps transcendent) way; participation, a personal stake in organizational ownership, whether literally or figuratively.

Confidence: The belief that the institution can be trusted in its stated policies and public pronouncements; a relaxed conviction that the organization is concerned with the welfare of the individual, that the group cares for the member. Related concepts: integrity, the honesty and fidelity of the organization; solidity, the consistency and reliability of the organization; fairness, the record of the organization in dealing evenhandedly without bias or prejudice.

Momentum: The forward motion of the organization; the energetic impulsion of growth and advancement; the sense of electricity and excitment generated by dynamic movement. Related concept: innovativeness, the pioneering of process and content, a venturing spirit, the intent to be in the vanguard.

Responsibility: The position of the individual in the organization; the degree of organizational trust given to the person; the expectational level of job performance. Related concepts: respect, the social standing of the individual; knowledge, how much information and feedback the organization gives the individual.

Accomplishment: The person's sense of reaching and attaining a broad and noteworthy goal, generally after significant effort. Related concept: fulfillment, the specific sense of task completion and a job well done.

TABLE 6-2 COMMITMENT BUILDERS: WHERE THEY COME FROM

Building Compounds	Elements/Factors (Antecedents)		
	Personal	Organizational	Organizational Experience
Identification	Transcendence Esteem Generalized Loyalty Materialism Education	Goal Structure Leadership Cohesiveness Organizational Esteem Permeability	Importance/Uniqueness Support Task Identification Investment Emotional Conditioning
Confidence	Affiliation Stability Structure Materialism	Leadership People Valuing	Reality Congruence Support Role Strain
Momentum	Achievement Esteem	Progressiveness Leadership	Reality Congruence Importance/Uniqueness
Responsibility	Power Autonomy Achievement Locus of Control Transcendence	Goal Structure Leadership Cohesiveness People Valuing	Support Status Rewards Role Strain
Accomplishment	Achievement Esteem Transcendence	Goal Structure Progressiveness Organizational Esteem	Rewards Importance/Uniqueness Task Identification

For each of the builders and breakers that follows, we use the same format. First we describe the concept, explaining its workings and import. Next we offer two case histories, one from religious organizations and one from business organizations. The purpose is to show the builder or breaker in live action, using the religious magnifying glass to see the business application.

IDENTIFICATION

What makes an individual allocate ego to an institution? Why do people exchange personal freedoms for organizational roles and exert private effort to achieve common objectives?

If the reasons found are ones of necessity, whether financial requirements or administered coercion, then the commitment can only be calculative or cog and the commitment can only be weak.

Most organizations have clusters of partisans and adherents. To build core commitment, to rouse partisans, it is necessary to form deep structural linkage between individual psyche and institutional essence. Individuals must extend themselves to embrace the organization. Identification is a merging of individual meaning and organization mission.

Identification comes in many forms. Most root for athletic teams, and when the spirit becomes strong, the rooting becomes strange. Sports fans in New York, for example, are not known for their lackadaisical reaction when their baseball or football teams blow a game; and soccer fans in South America have rioted in the wake of international championships. In the Olympics, Americans identify with American teams, as do citizens of other countries with their teams. In the best of circumstances, these feelings should not be unlike those between employees and companies.

Identification is amplified if importance or uniqueness is attributed to the organization. It is difficult to identify with an organization or corporation if the individual does not perceive the presence of something salient. Identification requires significance, a resonance with what's important to the person, even if that significance is simply to be on a winning team.

Identification is also related to participation, especially to a group that's cohesive. People will relate to an organization in direct proportion to their involvement. A high school student dropped from the football team will lose identification with the team and probably the school. Conversely, the surprise election of a new student to the governing council will increase that student's identification with the school.

When members identify with an organization's overall purposes, more is helped than just the organization. The process of transpersonal expansion, of sending ego out from self and joining with others, has an invigorating influence on the person. People fired up by causes are people energized for life.

WHAT AM I WORTH?

Bill Trillen was a proud man going down. A Midwesterner, he had worked for 20 years as a middle-line administrator in the personnel department of a medium-sized steel company. Steel had been the backbone of American industry and, though there would be peaks and valleys, one had never doubted the resilience of its strength and Bill had never doubted the permanence of his employment. But "Smokestack America," besieged by foreign competition and domestic recession, was becoming the "Rust Belt."

It was a month before his forty-fifth birthday that word came down. The plant was closing, and the company made it plain that it wasn't going to open again. "I was stunned, though not surprised," remembered Trillen. "We had been expecting it; but, somehow, like the death of an elderly parent, when it happens you feel so alone, so cold."

With a wife, three kids, and a mortgage, Bill hit the job market hard. Resumes were sent out by the boxload; calls and interviews were made at employment agencies without number. The toughest part, at least initially when self-respect was still high, was picking up his unemployment insurance. Waiting on those long lines was an embarrassment, not before others, but before himself. Bill was a rugged individualist, and prior to this he had never taken a handout.

Unemployment income ended too soon and job prospects were nowhere in sight. The number of resumes mailed hit 500; 12 form letter replies were all that came back — only two were promising but neither worked out. His wife, Judy, was forced into service. She took work as a waitress at a local bar. Bill buried his shame, but still they were living on dwindling savings and still there was no job to be found.

When the savings ran out, Bill became desperate. His oldest son, in his second year at a fine private college, was forced to transfer to a state school — and even then had to drop back to part time in order to work as a busboy full time. The mortgage payments were now six months overdue, and the bank was threatening to foreclose and repossess. If anything symbolized the meaning of Bill's life, it was the education of the children and the ownership of their home. Both were now severely endangered.

On the lowest day of Bill Trillen's life, when his wife was propositioned at the bar and the feared letter from the bank arrived, he pulled out his life insurance policy and checked the fine print. Suicide, it said, would invalidate the claim. He felt cheated by this trick and trapped on all sides.

He had never been a religious man, but with time on his hands, Bill had begun listening to some radio preachers while he filled out those endless mounds of futile applications. One evangelist intrigued him; he had a fascinating twist. This church emphasized the incredible spiritual potential of every human being through Jesus Christ and God's personal interest in everyone. Trials and tribulations, went their biblical view, are for our ultimate benefit. Spiritual growth takes place under physical pressure. It was for Bill Trillen a timely message.

Whether he was truly being "called," or whether just desperate without even suicide a way out, is not for debate. Whatever the driving motivation, the reportable behavior was clear. Bill joined the local congregation of the church. It was his last grasp at life.

In the church he found companionship, the support of a cohesive group, people who cared for his welfare — a vast difference from the cold rejections of hundreds of personnel directors. Though he could only donate the most modest money, he was dumbfounded that the church began giving him back far more money — enough, in fact, to begin meeting his mortgage payments. The bank agreed to postpone foreclosure, putting a moratorium on the payment of arrears — the timely intervention of influential members swaying the decision. Church members, though hardly better off themselves, began giving the Trillens little things to ease life. Some contributed food; others volunteered to fix appliances; still others organized a Sunday painting party to prepare the Trillen home for winter's onslaught.

Bill, in turn, volunteered for church work. Although he felt awkward, he surely felt thankful. He pulled together the church records, something that needed doing and something he was skilled to do. The simple job — it took about a week — gave Bill enormous satisfaction; it was his first work in 18 months, his first contribution to society.

The more he invested time, energy, and ego at the church, the more he came to internalize its teachings. He soon was helping the pastor with the logistics of speaking engagements, and he began counseling with prospective members. Within six months Bill was made a local deacon of the church, winning the honor and respect of the group.

In another six months, as the economy began to recover, a church member announced that his brother-in-law, who had a small manufacturing plant, needed an office manager. Bill applied, and radiating an inner confidence he had never before known, won the job with 20 percent more pay than he was expecting. Bill Trillen had renewed spirit in life; he had meaning and he was participating. Dignity and self-worth had returned.

MODELING BILL TRILLEN

The commitment model can be applied at three stages of the Trillen saga: the initial personnel job at the steel company; the dark period of unemployment; the revitalization period in the church. Each combines the elements of input in different ways. (Refer to Figures 5.11 through 5.14).

When Bill was working at the steel plant, all inputs to the model conspired to maximize commitment and generate full confidence — personal factors (affiliation, stability, structure, materialism, generalized loyalty); organizational factors (goal structure, cohesiveness, people valuing); and interactional factors (support, status, investment).

When Bill was unemployed, all elements were shattered: the stronger the commitment, the steeper the slide; the higher the confidence, the deeper the crash. Bill's whole personality, and the traditions of the company, combined to make the rejection stunning and the shame brutal. The humilation was so alien to Bill's esteem and locus of control that the role strain of an unsuccessful supplicant became more than he could bear.

When Bill joined the church, new organizational ties were created. The cohesiveness was strong; there was progressiveness; both self and organizational esteem were high; the goal structure was clear and the leadership was strong. Bill was rewarded for his efforts; he perceived significant importance in the church, had strong task identification and powerful emotional conditioning. Bill's commitment strength rose steadily — a healthy combination of both core and calculative — and so did his mission contribution to the church.

MONEY TALKS IN MANY LANGUAGES

Gary Roberts had been a consultant for Dan Nevin's engineering company for six years. Roberts's technical expertise had been responsible for several design breakthroughs that yielded substantial economic gains to the company. Nevin's ego, however, prohibited the acknowledgment of any genius other than his own, and therein lay a problem more serious than personality.

Roberts had always been compensated financially on a straight salary basis. Twice he had been given a year-end bonus, but those were exceptions — and they were based on overall company performance, not his own personal accomplishments. Sure, he received psychic satisfaction from his creative designs, but there was little praise and no recognition.

He liked working for the company, but had no great loyalty to it. Roberts would often listen to the high-note pitches of industry head-hunters, but nothing attractive had come along and there was no real hurry. The time had come, concluded Roberts one bright day, to be rewarded more adequately for his contributions.

Stories spread by senior members were not encouraging. All previous attempts to obtain profit-sharing or any progressive compensation based on performance had always been rebuffed by Nevin. Roberts knew this, but he also knew that his contributions far exceeded what anyone had ever made before. Nevin used to take pride in proclaiming that "I have created every innovative design in this company's history." Well, he couldn't say that anymore.

True, Nevin had founded the company, and was indeed brilliant, but the boss found it impossible to admit any creative contribution by anyone but himself. For this reason his company's business, always high quality, had leveled off in volume. Contracts were available, but just couldn't be fulfilled. A consulting business is directly related to the number of staff professionals, and many of his best had simply departed.

When Roberts met with Nevin he was hesitant.

> I wanted recognition, sure, especially some financial incentives for my developments. But, frankly, I didn't want a confrontation. I wasn't going to quit no matter what the outcome, and I'm a very bad bluffer. So the cards I held, walking in that day, could only win if the poker game was "Lo-Ball."

But Roberts found what he did not expect. Not only was Nevin listening to his request for "a piece of the action," but he was actively soliciting Roberts's opinion as to what would be fair. Suddenly the young engineer's commitment to the company soared. Maybe the rush of support resulted from Roberts's pleasant surprise, given his meager expectations for success. Maybe it was the dramatic increase in potential for financial gain. Maybe it was that the company was henceforth going to be partially his. Whatever the reason, the consequences of identification were enormous.

An introspective person, Roberts became preoccupied with understanding his change in attitude toward the company. His own surging level of core commitment fascinated him. It was with a flash of insight that Roberts realized what had happened.

> What is most critical in my increasing commitment to this company was that the president and founder, Nevin, has shown himself to be a leader who is responsive to me, to my personal needs. It's not just the money, it's what the money says. The financial benefits are important. But the symbolism

is more important than the numbers. I had always known Nevin to be committed to finding creative ways to solve technical problems in our consulting work, but what he has now demonstrated, in a significant and sincere way, is that he is committed to understanding my human problems, that he is progressive and willing to listen. I feel our future relationship will be based on constructing solutions to an ever-changing reality. I'm convinced that the company is moving in the right direction. We can attract and retain the best people. I can give deeper levels of commitment to a man and to a company that guarantees me that.

If a group member believes that leadership will make its best efforts to meet a changing set of higher-order, meaning-related needs, such a company will be viewed as solid soil in which to put down productive and permanent roots.

CONFIDENCE

Nothing promotes commitment more than confidence. Nothing holds the firm bond steadier more than the anchor of trust, the internal comfort of knowing that your organization will promise what is right and will do what it promises. Confidence underlies all elements of commitment and without it all else is for naught.

For a company to build confidence in its employees, it must be stable and consistent, predictable in its policies and fair in their administration. The company must treat all employees by the same standards. Nothing is more demoralizing that uneven compensation arrangements or overt favoritism irrespective of performance or seniority.

The company must also establish an image of integrity; in this manner personnel will believe what they are told and will act on what they believe. Leadership must establish a reputation as dedicated and forthright. When top management is suspected of softness or sluggishness, employee commitment follows suit. Confidence in the boss is confidence in the company.

Stability and consistency, we should note, does not mean stagnancy and torpidity. Creative companies can be stable, and innovative ones can be consistent. A firm that brings out highly original products radically unrelated to previous ones can certainly generate confidence among employees. The excitment brings its own consistency, and the new introductions its own stability. (Needless to say, these kinds of stability and consistency are more difficult to maintain.)

Confidence is easy for a company to keep when present but difficult to regain when lost. Employees have a natural tendency to believe the best, but become most suspicious once fooled. Confidence of employees is something that companies must not take for granted. It should be developed actively and monitored constantly.

NO RESPECTER OF PERSONS

Andrew Riley was pastor of an inner-city church. For five unheralded years he worked with the poor people of his forgotten neighborhood, exhausting himself to help the minorities and recent immigrants afflicted with the problems of unemployment, family separation, and drugs. He worked hard and without incident, the former a reflection of his character, the latter a tribute to his sensitivity.

He was fulfilling a rigorous and necessary assignment, but Riley felt as overlooked and ignored as the people he served. His career had veered off into an alley as blind as the ghetto was dank, and he was now sure that he would not be offered the prime pastorate opening uptown.

He hadn't even been asked to attend the recent conference on liturgy reform. Pastors from all over the country had been invited and he, in the same city, had not been. Though he was senior man on the list — he had put in his time and earned his distinction — he had a powerful rival for the important position. Reginald Smiley had been boyhood friends with the Right Reverend Smithton, and Smithton was the one who would make the decision.

His rival had been serving on the National Coordinating Board as chief liaison with the city government and other church groups. It was a high profile post, with frequent interviews in the press and meetings with wealthy parishoners. Smiley attended high-level political meetings with local officials, and organized ecumenical councils with other denominations. From what Riley heard from his inner-city billet — and it wasn't much — Smiley had dead aim on the upcoming appointment. And why not? It was the church's premier spiritual province, its pastor becoming a national figure.

Though Riley would never entertain notions of leaving the church, as it became clear what the outcome would be, his commitment began to shift from core to cog — not all the way, to be sure, not even half way, but movement nonetheless away from core. By background and belief it would be impossible for Riley to do anything else in life, yet he was lapsing from partisan to disengaged. Slight signs began to appear: a little less time with parishoners; a little more time with the bottle.

His confidence in the church was being shaken; though stability and consistency were there, fairness and integrity were not. Several of the experience factors of organization-personal interaction were altering his nature of commitment. Role strain, status, and rewards were pulling in one direction; while emotional conditioning, investment, and importance (of the church) were pulling in the other. The effect was not noticeable to others, but Riley himself sensed the shift.

And so it was on that fateful Sunday, at the yearly meeting of senior church pastors, that Andrew Riley, coming to church head-quarters for the first time in a year, heard his name called out, among all his peers, as the new spiritual leader of the most prestigious pastorate.

The Right Reverend Smithton congratulated Riley publicly, telling of his indomitable loyalty to the church and his selfless service to its members. He noted in passing, but it hit Riley hard, that never had there been any question but that the post would be his. Even Reginald Smiley, his face mirroring his name, offered his hearty congratula-tions and sincere promise of support.

The newly promoted Right Reverend Andrew Riley could never be shaken again. His commitment zoomed instantly back to core. His con-fidence in the integrity and fairness of the church had become im-mutable; and he would long remain a pillar in its leadership, steering the church into new areas of social responsibility toward its less for-tunate members.

DON'T ATTACK MY FIRM!

The Sloan Fellows Program at the Massachusetts Institute of Technol-ogy is offered for senior- and middle-level managers of exceptionally strong promise. The organizations from which they come are generally large. The average age of the managers is middle to late thirties and all are on their way up, some to the top. Each Sloan Fellow is an outstan-ding executive candidate, having been with his or her present firm for at least ten years.

Major corporations, national and international, sponsor these men and women for a year of intense study at MIT's Sloan School of Management. Here they learn modern theory and techniques for business management: economics, accounting, finance, decision theory, information systems, strategy and policy, marketing, organiza-tional psychology, and the like. It is estimated that each company will spend over $50,000 per executive attending, including tuition, moving and travel expenses for their families — in addition to their normal high-level compensation. Being chosen as a Sloan Fellow — first by their corporations and then by MIT — is a special honor, and con-fidence between the Sloan Fellows and their sponsoring companies is unusually high.

One of the authors recalls a minor incident while a Sloan Fellow that underlines the strength of commitment between manager and company when reinforced by both confidence and identification.

We were sitting together in a small coffee shop near campus. It was well into the first semester — during the summer — and we were settling into the rich and rigorous academic experience. Along with me were four other Sloan Fellows, three from General Motors and one from Ford. Since I enjoy stirring things up once in a while, and because I was genuinely unhappy with the quality of American automobiles — I had a BMW 320i — I put, after a beer, the following question to my classmates: "Why can't you guys make good cars? I'd much rather drive an American car, but nothing you're making can touch what I'm driving!"

Well, I couldn't have been less prepared for the onslaught. The response was instant; I was being attacked from all sides. "We make the best cars for the price." "We give Americans what they want." "We'd make better cars if Americans would pay for them." "You don't know what makes a good car." "You are just showing your ignorance of the automobile business." "It's people like you who are ruining this country. . . ."

I had thought I was bringing up an interesting question. I wasn't all that serious about the subject although I enjoyed driving cars that handled well. Frankly I really would have preferred to own an American car but felt that no American car could approach the road feel of the German cars. What I didn't get, however, was a discussion of the subject. I had inadvertently salted a sensitive wound. I was cavalierly attacking the companies that were sponsoring these fellows, companies that had earned the confidence and identification of these executives, companies in whom they had put their faith and their future — and they didn't like my assault one little bit. . . . I was more discreet in subsequent conversations with other Sloan Fellows.

GOING FOR MO

Forward movement is exciting; the thrill of high growth can energize anyone. Momentum is what happens when inertia is overcome through the application of constant force. Once started, it is hard to stop; once stopped, it is hard to restart. Corporate momentum is the exhilarating sense of company growth, with the payoff to employees coming in bonuses, promotions, and the personal pleasure of being a winner.

In Chapter 3 we described the positive thrust of organizational momentum in building commitment. We saw its power in Father Yun's "Cosmic House" and in several corporate analogues. We also saw the problems when momentum stops.

"Progressiveness" is more attitude than action, more a general state of corporate mind than a specific expression of company growth. A progressive company is never satisfied with the status quo, but never makes changes just to make changes. A progressive company is always on search for better products to market, more efficient ways to manufacture and distribute the product, more effective systems of internal control, better programs and benefits for managers and employees. A progressive company always wants to stay out front, if not number one in its field, at least very close to it.

Momentum and progressiveness are usually related, but either can be present without the other. Momentum without progressiveness will still stimulate employees into high commitment, but runs the risk of running wild. Progressiveness without momentum can also engender commitment, but it is only a promise of things to come and will falter unless those promises are eventually fulfilled. There is little warning in the former and little energy in the latter.

PUBLISH THE GOSPEL

Fred Neel was a member of a conservative church in eastern Pennsylvania that his parents had joined when he was an infant. He was nearing 25 and working as a computer programmer for a local bank. He attended Sunday services about once a month, no more. Though its doctrinal teachings he accepted, he couldn't relate to his church's old-fashioned style.

The congregation was large and its members well off. They could certainly have afforded to modernize facilities, if that's what they chose, but for some reason there was an unwritten rule against physical progress. Although members could work with all contemporary conveniences on their jobs and use all the latest marvels at home, none of these, it was felt, belonged in their church. God and technology, somehow, just didn't mix.

But why, wondered Fred? Was the Creator of physics really offended by microphones and amplifiers? Was there anything evil about radio and television? Certainly other churches were making good use of electronic media. Fred's church put great stress on preaching to the unconverted, but only did so on a door-to-door basis in their local community. Why not take advantage of all the resources available?

The question Fred was asking himself casually, the new pastor was asking the board seriously. There was no doctrinal proscription against technology, was there? Certainly the apostle Paul used every means available to him to preach the gospel. Why not, asked the pastor, enter the modern world where it lives?

The transition was remarkable: first came radio, a local station, and three months later two regional beacons. The programs were prepared by professionals with modern music and sharp scripts. The membership began to grow and the local papers took note. The church's income increased, old members were enthused, and new members participated. Soon the initial television programs went on the air. They were first-rate presentations, almost up to network standards, and they attracted wide audiences for religious programming.

It was as if Fred Neel had been "born again" again. Fred began attending church regularly, and even volunteered to help with some computer programs for analysis of media responses. Fred put it this way: "Sure, God said 'Cast your bread upon the waters,' but He never said 'Throw it into a sewer!'"

The church began using sophisticated ratings systems and response mechanisms. The trick was to determine the most efficient stations and times for their broadcasts. The message, however, was sacrosanct; "Christ and Him crucified" was the only part of the ministry not subject to critique and modification.

By this time, Fred was in charge of the computer department at the bank and conversant with the latest technologies. One day the pastor asked to see him. "Fred," he said after the greeting pleasantries,

> I want to go further. We've done well in radio and television, but we were always playing catch-up, imitating what others had been doing for some time. Let's play leapfrog and get out ahead! I want to experiment with two new media, cable and computers. We need to prepare for the time when cable is interactive, when people in their home can see and hear us, and we can see and hear them. And we also need to access home computers.

"I was on fire," reported Fred, carrying a bible and heading for his computer. "We had the message and I knew the medium."

Fred hurried down the hall where a modern room had been set up with 20 personal computers. No mere record-keeping here. These computers were strictly for the programming of bible-related software. Having resigned from the bank, Fred had been empowered to establish and run a software-development operations with a dozen programmers in his charge. He was not necessarily the most creative sort, but the progressiveness of the church combined with its goal structure and esteem to charge him with energy he had never known. Commitment "worm holed" from cog($-$) to core, with no intermediary stops.

Original programs of family entertainment and religious substance came out of his department. Software for teaching the bible to all age groups were written. Software patterned after popular interactive games — such as "Dungeons and Dragons" — were developed with biblical themes and using biblical examples. Software for instructing Sunday School teachers were already in use.

Fred's dream is now to have a "Biblical Network" tying together millions of home computers, a Dow-Jones News Service for the bible. "We want," he asserted, "the Ultimate Source!"

PLAYING LEAPFROG

Dr. Allen Stein, vice-president for research and chief scientist at Ener-Chem, Inc., a major petrochemicals company, was having increasing difficulty attracting the best young Ph.Ds. Ten years ago, at the height of the energy crunch, things were different. It's amazing how fast momentum shifts when a company loses its cutting edge.

Then he had the pick of the litter; he could chose the best researchers from the best graduate schools. And if he didn't find them, they'd find him. They would line up outside his office in the morning; they would wait near his car in the afternoon; they would even come uninvited to his home at night. EnerChem was the hot firm in those days, the one developing new methods for coal gasification, the one planning the new synfuel technologies. Everyone coming out of the labs wanted in.

But the energy crunch passed; the surplus of oil went up and the price of oil came down. Research contracts were no longer backlogged two years. EnerChem no longer cast a state-of-the-art image — the company had cooled — and students no longer sought Dr. Stein's office, car, and home.

Stein had a strategy, but would EnerChem's board be receptive? After all, the board only understood the energy business — geological tests, reserve estimates and the like — though several were good chemical engineers. Also, $30 million seemed an incredible price to pay for only 20 percent of a small genetic engineering company, even though they had two Nobel laureates and a dozen or so important patents. That put a valuation on the company of $150 million, and not dollar one had been generated in revenues and losses continued at several million per year! To present such an investment to this board, Stein realized, would seem harebrained.

But Dr. Allen Stein was prepared to put his corporate reputation on the line. He argued vigorously that the investment was not only worth the money, it was money better spent than five times that amount allocated to traditional projects. First, it promised a strong position in one of the leading companies in a dynamic growth industry. Second, it would give EnerChem an early window on new technologies, some of which would likely affect petrochemnicals. Third, it would put the company back at the leading edge of technology and make it an attractive place for the best young scientists to come.

It is difficult for large companies to change directions. Just as it takes a supertanker many miles to turn in the ocean, so it takes many years for a superfirm to change its products. Most never do it. In the history of business, new products are often created by new companies, organizations without tradition or inertia. Apple in computers, Diasonics in medical imaging, and Genentech in genetic engineering are three examples of new companies that pioneered and lead their fields.

General Motors, on the other hand, was the world's most dominant company of any kind for two decades — now they fight just to remain strong in automobiles, a mature industry. Polaroid was considered for years one of the world's most technically advanced companies; but by sticking to instant photography they didn't take maximum advantage of their position.

Xerox, losing its monopoly in copying machines, recognized that the office of the future would need much more than duplication equipment. They invested heavily in computers, automation, and information, and though the jury is still out as to ultimate outcome, the concept cannot be negated. Sears Roebuck began to lose ground to K-Mart, as the former remained static and the latter cut prices. But Sears recently embarked on a bold new initiative in financial services — Sears Financial Centers — by acquiring Coldwell Banker in real estate and Dean Witter in the brokerage business, and integrating them with Allstate in insurance.

RESPONSIBILITY

Responsibility is personal burden. It is being accountable for something within one's power. People react to responsibility in different ways. Some enjoy it — they like the power to do and the capacity to accomplish, and they like control over their personal path. Others do not enjoy it — it is weighty and onerous and taxes their freedom. In either case, however, when responsibility is given, commitment increases.

It is a curious thing, this responsibility. It carries with it more work and more anxiety, and all it can assure is more fear and more danger. If one does not have responsibility, there's no way to fail. Yet people seek it and pursue it with passion. Why?

Responsibility pulls one into many; it assumes a high degree of group trust and requires confidence on both sides of the bond. Responsibility heightens the exhilaration of achievement. Achieving something on one's own, however rewarding, usually means a smaller scope than achieving something with a team. Preparing a successful business plan is one thing; running a successful business is something else.

Commitment is built by knowledge and feedback. The more employees know what is happening, the more they feel part of the action. This applies to all employees, at all levels of an organization.

BELIEF UNDER FIRE

David Worshavski, a young rabbinical student with uncertain beliefs, had just been assigned his first pulpit. He wasn't happy. It was the summer before his final semester at the seminary, and he had serious questions about his profession. Nevertheless, when asked to assist at a local congregation, he reluctantly agreed. It was time, he was told, to put learning into practice. The year was 1939 and the city was Warsaw.

David's family had been part of Poland's intellectual Jewish society. His father, a rabbi and the descendant of rabbis, was a professor of Hebrew literature at the university and his mother was a fine actress in the Yiddish theater. David was the only son, and he was expected to become a rabbi and continue a lineage going back eight generations.

The young man was perceptive and sincere. He had studied torah and talmud for fifteen years. He knew all the traditions of the Fathers. But as he expanded his education, the more he learned about philosophy and literary criticism, the more the backbone of his beliefs weakened.

How, he wondered, could a beneficient God permit such suffering in the world? And how could He allow such misery to befall His people? How could one reconcile the fact that a God all-powerful and all-merciful would allow horrors unspeakable to consume the Jewish people, horrors without number, horrors without reason, horrors without end? (David remembered the joke about the old rabbi finally meeting God after enduring a mournful life of persecution and pogroms. "Is it true that we are your Chosen People?" the old rabbi asked God. "Yes," answered the Almighty. "Then, if you don't mind," responded the rabbi, "how about choosing someone else?" It was a joke, but it made the point.)

David began assisting the local rabbi with mixed feelings. His parents were proud that their son was entering the rabbinate, and they were sure he would become a great scholar and teacher of Judaism. David was pleased to honor his parents, but he felt he was living a lie. Judaism to him was a dead end, and the God of the bible a myth. He was teaching what he did not believe, and he was preaching what he did not practice.

Summer in Poland ended early that year. On September 1, one month before David was to return to school, the blitzkrieg began. A country of discipline and intelligence had given itself over to monomania and paranoia, and an unending nightmare had begun. It would be history's ultimate assault on the children of Jacob and, as a very minor consequence, the final blow to David Worshavski's belief.

During the first few weeks of the war, David was pinned down with his congregation. It was not where he wanted to be; comforting old women was not what he wanted to do. As soon as he could, he determined, he would volunteer for the army. But before he knew it, the battle for Poland was over — but the war against the Jews was not.

David, in fact, was a fine rabbi; he strengthened his congregants, he gave them hope. Though he believed not a word of torah or bible to be divine revelation, he rationalized that if the ancient writings could help the people, then who was he to deny them so little?

As time wore on, the mental conflict grew great and the physical suffering grew greater. Then, slowly, monstrous rumors began to circulate. Whispers in the street told of crimes beyond anything ever conceived by man, crimes so heinous that even the devil himself would cringe with revulsion.

Enough of this rabbi charade, David decided. He must pick up arms and fight back. If not now, he asked himself, then when? He was preparing to join a Jewish resistance group when the rabbi in charge of his congregation was executed by the secret police. It was the opening gambit of their beastly intimidation campaign; the occupiers were preparing their roundup, and they didn't want any annoyances.

Two hundred and seventy families, almost one thousand people, were now cut off without physical hope or spiritual sustenance. It would be the hour of their greatest need. "For us, Rabbi," an old member beseeched David, "we have no one else."

The Jewish people were in darkness. What would become of them? Their physical bodies would be destroyed, of this David was now sure, but who would care for human dignity and reaffirm spiritual worth? Who would guide them to look beyond? This, he now saw, was his calling, and he was determined to fulfill it.

So David put down his gun and took up his torah, thinking that in the long run he would do more good with the latter then he ever could do with the former. Guns would be coming on the shoulders of others — he could feel the pulse of history — and eventually the vile invaders would be destroyed. But his responsibility was here, and his mission was now.

David stayed with his people and did what he could, and in time his commitment to Judaism was reaffirmed. The responsibility he was compelled to assume forced a change in his outlook. The horror was so massive, he came to realize, that there had to be meaning and purpose involved. The reasoning, he knew, was inverted; but the reasoning, he knew, was right.

How could a well-working universe spew out such venom? David spent hours reading the scriptures, trying to comprehend the nature of God, trying to understand the mission for Jews, trying to believe. What possible purposes could God have in all this? David prayed and sought the will of the Almighty.

Then he saw it. It wasn't a vision and it wasn't mystical, but it was clear and it was sure. The ashes being scattered in Warsaw would soon rise in Jerusalem! The destruction of Jews in Europe would resurrect Jews in the Holy Land!

David read and he prayed, and he saw. Throughout the history of the Jewish people as recorded in the bible, God would bless them for obedience and curse them for disobedience; when they were scourged, He would again bring them back to their land. There was meaning here, meaning on a scale so massive that he could not comprehend it all. David, never a Zionist, took up the banner. David, never a believer, believed.

David Worshavski perished in the Warsaw ghetto. He was one of the last to die, giving comfort and vision to those few still fighting at the end. Of the 963 members of his congregation, 107 were shot in the uprising, 736 were gassed in Auschwitz, and 97 were asphyxiated in Treblinka. Of the 23 who survived, 20 made the hard journey south, where in the course of time four became generals in a new army, and one became prime minister of the new state called Israel.

THE "A TEAM"

"Do call me, because I'm not going to call you."

Those were the last face-to-face words Victor Simpson heard from his boss, Howard Blany, executive vice-president of a major computer products company. Simpson had been turned loose and told to design a "state-of-the-art-plus-one" computer targeted for the small business environment.

Simpson had heard of "intrapreneurs" — entrepreneurs *within* the corporate structure, but now he was one. He was responsible. He had the job and he could research, design, create, and test his products apart from corporate controls. He was given a large budget and a tight timetable. No other instructions were given and no other constraints imposed. It was as if he were running his own company, and his commitment, always strong, shot off the charts.

Three months passed. Simpson had called Blany several times to report success and "nonsuccess" ("failure" was an impolite work in the company's lexicon). Blany, true to his word, had not called Simpson once.

It was a heady experience. Never before had Simpson experienced such a commingling of emotions: confidence and fear, support and loneliness, power and impotence. He had carefully selected his project team and, no matter the outcome, the dynamics for the most powerful experience of his life were set in motion.

The responsibility Simpson had been given was in large measure the generator of his enhanced commitment. Furthermore, he had full knowledge and instant feedback. Virtually all input factors in our commitment model — personal, organizational, and interactional (see Figures 5.11 through 5.14) — were flowing fast in the same direction. Commitment strength was maximized, and optimum mission contribution would accelerate the accomplishment of critical corporate goals.

Many modern companies, especially in industries with rapidly changing technologies, have been forced by competitive pressures to experiment with intrapreneurship. In most cases the companies commission small strike forces to come up with product innovations. These elite employee groups are designed to more quickly, creatively, and resourcefully, without the shackles of corporate policies.

Companies in industries which do not use "A Team" structural designs can learn something from these recent developments in high-tech industries. Building core commitment is facilitated by giving key employees strategic responsibility, with all the trust and confidence that come along with it. Opportunities for breakthrough success are maximized in such relationships.

ACCOMPLISHMENT

Accomplishment, the concluding of noteworthy work, is the fulfilling of achievement, one of our meaning-related personal variables (see Chapter 2). It is completing tasks of personal significance, and the process itself carries its own reward. A more formal definition of accomplishment might be "bringing meaningful assignments to successful conclusions." Often it requires great effort and the overcoming of large obstacles. Accomplishment is more mental satisfaction than physical reward. It is the act of fulfillment itself, irrespective of benefits derived, that generates joy.

Doing things right gives an intrinsic kick. We all exalt in the feeling of a job well done, even if we are the only ones who know it is done. In many situations the reward can be eliminated without diminishing the feeling of triumph. (Take, for example, videogames at arcades; rewarding high scores with free games does little to increase playing or paying.)

Studies have shown the uniqueness of achievement as a mental phenomenon. Its independence from other desirables such as power and possessions is well established.[1] Achievement is desired for its own worth. Though financial compensation can be an "achievement," achievement per se is not dependent on financial compensation. Achievement is more than money or wealth. Achievement touches the human psyche deeply; it is part of what makes us tick.

Entrepreneurs as a class are the personification of achievement. They have a great need to see jobs completed and goals accomplished, and have little need for power or position.

Entrepreneurs are task driven and goal oriented. They are immersed in their work, yet can keep a critical perspective. They remain distant enough to see the forest for the trees, and yet are close enough to get hands on any of the wood.

Achievers are dedicated to finishing their work, which is often self-assigned and self-motivated. Achievers are compulsives, beset by self-generated passion to perfect and complete. Nothing makes them happier than to see the tough task done — but then again, they are not happy unless they are working on tough tasks.

WHAT A GOOD MAN NEEDS

Steven Locke was missing what he had had, and no amount of money could make up the difference. His family had come from West Virginia, miners all of them for a hundred years. His mother had joined a bible-believing church during the Depression, and Steven was not yet a teenager when he first attended services. The doctrines of the church gave great potential to human beings, and church members were eager to "spread the word."

Steven was a feisty kid who had little use for religion, his or anyone else's. It was only at his mother's insistence that he agreed to spend a few months at the church's fledgling seminary. He didn't like theology, and he certainly didn't want to be a clergyman.

At the seminary he met the church leader, an engaging fellow with deep convictions and enormous energy. Steven was impressed but not overwhelmed with the boss, and with characteristic honesty proceeded to tell him where he was wrong — wrong about some minor doctrinal issue and wrong about some major personal problem. Steven's challenge to some point of prophecy was no big deal but his meddling into nepotism was irritating. In spite of the latter — or perhaps because of it — the church leader came to respect Steven as a good and honest young man with grit and talent and a future that was bright.

Twenty years passed and the church multiplied a thousand times; the handful of struggling strangers became an international organization with high media interest and some political influence. Steven played a significant part in the church's growth. In the early days he was responsible for developing the internal systems of the church administration. Then he moved on to start two dozen local church congregations across the Midwest. When it came time to begin building the church overseas, Steven became point man and coordinator.

For ten years Steven managed the growth of the church in countries outisde the United States, returning home only for meetings and conclaves. Rarely was there a day when he worked less than twelve hours, and never a week less than seven days. Although the church taught the sabbath was for rest, that was the day ministers worked hardest, preaching and counseling from sunrise until midnight. The pattern continued unchanged for years, and it seemed it would continue forever. Steven was achieving in matters of high import; the church had a first-rate partisan whose commitment was all core.

When in the life-cycle of the church doctrinal conflict triggered internal strife, rebellion hit the ranks. In quick response, the now aging leader called upon Steven, his long-trusted servant, for advice and for help.

Steven Locke, as was his wont, immediately uprooted his family and brought them back. For three months he was on the road putting out fires and building up support. Throwing his own impeccable prestige into the breach, he held up the arms of the leader. Although he wondered about some of the charges, Steven maintained steadfast loyalty and worked till he dropped.

Six weeks it took to recover from total exhaustion. They thought it was a heart attack, but that diagnosis proved false. Once back on his feet, though his blood pressure remained high, Steven was at work once again, now directing church media efforts on radio and in print. But once again problems arose in the ministry, and the leader once again called upon Steven.

A perilously wide credibility gap had been opened, caused by overt discrepancies between what the leadership said and what the ministry knew. But Steven again put his reputation on the line. He rebuked the rebellious ministers publicly for their lack of loyalty and ethics, and he criticized the valiant leader privately for some of his teachings and some of his conduct. (Spiritual duty, biblical fidelity, and personal loyalty were Locke's only motivation.) The teachings needing changing were changed, and although many ministers still had their doubts, they could not contradict the eloquent, quiet integrity of Steven Locke.

For several years the church was peaceful — at least on the surface. The next time trouble surfaced, it took a nasty, virulent turn. Sides were not drawn so simply, and external elements entered the fray and augmented the confusion. In the panic, through the most ironic of twists, he who had fought so hard and so faithfully for the church and its leader was charged as an adversary.

A scapegoat was needed, and a scapegoat was found. Only one was big enough to fill the bill. The stage was set. Political gain was the hidden agenda, the obvious motivation, and those who sought control of the church had to remove the bulwark blocking the way. Only then could they take their prize and fill their ambitions.

The pitch was a simple one. They informed the aging leader that Steven was the covetous one, the one seeking to overturn, the one plotting to dominate. It was a time of trouble and Steven Locke did not fight back. He was defrocked without a hearing, then castigated, ridiculed and publically expelled. Vile propaganda was spewed out against him, but still he did not return one word for one thousand.

Though into his fifties and untrained for the outside, Steven refused all offers to start competitive churches. He was not interested in playing god games or church charades; he would maintain his original beliefs and not interfere with anyone else's.

He dropped out of circulation; he didn't answer letters or return phone calls. If God could get Jonah, reasoned Steven, he can surely get me. But no whales came to Nebraska that year, and for all practical purposes, Steven Locke the religious leader ceased to exist.

For two years Steven held various jobs. On each he did well, but on each he was unhappy. The money he made was reasonable, but the satisfaction he derived was not. Selling things that people hardly wanted and didn't need was not an achievement, irrespective of commissions generated and fees earned.

Steven grew depressed. He was a true achiever, needing more than financial reward, more than material gain. It was not until he was offered a job with a social agency of the state government that he brightened. The job was not very big, but at last he was again helping people, and only in helping people could his achievement needs be fulfilled.

AN ENTREPRENEURIAL SOUL

Daniella Kagan was a free spirit; vivacious and creative she always did the unusual. Whether it was a poem or a drawing in grade school, or a term paper or project in college, whatever she did was never expected. If the shapes were obvious, she saw the edges; if there were three ways to answer a question, she found a fourth.

Daniella wanted to be an actress, but she also had a flair for business. As a girl she had organized her sixth grade into a lemonade stand empire, monopolizing Park Avenue for ten blocks in New York. She saved her birthday and holiday money and bankrolled her brothers when they ran short for a weekend — charging exorbitant rates of interest that they were quite willing to pay.

By the time she graduated college she had started and sold three businesses: the first was a concept for selling ads in beauty parlors, the second an idea for a line of comic books, and the third a mail-order catalog for dolls of soap opera characters. Each was successful, but each she couldn't manage. Each developed operating troubles and had to be sold at an early stage. The prices she received, everyone reminded her, were substantially lower than the businesses were worth.

Money she had, but not success. Because of the forced sales, she was almost a failure, at least in the way that "success" and "failure" were commonly defined. Furthermore, although she was never short on ideas, Daniella still didn't know what she wanted to do with her life.

Friends and family advised her to go to business school or law school. It was the general consensus that she had to harness her talents and acquire the skills to *run* businesses, not just start them. Starting businesses and then not being able to manage them, in general opinion, was just about being a washout.

General opinion, of course, was wrong.

It is certainly true that starting businesses is not the same as managing them, but just as professional managers are respected for operating businesses that others started, so should professional entrepreneurs be respected for starting businesses that others operate. The successful entrepreneur is a much rarer species than the successful manager; the latter is a skill largely bred, the former is a personality largely born.

Achievement for entrepreneurs is a different characteristic than achievement for managers. Entrepreneurs don't give a hang about power or control; they care only about substance and content. Entrepreneurs are partisans to achieve their dreams. In them we see clearly the power of achievement in building core commitment. There is nothing wrong for entrepreneurs to concentrate on what they do best, and for companies to encourage them in that spirit. These are the people who build something from nothing, who carry society, and we are all in their debt.

CHAPTER SEVEN

COMMITMENT BREAKERS:
SEVERING THE BOND

Breaking commitment seems easy. It is not — it's just that organizations work so hard at it.

Commitment is broken by disturbances between individuals and institutions; the firm bond is severed by disruptions between personal meaning and company mission. It does not matter which side triggers the disturbance or causes the disruption. What is broken and severed on one side is broken and severed on both sides.

You would think that breaking commitment must be a high art, at least from the effort many groups devote to it. It is surprising the frequency at which reputable firms frustrate the strengthening of commitment. One might assume that Nobel Prizes were awarded for crippling relationships between employees and companies, or, better yet, tax credits.

In this chapter we pull the previous chapter inside out. What, we ask, are the mechanisms for *destroying* commitment, for shattering the bond between individual and institution? Though commitment is undermined gradually, the impact can emerge suddenly.

We examine situations where commitment has been ruptured, case studies involving both closed systems and corporate systems. We continue using the "lens powers" of total organizations. In each case we ask the critical questions: Why did it happen? What were the reasons? Were there underlying causes? Could it have been prevented? Can others avoid repeating it? Can the lesson be applied?

The answers to these questions are important for managers. Sometimes it is easier to understand what *not* to do than what to do. What are the danger signals for impending commitment collapse? What should companies be careful about not doing? What should they watch out for?

The commitment of employees, we should remember, is something an organization usually begins with; the firm bond normally starts out tied with some strength. For openers, commitment is a

126

given, almost like having products to sell. Commitment, at least at the calculative level, is something for companies to *lose*, not win.

FIVE BREAKERS

We will look at five ways that commitment is broken.[1] They are not the only ways, but they *do* work — and they're certainly tried often enough (Table 7.1).

TABLE 7-1 COMMITMENT BREAKERS: SEVERING THE BOND

Alienation

Powerlessness

Meaninglessness

Worthlessness

Anxiety

As with the "builders" of Chapter 6, these "breakers" are compounds distilled from the inputs to our commitment model — personal factors, organizational factors, interactional factors (organizational experiences) — see Table 7.2. Breakers are formed by combining and reacting these driving variables. Of course, when it comes to the formation of breaking compounds, the elements come together in unproductive, unmeaningful, or even damaging ways. (Note that several of the breakers are almost direct opposites of several of the builders. This was not intended; no effort was made to generate parallelism — but since both were derived from the same concepts, a few worked out that way naturally).

Alienation: The social separation between individual and institution, the estrangement between member and group; the feeling that organization and individual are moving in opposite and contradictory directions; the active rejection of organizational goals, values, essence, and substance. Opposite: identification.

Powerlessness: The belief that organizational events and outcomes are determined by forces beyond individual control; the feeling

TABLE 7.2 COMMITMENT BREAKERS: WHERE THEY COME FROM

Breaking Compounds	Elements/Factors (Antecedents)		
	Personal	Organizational	Organizational Experience
Alienation	Transcendence Esteem Generalized Loyalty Affiliation Structure	Goal Structure Leadership Cohesiveness People Valuing Permeability	Support Task Identification Importance/Uniqueness Emotional Conditioning Rewards
Powerlessness	Power Autonomy Achievement Locus of Control	Goal Structure Leadership People Valuing	Status Support Task Identification Rewards
Meaninglessness	Transcendence Achievement Esteem Education Autonomy	Goal Structure Organizational Esteem Progressiveness	Importance/Uniqueness Reality Congruence Investment Task Identification
Worthlessness	Esteem Materialism Education	Progressiveness People Valuing Organizational Esteem	Support Status Emotional Conditioning
Anxiety	Stability Structure Locus of Control Autonomy	Leadership People Valuing Cohesiveness	Role Strain Support Reality Congruence Investment

128

that what will happen to people is unknown and unknowable and they cannot change or influence future events. Opposite: responsibility.

Meaninglessness: The sense that nothing about the organization has any import or interest for the individual; the feeling of emptiness, the absence of significance in everything the organization is doing. Opposite: import and significance.

Worthlessness: The sense that a person is engaged in organizational activities devoid of benefit or reward of any kind; a depressed image of self and group. Opposite: esteem and pride.

Anxiety: The uneasy feeling caused by apprehension of trouble, danger, or personal misfortune; an unsettling expectancy of future events, a foreboding uncertainty about what might happen. Opposite: confidence.

In the examples to follow, we watch each of the above breakers fracture the firm bond and destroy commitment. The point for managers is to note the signs and avoid the path. In every case, options are discernible and alternatives available.

ALIENATION

Alienation was the buzz word of the 1960s. It was, we were told, what all institutions of society — government, corporations, universities — were doing to us. It was a "conspiracy," some charged, and others echoed the cry.

Alienation implies distance and disruption. As with many of the breakers in this chapter, it can be more easily defined in the negative. Alienation is the absence of identification. It is what happens when there is no positive relationship between organization and member, and it implies active rejection of all aspects of organizational essence.

When employees are alienated, they feel isolated and apart. The culture and society of the company become, in a very real sense, an "alien" world, a foreign territory in which people neither have nor want a part. Overt antagonism to goals and values is common, and ridicule of executives and managers is frequent. Alienated personnel — adversaries or disaffecteds — are a hard-bitten bunch to turn around.

Organizations do not have to be evil to turn off employees. In most situations, a part taints the whole. It is not that a middle manager at an Exxon refinery suddenly sees the entire company as rotten. It is more that he wasn't promoted or respected or given proper attention. Alienation usually begins as a small seed, but it is virulent and contagious and can grow anywhere.

WHAT'S IMPORTANT AND WHAT'S NOT

The most remarkable thing about the Kent family joining the church was that they did it together with unity and unanimous enthusiasm. Six months later you'd never have guessed this.

They began as a fine, hardworking family, espousing solid middle-class values. Their home was tucked away in a quiet suburb just north of Boston, where father and mother had been brought up since childhood. Richard Kent, the son of a dockworker, taught American history in high school and coached little league on weekends. Carole, his wife, worked part time in a bakery. They owned their own house, a modest three-bedroom colonial on a corner lot. Financially, it was a constant struggle, but a home of their own was certainly worth it.

Richard and Carole had two children, 17-year-old Cary and 15-year-old Susan. Cary and Susan were both good students and popular kids; Cary was a hot-shooting guard on the school basketball team and Susan was an all-city cheerleader. The family enjoyed each other's company and found it easy to spend time together.

There had been a fifth Kent, a sparkling 10-year-old named Nancy, and it was her death from leukemia that turned the family to God. For three bitter years, the Kents did everything possible to help their baby daughter — neither time nor money was of any concern — but the cancer just wasn't caught soon enough, and all that remained were the memory of her indomitable spirit and a backload of bills.

A family facing tragedy can go one of two directions: either they become cynical and separate, or they grow compassionate and close. The Kents did the latter, and so it was quite natural that when Carole first heard about the church from local friends, the four Kents discussed it together. Cary and Susan were serious minded and participated actively. The family sought understanding and meaning in life; they knew tragedy and wanted to know God.

The basic theology of the church was startling simple. There was, it was said, great mystery and purpose in human life, and Christ's sacrifice was the key for unlocking the former and fulfilling the latter. All human beings who ever had lived will have a full and fresh chance at salvation, and the God who created the heavens and earth will resurrect all for this ultimate opportunity.

The Kents were enthralled. The appeal was direct. "All human beings" would include their little Nancy, now encased in a cold dark box at a nearby cemetary. The impact was strong, the timing stronger.

The bible, it was taught, is the ultimate authority on all matters. Whatever the bible said to do, church members should do. No traditions of man should interfere with the doctrines of God.

After three months of almost nightly conversations, including several late-night sessions with the church's local pastor, the Kent family began attending services. It was a pleasure, said the pastor, to see a family come in together.

The Kents were estatic. Each began telling friends of the marvelous reality of God. Life was warm with purpose and hope. All their sufferings and struggles, they could now see, were part of a grand design. They were comforted in the knowledge that the God of the universe was also the God of their lives.

The first cool breeze came with the first service. Richard had noticed the middle-age man eyeing them all during the sermon. No small talk for this Guardian of Truth; right after the closing prayer he approached the family and came right to the point:

"You must instruct your wife and daughter, Mr. Kent," he said with a condescending clip, "that their earrings are too long and their dresses are too short. Both are the way of the world, not the way of the church. There is much in the bible that you do not understand."

Carole, overhearing the man, reddened with embarrassment. Susan, seeing her mother, reddened with rage. "What nerve!" exclaimed Susan.

"But he is spiritual, and we are still carnal," responded Carole softly. "We must appreciate his counsel and thank God for His Way."

In the ensuing weeks, the Kents discovered that there was much more "in the bible" that they "did not understand." Basketball, for openers, was out for Cary, along with his sideburns, jeans, and boots — competition was not part of the way. High school parties had to become relics of the past — no church member children could be allowed near such "conclaves of Satan."

Regarding books permitted to be read and movies permitted to be seen, the church's teaching were not so lenient. ("Controlling what goes into the mind," went the slogan among church leaders, "means controlling what comes out of the member.") The procedure was quite the opposite of a banned list; since the books and movies disallowed were far more numerous than the books and movies allowed, the church published an "Edification List" — only what was included on the list was permitted.

As for music, hymns, Bach, and Pat Boone were in; most everything else out. (In one curious twist, Paganini was out, but Rachmanioff's Rhapsody on a Theme of Paganini was in.) With art, Rembrandt was in and Van Gogh was out; Wyeth in, Picasso out. As for eating and sleeping and dressing and dancing and exercise and makeup and politics and economics, well, the church had teachings on every one — and every one in meticulous detail. A member had to have an encyclopedic memory just to remember what "God liked" and what "God didn't like."

Sexuality, of course, could not escape the rules. Restricting intimate relations to marriage, already a Kent family value, was just the beginning of constraint. Certain positions were "advised" and certain positions were condemned. Specific frequencies were recommended for certain times of the month and seasons of the year. Great pains were taken to encourage members in what they should do before (certain prayers) and after (detailed hygiene).

The regulations about food seemed endless. Using white sugar and white bread was literally a sin, consuming more pulpit time than, say, coveting or lying. Carole, selling cookies at her bakery, was under immediate suspicion. Historical interpretations were complex. Why one American hero was "good" and another "bad" Richard never quite understood.

Carole quit her job and Richard quit his coaching. Cary stopped playing basketball and Susan stopped going to parties. The house was purged of books and records and clothes and foods and whatnot. The Kents were spending so much time with the church's physical demands, that they began to forget their original spiritual needs.

Susan was the first to break. "I've now read the bible through twice," she announced while preparing for a party with long earrings and short dress. "What we're doing I can't find, and what I find, we're not doing!"

Her mother, fearing the damnation of hell, did everything to save her daughter from destruction. The fights were furious, but Susan would not relent.

Cary skipped one game, then chucked the church. He sought massive meaning in life, not miniscule directions for living. He thought his mother a fool, and put his thoughts squarely into words.

Richard was bewildered; he believed the primary doctrines of salvation and eternal life, but he never heard much about them anymore. What he was inundated with were trifles and trumpery. (The rigmaroles of sex were most disconcerting; it was difficult to retain interest after the preliminary prayers; the rest, pardon the pun, was anticlimactic.)

So Cary went away to college and Susan ran away from home. Carole kept demanding strict obedience. She and Richard began drifting apart. The core had been crushed by the edge, and essence overwhelmed by trivia.

Organizations alienate members more often for peripheral matters than for primary ones. It is surprisingly easy for institutions or companies to concentrate on outlying issues and ignore central thrusts. "We major in the minors," was how one employee described his firm.

There are natural processes at work here. If there is general agreement on matters within the organization, there is no need to speak of them often. If there is no consensus, if members or employees balk at certain principles however obtuse, then the organization must devote time to explanation and discussion. Thus begins the strange transformation. The more time allocated to trivial but controversial matters, the more valued these trivial matters become. The characer of organizational importance changes subtly but surely.

The end results follow directly. The original founding philosophy is pushed into a corner and ancillary matters move to center stage. Some members like the trend, needing more tangible symbols and boundaries to exercise commitment. Others become alienated and call it quits.

RUN OUT OF PARADISE

Marjorie Shilson was ecstatic. She had landed the job of her dreams: senior editor at Scholar's House, one of the leading publishers of academic books. Marjorie was only 27, but her reputation outshone her years and she was given charge over all literature and history.

Book publishing was a tough industry, the academic part particularly so. Competition for positions was fierce; the reason was the work — obviously it couldn't have been the money.

Marjorie had turned down a similar position with a large publisher of trade (bookstore) books at a guaranteed salary of 40 percent higher plus a generous package of perks and bonuses. At Scholar's House the perks were scant and the bonus nonexistent. (The "bonus" here, went the scuttlebutt, was keeping your job.) Security, surely, was no asset. Scholar's House was a small, minimally profitable subsidiary of a multinational communications corporation. Every month rumors floated out of headquarters portending cost cuts and personnel layoffs.

Salary, bonus, perks, security — taken together — mattered not in comparison with her new task. Marjorie would work with books she loved and authors she admired — topics in English history, criticism of the modern novel, and art in Western civilization. She would have edited these books for *nothing*; to be paid anything was bonus already. Marjorie Shilson had found her life's work.

Excited about the opportunity, she hardly noticed corporate policy. All employees, with no exceptions, were required to punch time-clocks. (She hardly noticed because she thought it a rather dry joke.) Such strict adherence to puntuality was unusual for a company founded on creativity.

Marjorie was a "night person," preferring to edit well into the early morning, often working three to four extra hours at home. She would then come to the office between 10 and 11 A.M., skip lunch, and stay til

6 or 7 P.M. Corporate policy said this was not possible. She had to be sitting at her desk, ready for work, at precisely 8:00 A.M."Sorry Margie," her editor-in-chief shook his head, "the rule book allows no exceptions. We've tried to get exempted. No luck."

She shrugged it off. Let the company have whatever policies they like, she thought. I'll try to conform — but not too hard. And if I miss a bit, no big deal. Besides, nobody'll ever know.

Her first "miss" was a bigger deal than she imagined. Several pairs of eyes from corporate staff had the roles of "efficiency auditors"; theirs was the unenviable task of monitoring work hours. Not five days after Marjorie began, she received a personalized (read: computer-generated) "MorninGram" from Personnel reminding her that work began at 8:00 A.M. The second warning, a week later, was more direct:

> It has come to our attention that you are in the habit of not complying with corporate policy regarding work hours. Tardiness, we remind you, is akin to laziness, and laziness will not be tolerated.

Margorie flushed with anger. In addition to the stupidity of the policy, two things really annoyed her. One, she had been averaging a good 11 hours a day editing. The time spent was certainly in excess of any of the other editors, and though much had been at home, it was first-rate work. Two, she resented being watched by spies.

The trend continued and Marjorie's fever rose. In virtually every area of worklife, the corporation asserted itself with arbitrariness and impunity. Employees had to take their vacations at prearranged times; they had parking spaces assigned by seniority; they had to comply with a rigid dress code.

When Marjorie's thermometer finally exploded, it was caused by a trivial irritation. Christmas parties were considered a major event. Held in the massive ballroom of a large New York hotel, the party was required attendance for all employees. (The highlight of the annual event, or so he thought, was the great speech of company history and projection made by the esteemed chairman.) The official invitation, sent to each employee, told of the need for a yearly renewal so that the "Chairman's Vision may become anew the Company Spirit." The enclosed RSVP envelope was designed to facilitate donation to the chairman's favorite charity.

Whether Marjorie really had a project more critical or was just plain fed up, she decided not to attend. Her work was individual in nature; not only would she be inhibited by a "Company Spirit," but she also wanted no part of the "Chairman's Vision." The more she thought about it, the more she realized how much she was thinking about it! Her life was being consumed with nonsense.

Within a week she received a notice of inquisition. Her absence from the yuletide festivities would have to be explained. So it was with great sadness that Marjorie Shilson, not three months into the job of her dreams, wrote out her letter of resignation. She enclosed it in that unused RSVP envolope — now that irony felt good! — and sent it to the chairman.

Alienation is an antagonist to *identification*. Although Marjorie identified deeply with her work, company policy had done her in. After taking some time to clear her head she accepted, with sorrow, a job paying 50 percent more money. At her new trade book company, the situation was the reverse. Although her specific editorial responsibilities — cookbooks, Hollywood biographies, romance fiction — were none too thrilling, the firm appreciated its creative members and catered to their habits. As long as the product was there, she was told by her boss, Marjorie could work on the dark side of the moon for all he cared. Identification with this company was easy. Companies, to be successful, must make it so.

POWERLESSNESS

"Powerlessness" as a commitment breaker is not the opposite of "power" as a meaning-related personal variable (see Chapter 2). Nor is powerless, in this context, the mere absense of power.

Having power is the capacity to command, alter, or influence the behavior of people and the course of events. If we choose to define powerlessness as the negative of power, then there is more here than common connotation.

Power per se is not a prime commitment builder. Power motivates inwardly, feeding the ego. Powerlessness goes beyond an individual's lack of capacity to command, alter or influence people and events. Powerlessness describes the *helplessness* of a person within an organization; it is the inability to make any dent whatsoever in matters of personal concern, especially those within one's own sphere of influence. Powerlessness for, say, a quality control supervisor in an electronics assembly plant is not the fact that he cannot change market strategy or affect compensation policy; it is the fact that he cannot make his job more effective or his procedures more efficient. His suggestions are requested, but never heard.

Powerlessness is that airy, aimless sense of no control when organizational forces dominate directly. Powerlessness is real when it is specific, personal, and close. Events seem to swirl around like a tornado without awareness or concern for the individual. (It is like the feeling one gets of trying to play a video arcade game when no money has been deposited. Although figures keep flying, there is no influence whatsoever. The image of involvement is illusion.)

"Learned helplessness" is a psychological concept discovered in animal laboratories and applicable, virtually unchanged, in human organizations. Picture two cages of rats, each with a two-sided electrified grid for a floor. In one cage, whenever a light goes on, a pulse of painful (though not harmful) electrical current is passed through one side of the grid. The rats, in this situation, are conditioned to run over to the other side whenever they see the light, and they learn quickly to avoid the shock. In the other cage, the lights and electric current have no relationship at all; each comes on randomly and it is impossible to learn how to escape the current. Wherever the rats run they get the shock and feel the pain.

The interesting point comes when both groups are placed in new though similar situations, this time, say, with a bell signaling the onset of the electrical pulse. The first group, successful with the light, is successful again, perhaps even a bit quicker in learning time. The second group, the one unable to learn with the light, is now equally unable to learn with the bell — even though it is fully possible to avoid the painful shock. The rats just freeze in a prone position. These rats have learned to be helpless.

This same attitude is all too common among people. "What's the use, it won't help anyway" is a typical response to many situations. When companies ask for new ideas, and none of them is ever considered, much less tried, employees are learning helplessness. They will be less responsive to future requests, and, if the pattern continues, eventually not responsive at all. A cadre of routiners and disengageds has been formed.

When managers are criticized constantly for performance (which, of course, can always be better), a "what's the use" attitude can be generated. Enthusiasm is destroyed; energy is sapped — commitment slides to cog. When companies teach their employees to be helpless, however inadvertently, it is trouble. Whether in religion or in business, the effect is the same.

RUNNING IN PLACE

Harvey Dickson ran Community Outreach for Unity Missions, an evangelistic program for South America founded by A. Simpson Davis, and managed tightly by him for 40 years. Dickson, at 37, was second generation in the Missions. His father had been a missionary in Bolivia for 20 years, retiring some years before.

Dickson had lived with his parents "at the Front" for ten of those years before coming to Davis's Mississippi-based Training Academy. There he learned doctrine and ministry, interspersed with assistant-ship outposts in Panama and Honduras.

Upon graduation — called "attainment" in the group argot — Dickson, a natural organizer, was sent to Venezuela to head

Mission activities. After a successful three-year stint, Davis called him back to the home office to head operational control of Outreach. He was the youngest member of the senior executive staff and was a personal favorite of Davis's. It was widely assumed that the present promotion would not be his last.

Harvey Dickson had all the builders of commitment pulling in the same direction. His identification with the organization was from childhood and his personal involvement had augmented it. Now he had the opportunity to put into effect programs and procedures he had learned from experience. He would be the first "Front-Pastor" to head Outreach, his predecessors having been elderly and sedentary bureaucrats, all long-time associates of Davis.

The founder gave Dickson his full confidence and authority. Dickson had power, though he didn't desire it. His focus was purely productive; he knew how to make Front operations more efficient for pastors and more helpful to parishoners.

Dickson's first move was to designate one person at the home office to coordinate all functions for pastors at the Front, thus eliminating confused communications. (Previously each pastor had constant need to touch a dozen different people — regarding church operations, liturgy, finances, conversion control, and so forth.)

The move was a good one, widely appreciated by Mission pastors at the Front, but not so appreciated by bureaucrats at home. The bureaucrats had access to Founder Davis (and to his relatives), and within a week Dickson's decision was publicly ridiculed and reversed.

Dickson was shaken but compliant. Their work was the doings of the Lord, and it was He who had ultimate responsibility. Dickson was determined to continue making progress; personal pride meant nothing when the souls of millions were at stake — he was committed to the core.

His next significant move — recalling a shaky pastor who had lost the confidence of his congregation — was again reversed, and this time the pastor, an old comrade of Davis, was *promoted* to head that country's Mission. When this pattern continued, when most of Dickson's major decisions were peremptorily changed, the young zealot began to tire.

His life was dedicated to Unity Missions; it was his world and his life and there was no chance of changing. Yet, like those rats in the second cage unable to affect their environment, he was learning to be helpless. He withdrew into a shell, made only routine decisions supporting the status quo, and no longer sought innovative action. His commitment, though still core in attitude, had been eroded to cog in behavior. No longer would he risk personal loss to achieve organizational gain. The partisan had become a routiner.

THE FEELING IS GONE

"I may stick around for a while, but I'll never put my heart in another project here."

When Connie Schmidt had started her assignment, she tackled it with her usual intensity. Twelve-hour days were the light ones, and all subordinates were energized by her enthusiasm. She had a track record for success in assignments requiring political diplomacy, and this one would be particularly sensitive.

A new magazine was to be launched; satirical it was to be, with a touch of the ribald. Market testing and focus group studies showed a well-defined, upscale audience, and authorization for the "go" came directly from the president of the publishing division. The "dummy issue" was a smash, though needing to be more risque to attract their target audience.

Therein lay the problem. Would the content be offensive to their conservative chairman? (It was rumored, though it may have been a joke, that he didn't like the "permissive drift" of *Reader's Digest*.) Connie had seen the chairman's flamboyant initials on the project memo, though she suspected that it might have been one of dozens floated by him in a fast-paced half hour. Had he caught the slant of the edit? His support for the project, she feared, was only perfunctory.

"You make the book; I'll play the politics," her president reassured her.

Connie had pulled off the impossible before. This creation would be her finest. The mission of the magazine, its superb editorial and graphics quality, and the sense of potency Connie brought to it — all combined to give the wallop.

The magazine's first issue received rave reviews. Reader impact was excellent. An audience had been identified, caught, and served well. Circulation bettered predictions by 10 percent for subscriptions and by 35 percent on newsstands. Advertisers, normally wary of new magazines for a year, came crashing in. She had the "hot book," and agencies were competing for space and position. Computer models predicted cash flow breakeven within less than 15 months, superb for a major new publication.

It was another success for Connie, and she was relieved when the president whispered that the chairman loved the "high-quality look" of the issue.

Connie became a celebrity in publishing. She was interviewed in newspapers and on television, the creator and spokesperson for the brilliant venture.

The second issue was even better than the first, a rarity for magazines: the wit was sharper, the commentary more incisive, the sexual allusions more refined. It was an editorial tour de force.

Circulation was higher; ad pages fatter — and the computer model now predicted 11 months to breakeven.

The magazine was a howling success, and so Connie treated the brief note from the "chairman" as a practical joke from her staff. A good forger she must have, since those garish initials looked real. "Cease publication immediately," the terse message read, "my company will never seek financial gain through immorality and treason."

Connie's first glance at her president's fallen visage, as he slumped into her office moments later, told her as no words could that the little missive was no hoax and her baby was dead.

"The irony," began the president somberly,

> was that the chairman didn't even catch the simple subtlety. He took the article "praising" communism literally, and missed totally the sarcasm and critique. It did no good to explain; he found ten other things he hated, including women's equality in sexual relations — and that one he read right! We could've solved most of his objections without compromising the book, had he not been so arbitrary. You're luckly he doesn't know you. I got the "credit" — and fired.

Connie was reassigned to the company's flagship women's fashion magazine. Her associate publisher's position was a powerful one, with opportunity for innovation. But Connie had been taught to be helpless in one intense learning trial. Her desire had been robbed and the feeling would not come back.

Managers and employees alike must have a clear sense of personal control to build commitment to an organization. Though critical for creative positions, it applies to all. At issue is a capacity to affect one's circumstances.

Connie stayed on the job, doing what she was told with a blend of calculative and cog commitment. After all, she needed some steady income while devoting her creative talents to devising the new magazine she would soon sell to a group of appreciate investors.

MEANINGLESSNESS

Meaninglessness is more empty than the mere absense of meaning. Its emotion is negative, not neutral. It connotes barrenness between the individual and the institution, and unbridgable gulf between the purpose of the person and the mission of the group. It means that nothing the organization stands for or is doing has any significance to the individual.

Meaninglessness is cold and gnawing. It eats away at the resolve of the group member or company employee, undermining dedication, destroying motivation, dissolving the firm bond. Its poison works without haste, building in lethal power. Like a slow-growing cancer, meaninglessness must be long present internally before its symptoms become readily apparent externally.

No antagonism is implied in meaninglessness; whether the organization prospers or falters makes no difference whatsoever. The company is a blank, a zero, as far as the person is concerned.

Human beings are motivated by diverse factors; but none as powerful or as robust as the search for meaning, the quest for cause.[2] An employee devoid of meaning will be, at best, a functionary (a routiner in cog position on our commitment scale), doing assigned work with minimum involvement and maximum aloofness.

Meaninglessness is hard to generate, but meaningfulness is even harder to *re*generate. Most people begin new work in new companies with a degree of enthusiasm and excitement — if only for the newness and uncertainty. It will require progressive and persistent pressure to suck out substance and leave in meaninglessness. But once present, meaninglessness is resilient and resourceful and extraordinarily tough to replace.

WHAT CAN I DO?

The most surprising thing about David Morgan leaving his church was that he still sought biblical truth. His church had been founded in the eighteenth century and was considered mainstream conservative in the evangelistic tradition.

David had been brought up in a casual church-going family whose allegiance, at least nominally, was to a large liberal denomination. It was during the late 1960s, when his college friends were making their decisions for protest and drugs, that David made his decision for the bible and Christ.

Meaning he was seeking, and meaning he had found. Personal salvation and the coming Kingdom of God were the most important concepts for human beings, overwhelming all other endeavors and activities. The church was the mother of those called to God, and the focal point of David's involvement in the world.

Meaning he had, but perspective he lost. David had come to the church's seminary after two years at Berkley (that being some 15 years ago). Energetic and committed, he had worked his way up in the service of the church, progressing from assistant pastor of a small community church to pastor of the large St. Louis congregation to regional director for the midwest.

All signs pointed to David as the next associate pastor of the entire American ministry after the "rotation," mandatory every five years (to prevent the building of "power and empire.") But whether he misread the signals or misplayed the politics, David was not chosen.

Personal pique began swamping doctrinal conviction and David grew bitter. His sermons contained double meaning, and time spent with congregants fell off sharply.

Bitterness is a virulent emotion, difficult to hide and easy to see. In a downward spiraling circle David was removed from St. Louis and shipped off to a small eastern town, a clear demotion. "Get close to God," his new superior counseled him, "Pull yourself together and you'll be back."

His new superior had been a year behind David at the seminary and soundness of advice was distorted by jealously of person. David moved east as he was told, but his path was predetermined. It wasn't long before David Morgan, gregarious and intelligent, found a reasonable outside job and one day departed. He rationalized that although the church "taught some truth," it was just another group of petty men without special calling or purpose. (It is remarkable, we have observed so often, how closely theological belief follows personal position. Doctrines of ultimates — purpose, life, death, God, man, salvation; universe — are tossed and turned, almost comically, by social standing and group recognition. It's a recurrent theme: the impact of personal status, however trifling or trivial, on systems of belief.)

A natural salesman with charm and flair, David was as successful selling diet aids and food supplements as he had been winning souls and converts. Within five months he equaled his previous year's income. But although his material needs were being satisfied, his religious needs were not. He had physical goods but no spiritual meat.

He could have joined other churches with similar teachings, but an odd reaction had taken place in his psyche. Call it cognitive dissonance or simple rationalization, the effect was the same. The longer Daivd was out of the church the less he believed in its doctrines. There was no spiritual substance to fill his spiritual void. So David went on search.

His first attraction was to a pentecostal group, with the full panoply of "speaking in tongues" and other "manifestations of the Spirit." The physical signs seemed good substitutes for spiritual vision, but soon the public performances grew repetitive and boring — and he quit. But the emptiness did not.

His next encounter involved a small, obscure group calling itself a "church," but teaching that Christ was a "mystic tuned into universal resonances," and that his miracles were performed by "rearranging rhythms." Intrigued at first, David lost interest rapidly. It was getting harder filling one void with another.

Then followed an eclectic combination of Hinduism and Buddhism, but the chants and meditations carried little substance beyond the initial high of forbidden territory. With each successive religious group, David developed higher resistance and shorter tolerance, and soon even his longing for purpose was wearing thin. Meaninglessness was swamping the search for meaning.

His final foray was the occult. Here, it was promised, would be ultimate meaning: a pipeline of communication to an unseen world teeming with beings most knowing and strong; signs from long-departed friends and relatives inhabiting dimensions beyond human understanding — here one could be knowledgable and control events yet future. The promise, of course, was empty, and David's hope in vain. With all the strangeness and portents, there was even less meaning in the occult. Whether predictions were right or wrong, they were always empty, always forboding ill, always multiplying complexity and obliterating any essence of truth.

David Morgan had come to the end of the line. He had allowed personal frustration to disrupt what had been important. While he searched for meaning, what he found was nothing. Only meaninglessness and dissolution were at the end of this line.

Now some would call it the "grace of God" while others might say "guilt." Three years after David Morgan began his quest outside his church, he repented of his transgressions and returned to the flock. Although personal bitterness had temporarily triggered meaninglessness and crushed commitment, the recapturing of ultimate meaning restored comfort and core commitment.

WHAT AM I DOING HERE?

Broderick Thorton ran the specialty paper distribution division of a large conglomerate. Into his twentieth year with the company, he was an aggressive executive and more than a competent administrator, having built the division into the second largest in the Southwest. For five years he had the capital and the confidence to build market share, and he fulfilled his mandate well. Recently, however, corporate priorities had shifted.

High tech was the new frontier and resources were being pulled from traditional businesses and poured into acquisitions in semiconductors and telecommunications. Thorton was largely left alone and, except for the quarterly budget reviews in New York, was rarely in contact with corporate headquarters.

The sketchy information from headquarters, official and grapevine, suggested strategic confusion. No one seemed to know what they wanted to build. A high-tech pioneer? A financially efficient conglomerate? A large share distributor? The strategies were as antagonistic as the board was politicized.

Thorton wasn't a maintenance man, nor was his style isolation from action. He was not satisfied to make budget and shovel excess cash flow into corporate coffers to be wasted by high-tech turks.

When asking for marching orders, Thorton was told to "build market share and improve return on assets." However, not one of his plans for building the one or improving the other was even considered. Patronizing comments from staff assistants outside the power train were the best he could get. The fact that capital was being regularly withdrawn from his division was dismissed as "not relevant." The contradiction in signals wouldn't be discussed.

Thorton grew restless, then irritated. The aimlessness of the firm and the uncertainty of his role were alien to his nature. Hard-driving and clear-thinking, Broderick Thorton was out of place. Though he had not the wandering eye, he became an easy target for an executive search firm on prowl. A medium-sized paper converter, intent on making the big leagues, was looking for a president.

Financial return was only a minor consideration in Thorton's decision to switch jobs. Security, for sure, was no incentive, since he was giving it away in the move, not getting any. What this company had was defined purpose, and Brad Thorton had his meaning.

Meaninglessness is a silent killer of corporate commitment, destroying the attachment between individual and institution, and sliding personnel from core to cog with only a brief stopover at calculative. Managers will give up much to find meaning, and companies must be sensitive to this uniquely human need.

What can be done to build organizational meaning for employees? First, goals must be set clearly, embedding excitement, participation, and reward. Next, and no less critical, personalities must be matched to jobs. Some executives enjoy managing a division for cash, squeezing costs out and shrinking assets down. Others need the prospects of expansion, and revel in becoming Number One in any definable sense. Still others find meaning in the nature of the work, the specific content of job tasks. It is vital that employees be put in the right positions. What is meaningless to one may be meaningful to another.

WORTHLESSNESS

Esteem and pride, though often berated, are important building blocks of commitment. Human beings need a positive sense of self-worth, and this applies both individually to the person and collectively to the group.

Nothing is more debilitating to initiative than feelings of uselessness and irrelevance, a low opinion of self relative to others. Depression is common to such persons; no one cares, they think, and nothing matters. A person feeling worthless will neither see any importance in life nor any reason to improve it. Worthlessness drains out energy and spews forth despair. Worthlessness is a circular system of thinking, vicious and virulent and very difficult to break.

Performance in any endeavor is dependent on confidence, and anything that undermines the latter will inhibit the former. Worthlessness can be the most deadly of the commitment breakers as it is one of the most subtle. It is highly protective of its existence, resisting conflicting evidence and seeking constant confirmation. (Extreme conditions of worthlessness, more than the other breakers, can trigger suicidal states.) Managers are often unaware that constant criticism of a subordinate, though done to correct and improve, can erode self-confidence and thus makes correction and improvement harder.

Worthlessness has a double punch. A human being submerged by waves of worthlessness is severely handicapped in modern society, yet modern society launches massive assault on the person's esteem. It is easy to be engulfed by overwhelming events and to see oneself as trivial and irrelevant within huge organizations.

ANY WAY BUT LOOSE

Sylvia Novak was a recent convert to a church that took issue, or so it seemed, with Paul's injunction that Christians should "work out their own salvation with fear and trembling." This church was determined to get all of its members into heaven, which meant doing all things pleasing to God.

The church had been started in Europe by a strict disciplinarian, and brought with it to America some very specific ideas of what was pleasing to God. These behavioral guidelines formed the backbone of the founder's revered book, *The Way Straight and Narrow*. Though hardly based on the bible, they were taught as if spoken from Mount Sinai, as Commandments 11 through 77.

Sylvia was a housewife in her early fifties with three preteen children and a truck-driver husband. He had been interested in her new religion until the time of her conversion which brought about the ever-present vigilance of the church-authorized "Helpers of Salvation." Though they irritated her husband, the Helpers were welcomed warmly by Sylvia. Each visit, no less frequent than weekly, was another confirmation of her righteousness.

Having been brought up in a strict religious family herself, with sins of the flesh categorized as the most terrible of all, Sylvia could readily accept the new church's emphasis that the human mind is "deceitful and desperately wicked." What she could not accept was her own "heinous sin," the one sexual experience she had had in high school, the night of her senior prom.

The fact that she was married now and had sexual relations with her husband (if without orgasm or pleasure) did not seem to matter. Though she prayed every day for God to forgive her "the disgust of that lust," she was sure that she could never be worthy of Christ's sacrifice or mercy and that some severe penalty would soon have to be exacted from her.

Sylvia prayed at the required times and repeated the required chants, yet every time the pastor preached on the evils of promiscuity and vice — which was often and powerfully — her face reddened and pulse quickened. Although Sylvia had never confessed her sin, she knew that he knew. Every time the pastor said the words "wanton lusts of the flesh," she imagined him looking right at her, exposing her sin for all to abhor.

Soon, she figured, the Helpers knew too. Why else would they look that way? They never said anything, of course — her sin was too horrible. It was the way they spoke, or didn't speak; what they said, or didn't say; the verses they quoted, or didn't quote.

Sylvia's self-worth was falling faster than the value of currency in hyperinflation. She was a sinner, probably the worst anywhere in the church, maybe anywhere on earth. Perhaps the problem, she started to think, was not enough prayer, not enough bible study, not enough fasting. Only continuous contact with God could erase so horrid a crime.

So Sylvia began to callous her knees and fray her bible in a frantic effort to appease God. The voracious demands of her religion were accompanied by a steady withdrawal from common patterns of life. Her house, always spotless, was now rarely cleaned. Her children she hardly fed. Her husband she never slept with. Maybe, she reasoned, if she abstained from sex altogether, God's wrath would be assuaged.

The Helpers, seeing the deterioration in the house, rebuked Sylvia for the first time, instructing her that she must care for her family as well as be devoted to God. Sylvia was mortified. She had never been so sternly admonished. All her intense efforts were having no effect. God was still angry. And those Helpers — now she knew they were her enemies, sent from Satan to stop her from praying to God. The church was false and her life was worthless. God had rejected her. There was so sense praying any more, no sense doing anything.

Sylvia Novak was a possible candidate for suicide. Her condition was not caused by this church, but flourished within its rigid system. She is an extreme example of worthlessness, and as such highlights aspects we can pick out in more normal situations.

In the actual case, the associate pastor was perceptive and sensitive, and had advanced training in pastoral counseling. When Sylvia missed several services he sought her out. After several difficult counseling sessions, she told him about her ancient sin, and he started slowly to soften her obsession.

To God, he explained, all sin is sin, and Christ's blood washes all sin. If there are any gradations at all, sins of the flesh are probably less severe than sins against one's fellows. The bible teaches balance, he showed, and that care for house and home, husband and children, are as important to God as prayer and fasting. Though the process was long and tedius, Sylvia was brought back from the brink. She stayed in the church and her self-worth was rebuilt.

WHERE DID YOU SAY YOU'RE FROM?

Not only individuals have self-esteem; organizations do also. Destroy organizational esteem and you destroy member commitment.

Elliot Graves, assistant treasurer of ValueMark Department Stores, had completed registration for the conference on Recent Trends in Cash Management and was filling out his name tag. Graves routinely printed in bold letters, but hesitated when he came to the company name.

ValueMark had just declared bankruptcy, putting itself into Chapter 11 and all the newspapers. The announcement, not unexpected, culminated a continuous stream of very bad press. The personal ethics of several company officers had been called into question.

Graves decided to leave "ValueMark" off his name tag. He went over to an empty table, sat down, and waited for the conference to begin. He hoped no one would ask where he worked.

On returning from the Conference, Graves decided to seek other employment. He felt like a failure, even a criminal. Though he had been hired only a few months before, and if anything had delayed the bankruptcy, not caused it, family and friends acted as if all ValueMark's problems should be laid at his feet. Enough of this nonsense, he concluded; there's a career to be built.

A week later, the creditors committee appointed a new CEO. Harold Jenkins was known as "the Fireman." He would only take assignments in "burning companies," and would only stay until the flames were out and the rebuilding under way.

After two days on the job, Jenkins called Graves into his office and laid out his plan for stopping the conflagration and reshaping the company. He intended stressing ValueMark's proven competitive strengths, especially its reputation for quality merchandise. There would be no more wanderings into manufacturing.

"Elliott, you've done wonders, though you've been barely appreciated." Jenkins was leading to some request.

I'm putting a new team together. I want a young, hungry group of first-rate pros. I want men who will stake their reputation on our success, who will take pride in resurrecting these ruins. I've asked Shapiro to become VP of Marketing and Riley to be VP of Store Operations. You, Elliott, I want for VP of Finance. You're all under 35, all ten years away from senior management under normal conditions. Well, these aren't normal conditions. We're going to have to work our butts off turning this billion-dollar baby around. But we'll do it. We'll take every opportunity for restructuring that Chapter 11 allows. We'll come out one hell of a strong company. I guarantee you that if we succeed here, you can call your shots anywhere; but I think you'll stay. Now, regarding your compensation package. . . .

Building organizational esteem is vital for executives, especially today when institutions face diverse and conflicting constituencies who are sometimes hostile. Graves caught Jenkin's vision, and personal worth overcame organizational worthlessness. Managers with the ability to impart self-worth to subordinates can surmount even the most difficult corporate circumstances. To fire the imagination, to induce self-generating dedication, to instill confidence — these are the rare qualities of organizational leadership.

The rise of entrepreneurs is a major cultural change in American business. The trend is caused, at least in part, by a desire to supplant worthlessness and build importance. It is difficult to see one's work making real impact in large organizations. The midlife decisions of stockbrokers and executives to change careers and own rare-book stores or manage ski resorts reflect a desire to establish such personal significance. In order to produce top performance and lasting benefit, personal participation must be grounded in personal worth.

ANXIETY

High anxiety is a general sense of foreboding, an unspecific fear of the future. It weakens commitment by breaking down stability, undermining confidence, and generating unease and uncertainty.

Anxiety is apprehension, and high anxiety is exaggerated or inappropriate apprehension. (We will use "anxiety" in this section to mean "high anxiety.") An employee wracked by anxiety will be in constant fear of organizational attack; there may be expectations of criticism

from superiors, failure on assignments, social ostracism, even ar-
bitrary termination or failure of the company. An anxious employee
has little psychic energy available for productive activities.

Anxiety can be defined as a present state of mind caused by the
possibility than an action of the past, present, or future might conflict
with the environment at some future date. Described in this manner,
anxiety encompasses Festinger's theory of cognitive dissonance.[3]
("Dissonance" means that two or more concepts are logically opposed
to one another.) Stated simply, anxiety is the anticipation of possible
dissonance.

Anxiety can be characterized from several viewpoints. In
psychiatric conditions, an anxious patient will exhibit pathological
alertness and tension. There can be extreme eagerness that results in
inept or awkward actions. The person considers each thought proof
that some dire event will occur. Sometimes this event will continually
change; occasionally all signs will point toward a single calamity.

Say a person has organized a club picnic three weeks in advance.
Many arrangements will have to be made. With the outing a few days
away, the weather bureau reports storm warnings. The picnic planner
is *now*, according to our definition, in a state of anxiety. There is a
possibility that his actions of the past (arranging the picnic) might conflict with the environment at some future date (inclement weather).
Anxiety would not be the present state of mind if the picnic had to be
definitely postponed for one reason or another. The emotion would
then be disappointment. Anxiety is present only when dissonance is
possible; if the dissonance occurs, anxiety is consummated and
another mood takes its place.

Anxiety is more serious when no immediate cause is apparent. The
person is in a continuous state of expectancy, waiting for some
disaster to befall. The awful event might happen at any moment, it may
assume any form. Perhaps financial loss will result from poor investments; perhaps one's job will disappear; perhaps. . . .

The magnitude of anxiety can vary widely. Apprehension is part of
our biological warning mechanism. A certain degree of anxiety is
valuable. We function better when we are more alert. Students do better on test, and athletes do better on the field, with *moderate* anxiety
than with either high or low levels. With the ill-fated organizer of the
picnic, anxiety is beneficial. The man will now be more alert to
weather reports and better prepared for alternative action. If,
however, this alerting reaction becomes inappropriately strong, normal functioning can be interrupted.

We can assess the magnitude of the anxiety by assessing the
magnitude of the dissonance since, by definition, anxiety is a function
of dissonance. If two elements are dissonant with one another, the
magnitude of the dissonance will be a function of the importance of

the elements. For the picnic organizer, the dissonance and hence the anxiety cannot exceed the level of resistance to calling off the entire event. A washed out picnic, however, is relatively minor compared with the anticipation of a cataclysm.

Anxiety can be reduced by reducing dissonance. How to reduce dissonance? The simplest way, though often not practical, is to alter the action. Call off the picnic. Since anxiety is the anticipation of possible dissonance, anxiety decreases as possible dissonance decreases. Although bad weather was forecast, the person might check other reports for second opinions. A humorous article recounting mistakes in weather forecasting will be read avidly, while other articles dealing with increased reliability due to weather satellites will be ignored. News reports of small craft warnings might be misinterpreted to mean that the storm was blowing out to sea. The person might begin to minimize the picnic by stressing the importance of the friends getting together irrespective of place.

A person with anxiety, expecting calamity, might be motivated to reduce anxiety by making the calamity *more* likely to happen. This is the strange part. Dissonance would be reduced since reality would then be in agreement with his feeling of imminent disaster. An employee overly anxious about being fired, for example, might start coming late to work or choosing projects more likely to fail. The reaction of superiors would then confirm his initial apprehension and justify his looking for other employment.

There is an inverse relationship between anxiety and security. A person rooted in a stable belief system and value structure will rarely suffer from inappropriate apprehension. Whenever such an individual confronts behavioral alternatives, he can evaluate them in light of a constant standard. He will be reasonably confident that the future environment will not be dissonant with his present behavior. Anxiety makes little headway with a secure person.

WHERE'S IT COMING FROM NEXT?

Richard Washington was a supervisor in a local branch of the U. S. Post Office. His work was steady and his pay was good. Security was what this 50-year old high school graduate had in abundance — a few more years and he would reach retirement with ample benefits. Yet Richard was beset by anxiety. The reason was his church, not his job.

Several years ago Richard had joined a prophecy-based church whose doctrine was guided by the coming "rapture of the saints." Church sermons had two primary themes: vigilance and preparation. Regarding vigilance, members were exhorted to watch world events and note calamities — the sure sign of the fast-closing rapture. Each week one or more of the feared four horsemen of the apocalypse (from the Book of Revelation) would be discussed in excruciating detail: false religion; wars and rumors of wars; famine; pestilence. Stories about declining reservoir levels would be interwoven with weather reports of floods and monsoons. Every dog bite, it seemed, was the beginning of bubonic plague. Armies moving into the Middle East would soon surround Jerusalem in ultimate confrontation at Armageddon.

Regarding preparation, members were admonished to be prepared to meet the Lord, to await the Lord who would swoop up the saints and save them from destruction. Every sermon was laced with the same exhortation. A constant state of prayer was vital and adherence to Church rules sacrosanct. Members were encouraged ceaselessly to build up their "treasures in Heaven" by giving generously to the church on earth. Its missionary work had to be finished before the rapture.

Richard believed in the accuracy of prophecy, the reality of the rapture, and the authority of the church. It was hard, though, to keep in the required state of "constant readiness and vigilance" that God apparently demanded. Every sermon was peppered with scriptures berating him. If Richard couldn't keep a perfect week — no beer, no lust, much prayer, and more offerings — he became agitated. He was apprehensive that the rapture would come and, not being vigilant, he wouldn't be ready. He would be left on earth, a sinner in shame, about to face the consequences of catastrophe.

Every time he put a dollar in anything but the offering cup each Sunday, he felt guilty. Each time he saw the newspaper he felt his stomach knot. Though the pastor kept setting dates, and the dates kept passing without fuss, Richard's anxiety kept increasing. He worried about everything he did, the foods he ate, the ideas he thought. He couldn't watch television or read a magazine in peace. Would God get him today? The attacks became more frequent. After several months, Richard was unable to eat or work. Holding down jobs or meals was impossible. Anxiety, not religion, monopolized his life.

At this point the road must fork. Either Richard would have to be put under medical care and perhaps be institutionalized, or he would seek to reduce anxiety by separation from the church. (The latter is easily rationalized; since he begins a sinner and reprobate in the church, he is hardly worse off leaving.) On either fork the church looses a member. Religious rigmarole hinders biblical belief; but biblical fidelity supports biblical truth.

Organizations must take care not to push members to the breaking point in the spirit of high dedication. Exaggerating group requirements or making unrealistic demands to achieve partial compliance is a strategy of risk — it might work with the lackadaisical majority, but it chances ruining a serious minority. Better is to state group requirements as they are, and make rules realistic. In this way, while less may be done, more will be accomplished.

WHAT'S GOING ON AROUND HERE?

Steven Hoag had all he could take. Enough was enough. He was a nervous wreck, never having had more than three months of consistent direction, never the same boss for more than six. ("If my boss calls, get his name," middle managers would tell their secretaries only half in jest.)

For three years Steven was supposed to be in charge of new product planning for a medium-sized conglomerate with diverse consumer businesses in tools, food products, garden equipment, and furniture. (Steven couldn't decide which part was more laughable, the "in charge" or the "planning.") The company had been run autocratically by the tough founder for 30 years, but since he died, his heirs and the board were split a dozen different ways.

Strategies were started and stopped. First "seasonal balance" was the guiding light (products with complementary timing, such as snowmobiles and lawnmowers); then "demographic growth" was the leitmotif (products tagged to the shifting age groups in the general population); then "synergistic channels" was the rage (products using similar systems of distribution). Each idea was good; but each idea was different — and the company leaped from one strategy to another like a drunken grasshopper.

Steve took each assignment to heart. He couldn't create a business plan unless he internalized its strategy and believed its prospects. But the frustration of having each plan torpedoed by a new board or a new boss was debilitating.

Senior executives often tried to coerce Steve into "modifying" (read *falsifying*) his projections as part of their political jockeying and game playing. Recently he had been seduced — the first time. He rationalized that it was in the company's best interest to move around top management. The fact that Steve was promised a promotion once the new boys took over was, he convinced himself, incidental to his decision.

Well, the plan worked — for a week, Steve's newfound friends were in and out so fast they didn't even have a chance to fulfill their Faustian promise — which, ironically, was beneficial since Steve would have been fired along with the rest of the blunders had he been given the promotion.

Anxiety hit record highs when the new president asked for copies of all business plans. Steve could hardly work; he dreaded the call from the executive suite, expected momentarily.

He was prepraring his resume when he received a "memo for managers." It came from the new president and laid out a blueprint for the future. First, he wrote, the board had given him a three-year contract, this to give stability to top management. He in turn pledged strategic continuity and administration consistency. Furthermore, company strategy would build upon the two areas of comparative strength and competitive advantage: home products and garden products. Other businesses, where the company didn't enjoy strong market position, would be sold off.

The memo concluded by giving specific times for private appointments for each of the recipients. "I want to know what you think," the president wrote, "and learn how you can make maximum contribution to the firm." Then, at the bottom, a handwritten note: "Steve, I've seen your plans. Excellent formulations. We're finally going to do some *implementation*. Looking forward to meeting on Tuesday."

Employees want to work. They want their companies to succeed. Uncertainty, unease, and the anticipation of calamity are not pleasant emotions. Although not wholly controllable, they can be stopped by consistency, stability, and reliability. In a word, managers who inspire confidence will eliminate the scourge of anxiety.

CHAPTER EIGHT

PERSONAL COMMITMENT: HELPING YOURSELF

Richard Schane had been a minister for over 25 years. His church maintained a rigidly constructed orthodoxy to which Schane had always conformed. Rigidity and orthodoxy fit his character well; doing things according to the book suited him fine.

Members were kept in line through a complex code of communal ceremony and private ritual. The Church had an excellent record of member retention, but was notorious for a characteristic grimness of member personality. Human beings, it was taught, must "toe the line" on earth in order "get in line" for heaven. Emotional affectations, like worldly possessions, were encumbrances to be discarded.

Schane had always personified such stolid, immutable righteousness, but tragedy shattered his granitelike adamance. After the sudden death of his wife, he experienced a period of heightened emotion not compatible with church practices. He felt more compassion for the frailty of members, and was much less willing to admonish others for sin. Personal faults, he now felt, should be worked with privately, mercy being a more effective weapon than punishment. Feeling guilty for months, Schane began to wonder if the church's rigidity was responsible for suppressing the proper expression of human concern.

Soon personal feelings could not be restrained. His ministerial convictions ran too deep. He could not withhold from his parishoners what he believed to be the truth of God. Schane, along with several other ministers of kindred spirit, started preaching their newly found truth that "the greatest of what abides is love." For them the inflexibility of law was out, and the sensitivity of love was in.

For the Church hierarchy, the only thing now "out" was Schane and his cohorts. They moved in quickly and excommunicated those who were threatening its orthodoxy and doctrinal control.

Richard Schane was not prepared for this moment. The axe fell swiftly. Though he was prepared to accept the consequences of his rebellion, the reality was jolting. He was out. He was counted among the condemned, separated from the church, avoided by all. The linear path of 25 years had been broken; his life snapped.

Schane knew what he could *not* do: he could no longer condone what he felt was gross insensitivity to human need. But he did not know what he *could* do. To his chagrin, few followed him in his brief attempt to establish an independent church. Worse yet, those few who joined him were "fringers" in their beliefs and behavior. What he got were the "weirdos." Schane could only blame himself: he had always been a good preacher, and church loyalty had often been his subject.

His breakaway church, for its several scant months of existence, was a congregation of miscreants and malcontents. Having tasted the blood of religious battle, they were eager to taste it again. Having rebelled once, they were ready to rebel twice. What began as a splinter soon degenerated into shards.

Schane struggled to reestablish himself. Religion, in such a crippled form, was pointless. He fought listlessness. He fought depression. He tried several jobs but could not focus his energy. Money-making ventures veered from scheme to scam: selling diet supplements in a multilevel pyramid one month to setting up tax-free "churches" the next month. Schane had no foundation, no roots. His separation from his former life had been too swift, too unexpected. "Cold turkey" had been a tough exit.

Schane cannot be faulted for his intensity and commitment in the service of his church and his beliefs. However, his example points out a major principle of commitment management for the individual: if you sense a "jump" may be necessary, at least have a parachute ready before leaping. Few jumps will be without psychological trauma, even if you have a fully functional parachute on your back. Without one, watch out for freefall.

HELPING SELF AND FIRM

A bond has two ends. The *firm* bond links personal meaning and corporate mission, and is our working definition of commitment. We built the model in Part I employing personal, organizational, and interactional elements. Thus far in Part II we've discussed some key builders and breakers of commitment. Now, in Chapters 8 and 9, we will apply what we've learned. Our objective is to benefit individuals and organizations.

Chapter 7 deals with commitment from the veiwpoint of the person — what the group member or company employee needs to achieve personal goals. How to arrange life to optimize talents and interests? How to structure job and position to produce fulfillment? How to get maximum value out of organizational relationships?

Chapter 8 moves to the opposite end of the bond and deals with commitment from the vantage point of the organization. How to optimize the fulfilling of mission and purpose? How to arrange structure to encourage productivity? How to get maximum value out of individual members and employees?

SACRIFICING THE CORPORATE MAN

John Kenneth Galbraith, Professor of Economics Emeritus at Harvard, calls organizations an "all-embracing force" molding "the life and larger social existence of the modern corporate man."[1] The perception is incisive; the image chilling.

"The counterpart of the modern executive's disciplined commitment to the job at hand is, however, an extremely severe sacrifice of the right to personal thought and expression. And also a wide range of personal enjoyments." Galbraith emphasizes the "ban on unlicensed expression," noting the media's lack of interest in executive communications — "there is no form of spoken literature, Sunday Sermons possibly excepted, that invokes such a profound silence." We are not left to wonder why.

What an executive says is "required by the rules and ethics of organizations to be both predictable and dull. He does not speak for himself; he speaks for the firm. Good policy is not what he wants but what the organization believes it needs. In the normal case, his speech will be written and vetted by his fellow organization men. In the process, it will drop to the lowest common denominator of novelty. Lindberg, as has too often been told, could never have flown the Atlantic with a committee. It is equally certain that General Motors could never have written Shakespeare or even a column by Art Buchwald."

Galbraith, not free enterprise's greatest booster, reflects on the best of the breed — graduates of the Harvard Business School. "All, with the rarest exceptions, will enjoy extraordinarily ample incomes for the rest of their lives. None, with only the most eccentric exceptions, will ever make any personal contribution in music, painting, the theater, film, writing, serious learning or the lower art of politics. Once, a good income was thought to allow such diversions; that was its purpose. From the modern business executive the most that can be expected is a check in support of someone else's achievements."

He mounts a piercing attack. The modern corporate executive, Galbraith reminds his readers, "has a more than modest role" in setting his own pay and perquisites. But what does the executive give up in return? Galbraith tags "personal identity." ("The organization takes over; the head is unknown.") The industrial chieftan commands respect and deference from all his minions; but on the day he leaves office, he sinks into "an oblivion that continues until the few touching lines appear in the obituary columns."

Galbraith concludes with an elegant absense of sarcasm: "I do not suggest that, given his sacrifices, the modern business executive is underpaid; there are millions more in line worthy of that concern. I do note that it is worth something to give up so much — considering recent state of knowledge on the matter — of one's only certain life."

The analysis is brilliant but betrays aloofness. There is little appreciation for "corporate creativity."[2] (The two words together, at least to Galbraith, might seem incongruous, even contradictory, like, say, "bright blackness.")

Galbraith is ignoring all the innovative activities that go in modern corporations. There are numerous companies turning out dazzling products, and innumerable executives in those companies who have tremendous opportunity for personal expression. To use the General Motors example, consider the new Corvettes, Firebirds and Fieros coming out their design studios. Surely, these are rich expressions of human creativity, feeding back fulfillment to their creators.

The corporate world generates enormous novelty. When a few American steel companies can beat back foreign competitors with efficient "minimills;" when video recorders transform home entertainment; when new forms and fashions of apparel, furniture, food, toys, electronics, machinery, services, make life more interesting — the *people* who generate this freshness are defining a new style of "personal thought and expression."

Galbraith fails, as he often does not, to sense discontinuity in historical change. The reach of human creativity has broadened, and the learned man has missed it completely. Social context is critical, and new definitions are in order. It is anachronistic, and perhaps a bit snobby, to limit "personal expression" to "music, painting, the theater. . . ." and to feel pity for executives who do not compose, draw and write.

What writing a piece of literature was a hundred years ago, designing a new software system is now. What sculpting a piece of art was in past centuries, bringing a new pharmaceutical molecule to market is today. Society is different; creativity has become more collective. But the change is more content and complexity than process and character. Take high energy physics research. In the early decades of the century, a single person working alone could advance the field. Today, two dozen scientists must handle a given experiment.

Human expression in the modern world has taken new shapes. Organizations are permanent entities, required by social structure and economic force. Their affect on members, however, is up for grabs. They can be either amplifiers or resistors, enhancing or inhibiting personal fulfillment. What business can learn from religion could make the difference.

A STRATEGIC FRAMEWORK FOR BUILDING COMMITMENT

The strategic framework is designed to give organizations and business optimum competitive position.[3] It is a way of thinking powerful and broad. We apply it here for the advantage of the individual, to optimize attitude and position, to build mental health, to strengthen commitment.

The system is a specific application, an extension of the scientific method. It uses the classic principles of evidence, experiment, and logical reasoning to ascertain truth. As such we can use the strategic framework to develop personal benefits for people, since such benefits build the individual end of the firm bond.

The strategic framework has several parts:

- Establishing overall purpose or grand design, sets of longer-term goals and subsets of shorter-term objectives.
- Assessing internal strengths and weaknesses in light of external opportunities and threats.
- Formulating and evaluating alternative strategies — by mapping the strengths and weaknesses on to the opportunities and threats.
- Implementing and monitoring chosen strategies.

ESTABLISHING GOALS

In establishing personal goals in organizational association, whether in business employment or religious membership, process is as important as content, somtimes more so. Process is what you *do*; content is what you *want*. The general vision one has for attaining long-range goals (content) must be articulated with the specific tasks one does in achieving short-range objectives (process). Process is what one does day-in and day-out, and the means are often more vital for personal fulfillment than the ends.

What elements should be considered in goal-establishment procedures? Some suggestions: What are your intentions in position, industry, company, personal finances, and perks — and what are the relative priorities among them? What financial minimums do you require, and how much financial potential would you sacrifice for desirable position, company, geography, and the like? What type work do you enjoy doing daily?

Try this approach. Look at the question in reverse. Take advantage of simulated hindsight. Picture yourself at the end of your career: What do you feel most pleased about; what work did you enjoy the most; what are your regrets; what would you change if you could do it all over again?

ASSESSING STRENGTHS AND WEAKNESSES

Assessing one's own strengths and weaknesses is no easy task. Accurate judgment is difficult enough. But there is an added problem. The job is easily confused with cataloging one's likes and dislikes. The two sets are not the same, though often related. We usually like what we are good at, and we usually do not like what we are not good at. (There are exceptions. Not a few successful businessmen would have liked to have been artists, musicians, and writers had they had the talent and the breaks.)

What elements should you include in the strength and weakness assessment procedure? Consider some common categories. How do you rate yourself? Sales? Technical? Analytical? Creative? Financial? Managerial? What about functions such as coordinating, control, production efficiencies, product innovation, product introduction?

The trick is to step outside of yourself and see your qualities as others see them. Strengths and weaknesses must be assessed relative to two standards: first, each ability must be compared internally to your other abilities; second, each must be compared to an external standard, to other people's abilities. Some subtleties (or oddities) may emerge here. For example, accounting ability may be your strongest point when assessed internally, but could become relatively weak if set against the standard of the Big Eight CPA companies. Similarly, human skills in personnel management may be weaker than numerical skills when compared internally, but relatively stronger when compared externally.

Don't overlook a built-in bias here. It is natural to assume that the things one does currently are strengths, and the things one does not do are weaknesses. Yet, there are many examples of secretaries becoming engineers and financial analysts going off to manage mountain inns.

One must try to be "honest and pure" in the self-assessment. It is easy to skew the analysis based on what one imagines others think is more important or prestigious. Don't confound the task. Avoid the pride trap. It's the pits.

Finally, don't fear the truth. There is no law that requires you to do what you can do best, if that wars against what you want to do best.

FORMULATING AND EVALUATING PERSONAL STRATEGIES

Though we combine formulating and evaluating personal strategies in one section, they differ cognitively and emotionally. Generating alternative strategies in the option-making phase is intuitive, holistic, expansive, and creative. Evaluating alternative strategies in the decision-making phase is analytical, fragmented, focused, and logical. The generation process is "right-brain"; the evaluating process is "left-brain." The former is done explosively with free association; the latter is done rigorously with honed analysis.

What elements are involved in formulating personal strategies? Try the following question. What job, within reasonable aspirations, would you most strongly seek (or desire)? To be effective, the generation of alternatives should yield ideas that are both unusual and contradictory, thus delivering real choice. If options are all tired and familiar, you've caught the wrong vision.

The key here is expansiveness. Divorce yourself from current patterns and ruts. Devise possibilities you've never thought about before. Consider all ideas open at the moment, then assume the occurrence of unusual events, most positive, some negative. For example, what would your employment options become if you inherited enough money to guarantee one-half your current salary for life? How about double that salary? On the other side of the coin, what would your employment options become if your present company went bankrupt and your job was lost? The answers, or possible answers, to both questions will help expand choices.

What elements are involved in evaluating personal strategies? The key is rigorous analysis. Each alternative must be subjected to a torrent of tough questions, all framed with specificity and incisiveness. Imagine each possibility actually materializing, and then test its relationship with your aspirations and abilities.

For each alternative: What skills are required? (Do you have them? Can you learn them?) What are the interpersonal relations? (With whom would you be working? Who would be your superiors and subordinates?) What about financial returns, the rewards? What about stability factors, the risks? What impositions would be made on yourself, on your family? What are the intangibles? (How much do you really want this job or membership, and what would you give up to get it?)

In making decisions, one must always consider the parameter of time. What works today might not work tomorrow. What is desired now might have to wait until then.

Consideration of the external environment is important. Where are the opportunities and threats out there? If your best skill is commercial art, but there is a surfeit of commercial artists, then your strength is contradicted by the lack of opportunity. Similarly, if setting up tax shelters is your specialty and Congress is planning new tax laws making such shelters more restrictive, that is a definite threat. On the other hand, if you are good with logical structures and there is a need for computer programmers, then even if you don't have the training there is opportunity. (One computer company built its technical staff strength on talmudic scholars needing commercial employment.)

IMPLEMENTATION AND MONITORING

Arraying ideas and making choices are theoretical; implementating and monitoring are practical. The former is done with minds and papers; the latter with hands and things. Never confuse the two.

Doing something is always harder than planning it. People are not totally controllable nor are events completely predictable. What works on paper may not work in life. Setting out to accomplish what one wants demands both prior planning and persistent pressure. If change is part of the preferred pattern, don't allow enthusiasm and impatience to overwhelm wisdom and common sense.

Monitoring is a vital part of the process. Feedback and control enable you to know what and how you are doing while you are doing it.

Using the strategic framework for personal guidance is a continuous, lifelong process. The results at all times must be fed back into the system. What is happening compared to what was expected to be happening? The real data may be painful but they are critical for progressive improvement.

What emerges is *refinement*: reestablishing goals; reassessing strengths and weaknesses; reexamining opportunities and threats; regenerating and reevaluating competing alternatives. The end product — what you do and where you are going — must be made constantly better.

Following are some vignettes. All portray one or more aspects of the strategic framework in action. The illustrations may be what the person did do, should have done, might have done, or could yet do. The reader is allowed the opportunity to decide without force or favor. Reflecting our framework, using "ultimates" and "closed systems" to highlight meaning and mission, religious and business examples are interwoven.

THE ARTIST

Brent Coleson reveled in the glorious doctrine of his bible-believing church. Everlasting life with God was a goal surmounting all others — it was a mission worth everything else put together.

He had joined the church in his native England where he gave up his promising career as a sculptor in order to study for the ministry. His first few years serving the British brethren were both engrossing and fulfilling. He was honored to help others share his great vision. His labor was long and his joy was sweet.

After about five years, however, Brent noticed a change in his own attitude, and he didn't like the drift. It wasn't that his dedication was in any way less, but an emptiness had developed where full-fledged commitment had been before. Even though he still believed the ultimate goal wholeheartedly and it still overwhelmed all others, he was feeling unfulfilled. And with the passing months, the emptiness was growing.

Unused ability is often a source of frustration. Brent had a strong artistic talent that was lying fallow. His sabbatical was upcoming and his superiors, with whom he discussed his problems, made an interesting decision. They sent Brent to the church publishing house in America for a working year, where he began illustrating church magazines, pamphlets, and books. He even showed some rudimentary editorial skills.

When the year was up, Brent was both given an American congregation and asked to continue his graphic designs on a part-time basis. It was hardly a year later that Brent was called back to work full-time in a senior position in church editorial. (Ironically, he now had to struggle to find expression for his ministerial interests. He eventually received an assistant pastorship of a small local church.)

Brent had put it all together. He was an excellent minister to be sure, but there were other ministers of equal excellence. He might even have been a better minister than artist, but in his particular environment he was *relatively* better as an artist. By making the shift not only did he fulfill his personal needs, but he also played his comparative advantage. Commitment never weak, was still strengthened, the product of achievement and self-esteem.

THE MINICONGLOMERATE

Wholeness — that's what Raymond Litte had experienced as a young man in his work. But wholeness was no longer satisfying.

Litte worked as fiction editor for a small literary magazine in Texas, and all that he had needed in life was provided by his editorship: creative expression, personal writing, artistic association. Everything he wanted he had. Why this changed is only part of the story. What happened after Litte lost his Camelot is also important.

As Litte moved into his forties, he felt a small void starting to expand. He wanted part in more mainstream activities of society; he wanted to make more money; he wanted more security; he wanted to experience new areas of the work world. But he also wanted to maintain his contact with publishing and he wanted to remain a writer. He wanted; he wanted. . . . So many pieces making up Litte. Why, he wondered, couldn't it be as simple as it once was?

The reasons could be complex, but in all likelihood they related to the phases of life, the flow of adult-development stages that shift with age and shape one's needs. What works when young may change when older.

Having clarified his expanded goals, Litte tried to achieve them. His approach was systematic. All goals could no longer be found in one place. Community involvement in local politics brought him into the mainstream. A consulting business on the side, helping companies with their in-house publications, brought in extra dollars and generated fresh areas to explore. He maintained his editorship, using his new experiences to enlarge the scope of the publication. And the whole package brought security and fulfillment. Personal autonomy had augmented organizational commitment.

One unifying whole is not always to be. Some people need several simultaneous activities, whether all business or part vocation and part avocation. The whole is sometimes constructed by accumulating diverse pieces and putting them together.

THE PROFESSIONAL

Donald MacDougal had been a dynamic young executive before religious conviction caught hold of him. Spark and spunk were his assets. Though he had been without prior means or political pull, he had worked his way up to running a sizeable dental distribution business with large foreign sales. A fine salary was augmented by options to acquire 10 percent of the company. Never one to do things halfheartedly, Donald gave it all up to enter the ministry of a growing denomination with international missionary activities.

Though Donald's ultimate goals changed dramatically, his shorter-term objectives changed hardly at all. This is important. Continuity of ability and personality assured consistency in "process" (if not "content"). He was soon running the church's overseas publishing arm, specializing in Africa, South America, and the Far East.

Why Donald eventually dissociated himself from the church is not the issue here, though we note that his leaving was not a solitary act. What to do now? Since he had not been concerned with either financial security or professional growth, Donald found himself, some ten years later, well behind his previous business position.

How to start from scratch? A personal inventory should be taken. Strengths and weaknesses were easy. He was a people person, not a technician or financial analyst; he was an outgoing manager and team-builder who gets the most out of his employees; and he was a fiery personality who cuts a first-class public image.

Alternatives were plenty. New church? Tried one offshoot; didn't work well. New business? Where to begin at almost 40? Old business? He was far outdated in dental supplies. Publishing? Tough, incestuous industry — but he was somewhat known and better liked.

After a year of search and struggle, Donald MacDougal was offered the presidency of a fine regional publisher with ambitions in international distribution. Three years of dynamic success later, having restructured the company and now owning 20 percent of it, he would joke that he had worked for 15 years to get back to where he had been. More than money was involved — he loved publishing and was earning substantial psychic income — and that was the only reason the joke was funny. The spark and spunk had not departed.

THE BANKER

Charlie Amato was a respected banker heading up business loans in one region of a large midwestern bank. He had started at the bank at the bottom, when first out of high school. He was diligent but low key, and although he had earned bachelor's and master's degrees at night, and although he had compiled an enviable book of financial returns, he never quite caught the eye of senior managment. To the top brass he was still "just a kid."

Perhaps he was too conservative in personality; perhaps he wasn't much of a politico or into the social scene. Whatever the reason, Charlie saw others with notably inferior track records being promoted above him. He also saw some of his customers — entrepreneurs no older or smarter than he was — accumulating substantial wealth. He watched both for years. No quick moves for Charlie.

Crossing that "magic 40" triggered decision time. His bank career, though successful to others, had stalled to himself. Others thought him most content, but his internal clock struck midnight. He had high ambition, both financial and managerial. His contacts were broad and loyal, especially in several industries with which he worked (machine tools and die castings). The strategy chosen was an honorable one; he gave notice to the bank without having made an external contact. Never would he use his office in the bank to feather his own nest.

As soon as his pending resignation became known, Charlie was approached in short order by several groups. The most attractive offer was from the founder of a metal-stamping firm (the company had been one of his long-standing customers at the bank). The company had languished under current management, and the founder decided he needed the infusion of strong leadership. Charlie was given a substantial piece of equity as incentive.

Though it would be unfair to state that Charlie's dedication running his new company was greater than it had been at the bank, the intensity allocated and the hours spent were demonstrably more. The company flourished and Charlie prospered. Task identification and achievement had combined to build powerful commitment.

THE STEADFAST SERVANT

Clarence Scott was a "clear tracker." He had made his dedication decision years ago, and had stuck with it ever since. Never think the sticking was easy.

The reason Clarence joined the church, he believed, was God's Divine Call, not his own personal choice. This foundation proved critical. Throughout his church career Clarence had been treated to a stomach-churning roller-coaster ride, with the precipitous falls steeper than the occasional climbs. Although public embarrassment outweighed private praise, he had signed on for the long haul. No short trip this journey.

In building the church, Clarence developed a reputation for hard-driving rigidity. In the process, he was often oblivious to the feelings and frailties of employees and members. He adhered to church teachings strictly in his personal life, and he expected everyone else to do likewise in theirs. Humble before God, he earned the image of a stern authoritarian before man. People would fear an encounter with him. Yet those who knew him well — whether they agreed with his positions or not — would always acknowledge that Clarence was forthright and direct, with little guile and no deceit. One never had to wonder where Clarence Scott stood.

After two decades of faithful service, a typical palace coup — more common in religion than in politics — brought Clarence down. A consortium of ambitious clergymen and servile assistants, trumped up charges and politicked his conviction.

Clarence was stripped of his position and exiled, quite literally, across an ocean. The banishment was so sudden that uninformed congregants suspected severe problems of a moral or criminal nature.

The alternatives before him were clear. Quit the church and forget religion? Quit the church and start a competing church? Stay in the church and lobby for counterrevolution? Stay in the church and be quiet and loyal?

His choice was self-evident, little evaluation was necessary. Though others would choose different strategies in similar circumstances, Clarence did not waver. God was in charge — that was his credo — and what the Creator was deciding or even allowing, man must not contradict. Clarence would remain steadfast and firm and await His Will. (Transcendence, affiliation, and generalized loyalty were personal variables of import.)

The decision was the only one compatible with his whole understanding of God and bible. If God be in our church, Clarence reasoned, He not I must make all judgments and right all wrongs. If the work of this church be God's mission, my commitment must remain sure (core). No parachutes worn around here.

He was watched like a thief on probation, meetings were monitored and conversations checked. He discovered the difference between friends of position and friends of person. The former would turn him in for personal gain; the latter would protect him at personal risk. He found himself buckling — could he withstand the pressure?

A man subjected to such trials might become hardened, even vengeful and bitter. Yet Clarence learned from his troubles. He grew more understanding of people's faults and frustrations, and more compassionate toward those unable to live up to his own high standards. He came to realize that his concept of "righteousness," while true, was not Truth; that there were internal attitudes of mind not expressible in external modes of behavior. "God looks on the heart" was a scripture he had always quoted. Now he finally knew what it meant.

THE STEADY MANAGER

For 27 years, since before he was 20, Ralph Richardson worked for a large packaged goods company. A steady, reliable sort, though surely no superstar, Ralph was promoted regularly and five years ago was put in charge of a $250 million division. He never took advantage of his longtime association with the company founder, but the fact of the friendship was known and it didn't hurt.

Two years ago the founder died, and Ralph's fortunes began to dip. No doubt he was competent, but the torch had been passed and a new generation came to power; and just as a new pharoah of ancient Egypt "knew not Joseph" and thus made trouble for the Israelites, the new president "knew not Ralph," and would make trouble for his career.

Though at 45 Ralph was only a few years older than the arriving top management, he symbolized the old and had to be moved. The new group had to establish their presence in the eyes of employees, and all remaining vestiges of the old order had to go.

Going, however, would be neither quick nor easy. No one wanted to hurt Ralph's feelings, and thus the situation was set for worse. Trying to ease the pain, they exacerbated it. The first step was a "promotion," though no one believed the doublespeak announcement. Ralph was thrust into a makeshift "Office of the Vice-Chairman" with several other "lateralized" VPs, each with vague formal responsibilities and little actual work. It was the beginning of severe frustration.

What were his alterantives? Every year added to his very nice retirement package. Yet more important than money and security was his sense of self-worth and self-control, both of which were taking a terrible beating. He was young for a senior executive, at the prime of his career, and if he waited many more years he would lose any value for another firm. The clock was ticking.

Ralph Richardson decided to stay. Though fear of the unknown played a part, stability and structure were more controlling. He decided to cope in different ways. He began developiong some avocations. Not a big sports type, he took up woodworking and dabbled in real estate, doing well enough in the latter to beat back defeatism and build up confidence.

The story ends with a twist. The new management team failed and were replaced from the outside by a still newer group. The outside CEO asked Ralph to take over his old division, but only to bring it back to form. After a year or so, the CEO stated upfront, Ralph would be asked to take early retirement (with some financial sweeteners).

Ralph was pleased to have a real role in the company, and even more pleased to be treated forthrightly. In under a year, having accomplished all he was asked, Ralph took his retirement and went on to a successful second career in real estate.

THE SOCIAL WORKER

Leslie Irwin's chief asset was his chief liability. He was Midwest regional administrator of the ministry for a dynamic growth church that was just gaining national prominence. Irwin was only 34 — the youngest administrator in the church — and was a marvelous counselor of clergy and laity alike. He radiated compassion and confidence, and combined an easygoing manner with human insight. He was the minister of choice whenever someone's problems were serious. But what helped members hurt Irwin. Empathy and sympathy for the people triggered conflict and turmoil in the church.

At issue were a number of doctrinal teachings that caused hardships for the brethren and their families. The subtle pressures to limit the use of doctors in illness, for example, worked well on minor members while being ignored by major ministers. When Irwin could no longer stand the suffering, he could no longer believe the church.

What to do? Autonomy was the chief driver. Financially his family was in trouble. Wholly dedicated to the church, they had sacrificed everything for its success. They never saved, never accumulated; any excess salary was always given back in offerings. Money, of course, was now an issue — but so was mission. Irwin was no longer in the church, but his concern for people was still the essence of life.

He loved working with people, helping the troubled with their problems. Social work with the disadvantaged was what he would do. He would devote himself to the poor, the widowed, and the orphaned, and thus fulfill the biblical injunction.

Irwin decided to go back to school. It would not be easy. He had to start from zero. An excellent teacher, he anticipated applying his natural abilities.

How to support the family in the interim? Both he and his wife took to the marketplace. Industrious and energetic, they worked together in building a small company, specializing in group insurance. The wife, in addition, found a part-time job; within six months she was office manager.

There would be years of strain and struggle, working hard days and studying hard nights. But Irwin would climb the multiple mountains, take advantage of his strengths, and become a superb social worker and later a well-respected lecturer.

Financially the family would do very well. Husband and wife would prosper in their three jobs, one each separately, one together as a team. Mission, money, and family make a nice combination.

THE RISING STAR

Choices were what Ed Goldstein had in abundance. At 32 he was in line for partner at one of New York's most prestigious investment banking houses. His salary, already six figures, was likely to skyrocket in the next few years.

He had come from a poor Bronx family and had elderly parents and a young family to support; he was well off but not yet wealthy. In five years he would be financially independent, but he was considering a radical career shift now, and money would be one element dramatically affected. How important, he asked himself, was personal wealth?

What was turning Ed's head was an offer from Washington. The new adminstration was considering him for deputy director of an important White House staff office. Offers were nothing new to this astute financier; he was on the hit list of executive search firms, and every month he was turning down senior management positions with major corporations. This opportunity, however, was different.

Though not a politician, politics fascinated Ed. More interesting was the potential to apply his sophistication and insight to a host of significant national problems. Here was real meaning, well above the linear thinking and parochial penchants of Wall Street.

Money, unfortunately, was the immovable object. Money, not wealth. Wealth, Ed was more than willing to forego. But basic support for basic needs? The only way he could support his family on government wages would be to go into debt — and even that might not be enough. Parents in hospitals and kids in private schools pile up hefty bills.

After much agony, Ed turned down the Washington position. Locus of control, not materialism, was prime driver. He hoped to be able to go into Government in a few years, he told himself, but that did not alleviate his frustration.

THE CHIEF EXECUTIVE

Forrest Hudson had just been fired from his position as president of a huge Fortune 500 corporation. Within two weeks he received five serious proposals to run substantial companies, from high-growth high-tech to a major diversified conglomerate. Why he was fired is interesting. Why he refused all offers is important.

Forrest had been the protege of, and heir apparent to, the eccentric founder of the firm; the man was 80 and still controlled the board as if they were his serfs and the company as if his fiefdom. The founder had chosen Forrest for his vision and toughness. But the old man's feelings changed quickly when the "prince" did not defer to the "king." When Forrest decided to prune back some of the founder's favorite (though unprofitable) acquisitions, the founder decided to prune back Forrest.

For 15 years Forrest had worked for the company, 10 in senior management. Now he was out. It was time for a fresh look at the world — and at himself.

Though he was only 43, he felt out of touch. He had become rusty in product planning, cash-flow projections, manufacturing efficiencies — all the elements needed in running modern businesses. Strategic planning is great, but too much of it can lock you in an ivory tower.

Forrest was going through a crisis of confidence, though no one would have suspected it. He liked making things happen, and he didn't like uncertainty. It was almost as if he were a paraplegic who ordered others to do what he could not do himself. To regain self-confidence he needed that hands-on sense of control. He would go back to the trenches. All inquiries for chief executive positions were politely but firmly turned down. (Locus of control and task identification — certainly not power or materialism — were motivating. Autonomy and esteem were also involved.)

Forrest began to look for small companies needing broad-based assistance. They came and he dug in. He involved himself in all areas of the business: he prepared the financial statements; he worked the plant floor; he planned the marketing strategies. He was feeling good.

"I wouldn't even take over several venture capital investment funds thrown at me," Forrest commented, "at least not until I reproved myself by building some companies on my own. If money is needed, I'll invest my own."

THE LOYALIST

It hurt deeply, but James Turner accepted without question his church's decision. The pastoral council had decided, without asking his opinion, to move him out as director of data processing and into a local pastorate. He gave little thought to the fact that he was the one who had founded data processing, installed the first computer, and built the department into a national showcase. He was both a minister and a technician, and if the church hierarchy, for whatever arcane reason, concluded that he could better serve in a strictly spiritual role, so be it. The content of ultimate purpose overwhelmed the process of job satisfaction. Goal structure and emotional conditioning bested task identification and status.

Yet process, for all one considers content, must make itself known. Its pressure is inexorable. Within several months, James became uneasy. There was a definite void in his life, and he decided to fill it with personal computers. He became an expert in programming, and even sold a few utility programs. Later he devised a simple "ministerial network" for transmitting sermon ideas. Avocation had supplemented vocation, and then complemented it.

When insurmountable circumstances prevent ideal expression in one's primary job, all is not lost. There are alternative strategies for those with ambition and persistence. Fulfillment can be achieved on multiple levels.

THE MUSICIAN

Though piano was her passion, there was no way that Susan Feinberg could support herself in her art. She didn't begin serious lessons until she was 15 and never really had a chance at a career. She had half a dozen students who were mostly weak, and she accompanied struggling violinists who were always mediocre.

Susan was both poor and frustrated, a sorry combination. The more she practiced — upward of six hours a day — the more depressed she became. Her dream had become her nightmare; her love had become her chains.

It was a chance article that triggered the turn. It reported a high correlation between musical talent and computer skills. Susan was intrigued, though she had never considered herself scientific in any way; math, she recalled, was far from her best subject.

Within two years Susan was a leading applications programmer at a large software house and was in training for systems analysis. She was being targeted for management, perhaps in marketing where her sensitivity to people would be supported by her strong technical skills.

(Achievement and materialism had gained on transcendence and education — which, we should stress, makes good sense here for Susan.)

And the piano? Now that it wasn't a poor means of support, it became a marvelous source of joy — the hour or so she played a day was both relaxing and invigorating.

THE CREATIVE CRACKUP

Don Hall was one piece of work. He would have stood out in any organization. In a religion he was unique. As a minister he was cut from different cloth.

His ready wit complemented a magnetic personality. He had a hardy laugh with a girth growing to match it. Everything he did he did with all his might. "When he works, he works hard," said a subordinate, "when he plays, he plays hard."

There was the time he ran up to the denomination's leading scholar and said, "I don't care what Heaven will be like, just tell me whether I'll be there." Another time he was confronted by an irate husband of a woman seeking baptism; this mountain of a backwoods man approached Hall with teeth clenched and shotgun loaded.

"I suppose you'll go straight to Heaven if I pull this here trigger, preacher boy," he said.

"No sir," shot back Hall without a moment's hesitation, "I'll go straight to hell" — using this term in its literal biblical meaning of "grave." The man was so flustered that Hall had time to make tracks.

Hall was not afraid to expound freely on human frailties of the prophets and apostles nor was he embarrassed to preach frankly about sexual allusions in the Song of Solomon. Describing in explicit detail the first marital encounter in the Garden of Eden was a particular favorite. One thing about his preaching, it was never dull — and never like anyone else's. He was a legend.

Jack — he was known by his middle name — was renowned for clever speaking and original thinking. He was continuously breathing life and energy into sanctimony and ritual. He could really uncork a sermon and move an audience. The Kingdom of God came alive with his words, the bible became meaningful for modern life. Some said Jack was the finest preacher in the church; others called him unfit for the ministry — there was never anyone neutral about Don Jack Hall.

Sensitive and sincere, Hall cast the image of boisterousness and hedonism. "Other people hide their sins," commented a friend, "Jack parades his."

He was certainly no ascetic, but his reputation far exceeded the reality. It was Jack's fault, really, since if someone suspected him of any fleshly excesses, he would go out of his way to *reinforce* not reduce the suspicion. (He'd pile up half a dozen beer cans on his desk, though he'd drink only one — especially if one of his critics would be coming to see him.)

Jack had come to the church as a teenager, and a more naturally creative character you never could find. He was given a host of jobs in building the church, ministerial and administrative. Into each he threw himself with vigor and brilliance. He'd not always do what he was told, but he'd always produce what was needed. He stood out with special strength in publishing, where his feeling and flair radiated to readers. It was his sudden demotion from a desired editorship that began Jack's slide downhill.

Why he was fired is not important; even the next day those who made the fateful decision would offer opposing reasons. Some said Jack was needed in the active ministry; others said he was injecting too much personality into the publications; still others mentioned his liberal life-style.

Other positions followed. Into each Jack put his full energies, only to have some circumstantial event or political storm wipe him out. Jack appeared indestructible outside, but each setback broke something more off inside. (Role strain and weakening support were swamping transcendence, affiliation, and perceived organizational importance.)

It was as if life and church had conspired against him. His wife, with whom he was so close, died young; friends deserted him as they saw his influence wane; the new leaders of the ministry forgot his sacrifices of old.

The cycle became vicious. His prior image as a heavy drinker became, tragically, a self-fullfilling prophecy. Then followed a devastating sequence of job loss, excommunication, personal difficulties and financial ruin. Jack had nothing left. Everything was gone.

Rumors about Jack would surface from time to time. He was hiding in the mountains. He was working on the Alaskan pipeline. He had lost weight, stopped drinking, got his head together. He was beginning to write again — what, no one knew. Some reported that Jack, like his biblical counterpart Job, blamed God for his misery. Others would wager that there was no one on earth whom God would show more mercy.

TAKE CHARGE

Two principles emerge supreme from these sketches: personal *awareness* and personal *control*. Both are essential for assuring a life well lived and a job reasonably fulfilling. Both are key adjuncts in the management of individual commitment and the strengthening of the human end of the firm bond.

It is not always possible to direct one's destiny, but with conscious effort it is surprising how often such active control *is* possible. The process, however, is not easy, and will at first seem awkward.

To make a conscious assessment of one's goals, strengths, and weaknesses, and as well as one's alternative strategies, may cause some disorientation — a touch of psychological dizziness, even a case of career vertigo. It's almost like relearning your stroke in tennis or golf; it's vital for your game, but it sure messes you up for a while.

All should strive for fulfillment. One dynamic chief executive defined the ideal: "My days are too short," he noted with eyes dancing. "I can't wait to get up in the morning, and I am frustrated when evening comes so quickly."

"Change" is an important consideration in most careers; even if no change is ever made, it is always present as a standard of comparison. Change was indeed a major element in all of the above cases. This is not meant to imply that change is necessarily either widespread or good, but rather that it is fertile soil in which to study the personal management of commitment. (Change is in fact becoming more widespread, with cognitive and emotional benefits.)

Since change is so important and so common, it is wise to understand what makes it successful. What elements should one control when changing organizational membership or company employment?

One critical factor is to maintain or build some strong alternative support groups during the transition. To make the point in reverse, it could be devastating to change jobs in the same time frame when one quits a church and divorces a spouse. One must feel "legitimate" in making the transition, anchored by the security of some group permanence.

Personal control does not demand working for oneself instead of an organization. It does require conscious awareness of what one is doing and how one feels about it. If job satisfaction is poor and you acknowledge it to yourself, you will be better able to cope with the problem. Not having such overt awareness will cause sublimated frustration to fester and ferment and probably erupt in an inappropriate form. Such sudden transformations can be ruinous. Frustration untethered runs wild.

"Take charge" is not some macho battle cry. It is practical advice for everyone who seeks fulfillment in organizational memberships and company employment. Whatever you do, wrote some sage, always paddle your own canoe.

CHAPTER NINE

CORPORATE COMMITMENT: PULLING TOGETHER

The executive council of Modern-Day Elders was tense. It was showdown time. The meeting had been scheduled for weeks and anxiety had been building steadily.

The dynamic fundamental church, known for its rigorous admission criteria, had been wracked by several years of organizational dissent and personality conflict. Some called it "maturation pains." Others cried "apostasy." At issue were recent policy changes championed by the more liberal wing. What had been hailed as "revolution" was now being challenged as "revisionism."

"The people who come to church these days don't know anything about church doctrine," complained a conservative spokesman.

> They're bloating the membership up front and causing spillage out back. We're losing as many members as we're gaining, and we're watering down fervency. Zeal, not numbers, is what counts in the church. God would rather have a few good people, hot and wholehearted, than thousands lukewarm and half-hearted.

Up until two years before, all prospective members of the tightly knit church had been screened and questioned carefully. There was a mandatory probation period of nine months. There were required correspondence courses to prepare and a formal series of counselings to complete. The oft-repeated phrase to these prospectives was "Count the Cost."

Local pastors had kept watchful eye on those who wanted in. These shepherds of the flock were waiting for the prophesied entry of "wolves in sheeps' clothing." Frequent warnings by superiors told them to beware and guard their church. Every new person was looked upon with suspicion.

Two years ago all had changed. Church growth had been slowing and this gave the liberals their shot. Courses and counselings prior to membership were shortened; and, reversing the church's long-standing insistence on simple services, hard-sell advertising was placed in local newspapers soliciting people off the streets to attend with the brethren.

Curiously, the open doors did not much increase membership. For a while there was a rise in church attendance, but "attending" was not "admission" — church teachings put a vast chasm between the two.

Most of the attendees didn't attend very long. Once the novelty wore off, and especially after they got a whiff of the church's strictness, they were long gone. But what was even worse was the effect on real members. The temporaries sapped spiritual strength.

Previously, church members had been zealous and dedicated, each encouraging the other to attain higher levels of commitment in prayer and meditation, donations to the church, and in the allocation of voluntary time for church activities. Members had been an elite group.

But the avalanche of amateurs changed essence and style. By sheer weight of numbers, the character of the congregation shifted. Whereas in the past the apprentice member was surrounded by a dozen or more older members, now the odds were more or less even. And the recent additions were aggressive. Conversations became skewed to more worldly matters, and questions were asked with skepticism and doubt. The sharp identify of the group became fuzzied and older church members started to waver. As many were lost as were gained, and the velocity of member turnover generated further uncertainty.

The time was ripe for a conservative resurgence. The old boundaries were restored; the newspaper ads were softened and public solicitations modified. Selection criteria were tightened and the nine-month process reinstituted. Ministers again worked closely with prospective members. Most requirements were back, and formal attendance was again tightly controlled.

After a period of adjustment, commitment levels rose, followed closely by the stability and strength of the membership. The gates were guarded and the church was solid.

WHAT RELIGION TELLS BUSINESS ABOUT BOUNDARIES

Profit-making commercial corporations have much to learn from not-for-profit religious organizations. The above example, while not presented as a paragon of what churches should or should not do, does illustrate an important principle of group sociology. Individual commitment is strengthened by institutional clarity. The sharper the focus of the group, the easier the identification of the member.

The applications for business are direct, the controlling principles clear. Elements include the following: defining and tightening boundaries; designing selection criteria for strategies; designing selection criteria for executives and employees; the strategic planning of permeability; the sharpening definition of purpose. Such techniques, employed intuitively by religious organizations to establish group solidarity, can be used deliberately by business organizations with equal effectiveness.

A company that understands internal image will establish independent identity, setting it apart, making it distinct. The results, even for companies marketing common commodities and uniform products, will be greater productivity and smaller employee turnover, both of which translate into higher profits. Tightened boundaries and sharpened focus can be the difference between flourishing and floundering.

Issues of separation and distinction are critical. Where does one group end and another begin? Companies with ill-defined boundaries cannot generate strong employee commitment. Workers, if you think about them, have little to commit *to*. For optimum effectiveness, a company should have a corporate purpose that is carefully defined and clearly distinct.

There should never be confusion between companies, even if they produce similar products. Establishing sharp corporate purpose and setting high company boundaries can shoot more for perception than reality. It is as much a matter of attitude and form as it is product and substance. Even if the products are common, there are numerous ways to establish independent identity.

A company can tighten boundaries by making the firm's purposes and policies explicitly different. A new employee, no matter the level, should immediately sense the difference. From company orientation to first day on the job, the organization must fashion a unique image.

Employee policies are critical. Compensation programs, for example, can encourage genuine participation. Benefits and retirement programs are equally important. The differentiation achieved can increase productivity, reduce turnover, and generally make the difference between consistent profitability and just muddling through.

Having an employee-selection program that seeks out special sorts of people, going beyond the normal needs of specific jobs, has multiple benefits. First, it shows each prospective employee that this firm is unusual. Since the interview will constitute that employee's first association, the impression will be a lasting one. Second, it sends a message to current employees: they are part of a special organization that has high standards and specific criteria. Third, the image will generate the reality; the selection criteria will sculpt the character of the company.

The strategic planning of permeability is an interesting issue. Permeability, remember, describes the ease of flow between organization and environment. Too much permeability, as with the above religious example, and the organization loses its uniqueness and cutting edge. Too little permeability and the organization becomes isolated and insular and unable to grow.

Though there are differences between religious and commercial organizations, the application of principles is similar. It is often important to control the direction of the permeability, to make company boundaries semipermeable. More flow, for example, may be allowed out — from organization to environment — than allowed in — from environment to organization. Mechanisms for controlling permeability include the above guidelines for maintaining a special internal order while encouraging sustained external drive. In this manner, the group's growth objectives can be sustained without disrupting the organizational atmosphere.

WHAT RELIGION TELLS BUSINESS ABOUT COMMITMENT

We seek to improve ties between individuals and institutions by bringing the benefits of commitment to both sides of the firm bond. Businesses have much to gain from enhancing the dedication of their employees, and should be on watch for helpful ideas and techniques.

The traditional approach in discovering optimum business practices is to study companies which best represent those practices. If one is interested in learning about marketing, for example, one should examine those firms, like Procter & Gamble or IBM, that are considered to be premier marketing companies.

The approach here has been different. Though interested in commitment for business, we have not used settings in business as prototypes. This most peculiar characteristic, we decided, demanded a fresh approach and a novel setting. We sought the essence of commitment, and so chose those organizations that personify it.

Religious organizations thus became our "living laboratory" in which we investigated commitment. We further refined the approach by choosing those kinds of "closed system" religious organizations in which beliefs were more intense and commitment more extreme. These "special lens" situations became our "magnifying glass" to examine elements and aspects of commitment not easily visualized in normal business environments.

The results, we trust, are both interesting and useful. We discerned key elements of commitment in religious organizations and then searched for them in business corporations. The transference, we believe, has been good. What is present in one is also present in the other. Whether one is preaching the Kingdom for God or building the market for General Motors, the thrust is the same. Similar forces are working in building or busting commitment. (Differences are a matter of intensity and degree, determined as much by individual personality as by institutional objectives.)

The search for "transcendence," discussed in Chapter 4, is a prime example of an organizational characteristic seemingly unique to religion that can be used effectively by business. The effort cannot be artificial, however, nor the effect canned. "Reality congruence" is ever-present, keeping the company honest.

The kinds of commitment types — whether partisan, adherent, routiner, disengaged, disaffected or adversary — are applicable for business as well as religion. We've all seen each of these types, though hopefully more partisan than adversaries have crossed our paths.

The styles of commitment — core, calculative and cog — are expressive of attitudes among employees of companies as well as members of religions. What we find in one we locate in the other. What we learn we apply.

STORIES AND CULTURE

Stories of commitment, stories of sacrifice — both build the coherence of the group. Told over and over again, the narratives tie present to past and ground members into a common culture as if in parallel circuit on an electrical grid. (The term "myth" is often used to describe traditional stories of earlier times.)

The effect is almost mystical. Organizational memories are transplanted from historical chronicles into collective consciousness. Present members come to feel as if they were actually there at the beginning, that they helped the founders lay those first bricks.

Legends of old: heroes arising to save the organization; founders working with cleverness and cuteness, fulfilling a mission of transcendence. However that transcendence is defined, whether theological or commercial, it is always there with the founders. These are the basic elements of culture and commitment.

Group uniqueness is founded on group culture. Linking past with present is an integral part of that culture. What are the historical roots of the organizations, and how can current members be grafted into them? The way it is in religion is the way it is in business.

RELIGIOUS STORIES ARE NOT JUST FOR BEDTIME

I want to tell you brethren that starting God's Modern Mission wasn't easy. We didn't have the blessings of church buildings across the country that we have today. And who ever heard of television to broadcast our message around the world? There are many nights when I wished that God would take my life. The pressures were enormous.

Money was always a problem in the early days. When I signed the agreement to purchase our very first building, where for many years we held our services, I didn't know that I was dealing with a shady character. The seller had his lawyer place a clause in the contract which required that the mortgage be paid off much faster than we had originally agreed. Well, in those days, I couldn't afford the services of an attorney, and I didn't notice the change. The seller intended to force a foreclosure and take both our money and our building.

But I'm afraid the seller didn't understand that although I didn't have a lawyer, I did have Someone Else. *God* was on our side and He wanted us to have that building. He was providing for our needs, bringing us pioneering church members who were wholly dedicated to His church. There was Robert Hughes. Do you know what he did? We didn't even realize he had any money at all, and so he shocked us by contributing his life savings. His bank account was exactly what we needed to save our building! Now some may call it "coincidence," but I know better. I've come to recognize the Hand of God.

God's people have always rallied to His cause. Even today our bankers are amazed that whenever we are in financial straits, God and His people always come to the rescue. You brethren are no different from your predecessors. All of us are dedicated to the same goals, building this mission of God to preach the gospel.

BUSINESS STORIES ARE NOT JUST FOR BOARDROOMS

"Commercial transcendence," we should note, must be framed conceptually not financially. Proper goals are pioneering (new products) or forging (new markets) or building (largest share) or creating (a special corporate culture). It is hard for employees to identify with a compound rate of return of 25 percent, though not hard for stockholders.

I want to tell you executives that starting this company was not easy. We didn't have the benefits of bank lines and equity markets. We didn't have R & D departments, manufacturing controls, and international sales. We didn't have *any* market share, much less dominant product areas. There were many nights when I wished for the security of my old engineering job. No payroll to meet; steady salary; deep sleep. Cash flow was always a problem in the early days. The pressures were enormous.

When I signed the agreement for our first supply contract with a major defense contractor, I couldn't afford the best legal advice. We had a new product for aircraft control systems and they wanted it. I thought it was simple. What I imagined the contract said, however, was not what it did say. I had never negotiated a business deal before. The fine print put punitive penalties for not meeting an extremely tight schedule. And "punitive penalties" for a poorly capitalized company was a death sentence.

Well, we were new to the business. We had a great design, better than anything else around, but we had never actually manufactured and delivered anything, much less a steady stream of products. A million things could go wrong, and in the first month they all did. There was no way we could meet the schedule. I think that giant company wanted to buy us out on the cheap.

I was desperate. Yet our pioneering employees were something special. They didn't know what they couldn't do. Richard Holden, never having dirtied his hands before, took over the shop and in three weeks accomplished the impossible. I don't think he went home at all. He never saw the sun. He put a cot in a back closet, worked until he dropped, caught a wink or two, then went right back at it. I think he built every control system himself. We made the schedule. The paint was still wet — but they all worked and we've never looked back since.

That same attitude, men, must be present today. We live in a highly competitive world, and we must do more than survive. We must prosper. And this company must have a hundred Richard Holdens — and we do!

Stories are told in all organizations. To a large extent, it is through such tales and legends that organizational culture is formed and organizational commitment is established. These stories must be loaded with emotion and pathos; the pioneers must struggle to achieve what is commonly accepted today. But the stories must be genuine; though some historical liberties can be taken, truth is vital for continued confidence.

MANAGERIAL ATTITUDES

In today's bookstores there is no dearth of help for managers. Advice is offered abundantly, if not freely. Promises made are usually extravagant; but hype is hep — exaggeration is the way of business life and so no one really minds. "If a book can give me one piece of practical advice," commented a senior executive, "it's worth the full price of admission."

The one piece of practical advice offered here is "Look to Religion." Not for spirituality or morality — that is the subject of another book, not this one — issues of ultimate cause or proper behavior go well beyond our current scope. We are not concerned with religion per se. What we are concerned with is more mundane in the overall scheme of things, but quite germane for the conduct of daily life.

Organizational direction and managerial control are the nerve centers of modern corporations, and lessons about both can be gleaned from religious groups. If success and not ego is of primary import, then managers will listen and learn.

Those who lead religious organizations put great emphasis on strengthening the commitment of their constituents. Members' *attitudes* are their target. It is not overt behavior, what they *do*, that counts, but inner motivation, what they *feel*.

More than one church group stresses the need for its supporters to be "cheerful givers," not just "grudging contributors." The money of course is important, but the posture is even more so. A cheerful giver is more committed and will continue giving without constant outside pressure. The money is shortterm; the mind is longterm. Behavior is for now; attitude is forever.

The example applies directly to business management. Employees controlled by coercion must be controlled continually. Employees, on the other hand, who have internalized the values of the company and the meaning of their jobs, will be self-regulating. They will accomplish organization goals on their own, without external compulsion — because that is what they *want* to do.

How to make the transition? Try the following trick. Business executives can imagine subordinates as if they were "associate pastors" and employees as if "parishoners."

What sensitivities would be developed? Surely there would be a concern for frame of mind, not only performance of job. How employees feel about things — and why — would become increasingly important. Does each subordinate see the big picture, and how his or her part fits into it? (Japanese companies, we have been told, stress communal attitude; and rather than calling this approach "Japanese," one might rather label it "religious.")

Please do not misunderstand. We do not advocate business as a substitute for religion. Not at all. Business and religion each weave separate strands in the elegant tapestry of life. One is economic, the other is spiritual. Together they form a pattern most intricate, a design most beautiful. We do advocate that understanding religious organizations can offer insight into people's fundamental nature — especially regarding commitment — and that such commitment can be effectively applied by business for the good of both the institution and the individual.

RELIGIOUS TECHNIQUES

Things are done in religion naturally that might seem offbeat in business. Take for example, the common religious practice of "calling those things which be not as though they were" (Romans 4:17). In theology, liberties of logic can be taken because, with the power of God, they are acceptable. Believing the effects before knowing the causes (such as life beyond the grave) can be trusted and internalized — but only with the divine factor involved.

We do not advise companies to dissimulate or restructure truth.[1] What we do advise is awareness of individual aspirations, a sense of what employees want in planning their lives. Satisfying ultimate needs is a major strength of religion, and although businesses cannot go beyond death, they can give the confidence, security, and excitement desired in life.

The linking of danger and trust is another path well travelled by religion. Whether describing conditions of the afterlife or prophesying events of the future, religious organizations become associated strongly with information of the most vital kind. The prospect of missing heaven or falling into cataclysm is indeed terrifying. Likewise, the trust built between the individuals fearing this danger and the institution saving them from it is powerful.

While commercial companies cannot compete on such grand landscapes, the key elements of danger and trust are often linked by circumstances. Situations requiring mutual confidences can arise among peers or between superior and subordinate. Such situations offer rich opportunity for building commitment.

The formation of trust is catalyzed when people run risk in what they are doing together. There are many examples: a corporate team whose collective success rides on the fortunes of a given project, say a new product development or sales campaign; or a boss who "goes to the wall" to protect one of his people, putting his job on the line; or the secret sharing of potentially damaging information in the subculture of company closets.

Such trust is delicate. Constructed with care and risk, it is easily trashed. Most employees are presented with occasions where political advantage can be achieved by self-serving shaft or simple betrayal. The advantage, of course, is often short-lived, and those who step over people on their way up the corporate ladder often meet the same people on their way down.

It is unrealistic to expect that even perfect managerial attitudes can transform an adversary into a partisan. (Such conversions, rare under any circumstances, are much more likely under religious conditions — recall the apostle Paul.) What is realistic is to move people up the commitment scale, perhaps even changing their type.

A good manager should have as a goal the upward movement of at least one category for most subordinates. Such improvements — from disengaged to routiner, from routiner to adherent, from adherent to partisan — would mean major enhancement of total commitment strength and mission contribution when summed across the entire workforce. The effect on the bottom line would be demonstrable and potent.

Caution must be exercised. Rapid conversions must be assessed skeptically. Sudden, spectacular changes in commitment, even under ideal conditions, must be reenforced over time for lasting effect. Don't be beguiled. It is deceiving and dangerous to accept the permanence of quick, quantum jumps.

WHEN TRUTH MUST CHANGE

Which pieces of the past do you honor? Which are so sacrosanct that they are forever above challenge? Such questions are addressed at critical times during the life cycles of both religious and business organizations, and the sets of answers that emerge have much in common.

Framing the issue for religion, when are doctrines and dogmas still fluid? When do they solidify? When do they ossify? How do beliefs define the boundaries of groups with spiritual purposes, and what happens when some of those beliefs must change?

Framing the issue for business, when are strategies and policies still fluid? When do they solidify and ossify? How do corporate goals and business objectives define the boundaries of groups with commercial interests, and what happens when some of those goals and objectives must change?

The alteration of fundamental doctrine or strategy, whether for a religion or a business, is a radical inflection point for an organization. Often such shifts are not difficult to make in the formative stage of development. But after a time, change in fundamentals becomes extraordinarily hard to accomplish. (Note the fact that more than half of the top American companies of 50 years ago are either nonexistent or unrecognizable today.)

The following case histories illustrate the problems and opportunities when foundations must shift and fundamentals must change. The parallels are powerful. What happens in religion happens in business.

WHEN DOCTRINE MUST CHANGE

The devoted followers of Rabbi Gershom Mandlebaum considered themselves the truest spiritual interpreters of the holy Hebrew scriptures. They alone had the "spirit of knowledge," hidden for a thousand years. The rabbi, born of generations of rabbis in Poland, claimed direct physical lineage from the ancient rabbis whose teachings were prodigious and expositions legendary.

The rabbi himself never claimed infallibility, although his devoted disciples all but labeled his pronouncements perfect. His teachings, they whispered, were as if dropped from the lips of the Almighty. So trusted and honored was the rabbi's scriptural understanding that his every word was recorded, transcribed, published, and studied. Nothing the learned scholar ever said was allowed to be "spilled."

Great energy and growth characterized the movement within the ultra-orthodox segment of Judaism. Men and women of intelligence and dedication were attracted by its clear cosmic call. No other group in all Judaism, said the rabbi, not for a millenium, had such all-encompassing answers to the basic questions of human existence. Many were intrigued by the rabbi's constant challenge for proselytes to read the holy scriptures for themselves and discover the truth of everything he taught.

In the second decade of the movement's mission, as more converts took the rabbi at his word and read the torah and talmud in translation and in the original, a small number of minor doctrinal questions began popping up: nothing major, nothing shaking the basic belief structure, but problems nonetheless.

One concerned the specific calculation for a prophesied epoch of time. Another dealt with when to celebrate a certain holy day. Still others concerned the kinds of clothing and facial adornment permitted men and women. In each case, the primary issue was scriptual fidelity. Would the rabbi follow the torah and admit error?

The way the prophets and rabbis counted time became an issue loaded with emotion. Whether the Golden Age would *begin* 1,000 years after the Messiah, or whether it would *last* 1,000 years after His Coming, hardly seemed to affect current affairs. ("When He comes, we'll know," whispered one wag on the underground; "I worry about whether it'll be before my teeth rot, not what'll happen afterwards.")

Nonetheless, the issue of the 1,000 years became important. It was the symbolism more than the substance. The rabbi said he would instantly change his teaching if it could be proved that the scriptures said differently. God, he claimed, was inspiring him to reach deep understanding, but that if God permitted him to err — which, of course, He had not — then the congregation would be quick to repent and change.

The calculation of the holy day observance referred to a possible double meaning of a certain combination of words. The overt reading seemed simple enough, but the rabbi saw complexity in later renditions of the specific texts. There were other hints by earlier scholars, but Rabbi Mandlebaum had come to a conclusion no other interpreter of the Hebrew, though there had been innumerable rabbis before him, had ever come to before. Mandlebaum's followers used this example, as one among many, to prove the unique inspiration of their leader. This explains the emotional impact of the challenge. If the rabbi could be wrong here, where else might he have erred?

Those who made the challenge were not doing so to be either antagonistic or combative. They had learned Hebrew and wanted help understanding what they were reading. But stock answers wouldn't work. The words were plain and the interpretation self-evident.

The Rabbi's associates took to ridiculing the questioners, twisting their sincere inquiries into buffoonery. The rabbi's scholars came up with complex "proofs" of his alleged inspiration, but the reasoning was circular and the logic tortured.

When after a Doctrinal Conclave a senior member of the congregation was asked which of the many arguments he believed ratified the rabbi's position, he answered, "It is not for me to understand; the rabbi pronounces, the scholars support, and I believe."

Such uncontested belief may have been fine for an acquiescent old-timer, but it didn't satisfy the more literate converts. It plainly contradicted the slogan of the movement: the rabbi had said that each student should study and prove all things for himself.

Many of the associate rabbis surrounding Rabbi Mandlebaum became deeply affected by the challenge. Rippling divisions opened among the group. Most defended Mandelbaum's position, claiming inspiration for their leader. Others would see the problem one day and support "our honest petitioners," only to swing suddenly the next day and condemn "these brazen heretics." (Such "swingers" were called "180's" — after the number of degrees separating North and South, and the high frequency of their polar flips.)

A smaller contingent believed that the only way to truly support the rabbi was to support him with truth. Wasn't that the master's own approach, they asked their fellow rabbis? Wasn't that what the Rabbi had always taught? How could one claim to be loyal to the master and let him remain in error? How could one allow the rabbi to be exposed to external ridicule? Better is to brave confrontation and protect his honor! Better is put life on the line in service of The Almighty.

The defenders of the status quo took violent exception to some of their number who, it seemed, were siding with the critics. This was a good opportunity, they thought, to attack and solidify their own position. The battle raged on, with skirmishes being fought in open sermons and secret encounters.

To the rabbi's credit, and to the consternation of his more virulent defenders, he finally changed his teaching on several sensitive issues. How difficult it must have been! How strong his belief in scripture! (His retinue of associate rabbis of course changed too, although some, having spun around so quickly, were no doubt treated for whiplash.)

Those associate rabbis who had encouraged doctrinal change were pleased that their movement would no longer be subjected to attack and ridicule. Protecting the movement was worth personal pain and prolonged anxiety.

It must be said, however, that those who promoted scriptural truth were always grieved by continued suspicion. Their rabbi, though he recognized the accuracy of their arguments, could not overcome the heat of their logic. He continued to believe, though he could not have been more wrong, that they were more against him than for him.

Those whose support went deepest were those whose motivations went questioned. They had defended their rabbi at great peril to themselves; they had borne personal hardship to support the movement's beliefs — and yet, though successful in defense, they remained under a cloud.

The status quo defenders, on the other hand, always remained in the purest of light. They supported the rabbi when he refused to change, and they supported the rabbi when he decided to change. They were always "in support," always "loyal," and consequently always in favor.

One might look at the issue of doctrinal [and also strategic] change within the context of the organization's life cycle. In the early days of the movement, there was free discussion between Rabbi Mandlebaum and his first believers. Many doctrines were openly and freely contested. Associate rabbis were encouraged to argue with their teacher and confront his views. That way, the rabbi said, his arguments would become tested and his techniques honed.

Yet something happens as an organization matures. Doctrines [or strategies] stiffen, then harden. What was once considered loyal gradually becomes disloyal. Whereas at first it was supportive to challenge and prune, later it was supportive to defend and preserve. The more success an organization has, the more immobile its positions become. The path becomes cyclical and turns on itself, since such rigidity often facilitates fracture.[2]

WHEN STRATEGY MUST CHANGE

ChemTech had been the darling of a generation of investors; its stock had been one of the highest flyers in market history. No one had carried more clout on Wall Street than its inventor-founder, Mark Chinn.

Chinn was a genius. He had come out of nowhere in the early 1960s and personally revolutionized the specialty chemical business. He turned out, almost singlehandedly, a continuous series of patented products that dominated markets.

ChemTech became Mecca to a generation of the brightest scientists and engineers graduating from the leading schools. The company was the hottest in the firmament. With its talent, it was said, it could become one of the leading science powerhouses in the world — and its price/earnings ratio reflected that expectation.

By the early 1970s, many of ChemTech's strategic planners were foreseeing an end of high growth for their current businesses. It was vital, they wrote, to move ChemTech into the new high-growth areas of the 1970s and 1980s. The future, they warned, would not reflect the past.

Chinn dismissed them all. "We are a specialty chemical company," he insisted, "and we will continue to develop new molecules to serve the needs of our markets."

In the late 1970s ChemTech's basic businesses leveled off, and in 1980 the company suffered its first loss in 20 years. The recession had affected its primary customers. ChemTech was tied to Smokestack America. Its stock, of course, plummeted, and there was talk of an unfriendly takeover. Throughout the tailspin, Chinn kept insisting that ChemTech would stay in its corporate niche, and that he would stay in his personal lab.

Though he did continue creating marvelous molecules, some became commercial failures. Furthermore, many of his managers did not remain. Frustrated with corporate stagnation, many of Chinn's first-rate executives resigned to start the new generation of high-technology companies sprouting in electronics and computers.

Only in 1981 did Chinn agree to a major diversification. Following some agonizing restructuring and cost cutting in its traditional businesses, ChemTech bought a 30 percent interest in an emerging software engineering company. It also began producing discs and other technical accessories for the personal computer market. In each case, it sought some synergy with its own internal areas of expertise.

Chinn made the moves — retrenchment and resurgence — and the company remained strong. But the moves were late, and the company forever lost its chance to become one of the true giants of our age.

REWARD FOR ITS OWN SAKE

Whether directing a business or a religion, managers must motivate. The methods involved are often similar. Material and financial incentives may keep employees committed in the calculative range, but will never move them up to core.

Religious organizations, on the other hand, hardly worry about such incentives. They make membership its own reward — being allowed to join the group is itself something special, a privilege, a calling by God.

Can business play the same game? Not exactly, but it may come closer than you think.

People do not give core commitment because trinkets are dangled. Formal rewards are more company tools to get people on board than incentives to encourage them to commit. Galvanizing employees to put optimum effort into projects requires sensitivity and skill.

Rosabeth Kantor, in her book *The Change Masters*, reports that in innovative companies, motivation does not come from traditional reward structures.[3] Instead of rewarding after the fact, innovative companies invested in people *before* the projects were carried out. The reward was being chosen to work on the project in the first place! And the reward for success on the first project was an opportunity to work on a second project, bigger and more exciting. One manager likened the process to playing pinball: "Doing well enough to win a free game, getting the chance to play another one."

TITLES BY THE BUSHEL

Without the financial means of commercial enterprises to induce calculative commitment, religions have developed other mechanisms — often appealing to higher-order needs, and often winning higher-order commitment. Appointing members to prestigious positions, as an example, has long been a well-honed art.

Personal titles in religion are always interesting and often elegant. One has to be in close touch with a denomination to know whether "Very Reverend," "Right Reverend," or "Most Reverend" is, well, *most* reverend. The connotation of "evangelist" in some churches is a powerful confirmation of spiritual preeminence. The title of "rabbi" in Judaism brings with it generations of rich tradition.

Experienced executives are fully aware of the personal attachment to titles. Lateral moves of managers can often be made less traumatic by appending a significant title to the change. (Don't try it on entrepreneurial types; they would rather work on substance with no title than have the big title and only form.)

INOCULATION TO BELIEVERHOOD

Exposure to the mild form of certain diseases can trigger the body to develop an immunity to those diseases. (Vaccinations are based on this principle.) An analagous phenomenon is at work in social settings.

Children brought up in religious environments that are part core and part calculative (or all calculative) often develop an immunity to the religion. Such immunity is more frequently found in such lukewarm environments than in either of the surrounding extremes; we would expect, for example, less immunity and less antagonism toward religion in environments composed of either core believers or no believers at all.

Applications of this to corporate environments are direct. The likelihood of someone "catching" commitment to company mission is related to that person's exposure to employees previously "infected" with it. Exposure to employees with mild (or calculative) forms of company commitment is far worse than exposure to people with no knowledge of the company at all.

Managers should plan their personnel introductions with this phenomenon in mind. Without becoming too Orwellilan, it would be a mistake to allow current employees of the calculative type to cause "mission immunity" in new employees. Conversely, by surrounding potentially important personnel with core commitment partisans, a manager can maximize the chances that these employees "catch the vision."

HYPE HURTS, RELIGIOUSLY

A factor common to many fundamental religious groups is an interest in prophecy. The setting of specific dates, though contradictory to the message of Old and New Testaments, seems a special predilection of certain churches. Perhaps it is a desire to quicken the advent of the kingdom. Perhaps it is an effort to keep members in a state of perpetual readiness and sacrifice.

No matter the intent, the results are the same. People are at first excited; exhilaration is mingled with fear, secret knowledge mixed with special calling. But after one or more disappointments, disillusionment must set in. (The "Boy Who Cried 'Wolf' " is a classic myth of overworked and inappropriate calls of alarm. If such prophecies are ever to be known in advance, the constant setting of dates will stop the ear and cloud the eye.)

Though often constructed through the most circuitous calculations, with unproven assertions piled on arcane assumptions, such dated and detailed prophecies continue to attract unfaltering interest. Why is no mystery. Foreknowledge, transcendence, and special calling are essential human needs being satisfied by these prophecies.[4]

HYPE HURTS, COMMERCIALLY

It is erroneous to think that only religions predict future events, with all the attending upkick of prophecy and all the subsequent letdown of nonfulfillment.

In June 1983 the president of Coleco Industries announced that his company was producing a home computer that would sell for $600, yet would be capable of doing what most $3,000 machines could do.[5] The computers would be arriving in stores by August and an incredible 500,000 of them would be sold by the end of the year. Coleco, he assured all, was quite capable of producing such a prodigious amount of the untested machines. The stock of Coleco rose rapidly in response, going from $40 to $60 a share.

In August 1983 rumors begin to circulate that the "Adam," a catchy if somewhat arrogant name for Coleco's creation, was running into production problems. The president's lofty predictions were questioned.

In September 1983 the production line yielded its first Adam (rather more than six days after the Creation). But the Federal Communications Commission's approval was needed before the product could be sold. More technical problems followed. The first showings to reporters were less than spectacular successes. Bugs could not be squashed. Coleco slid its initial date to October. Financial analysts lowered projected earnings and the stock price dropped.

In November 1983 Adam finally reached a few stores, but in very limited quantities. Some units didn't work as claimed. Coleco's stock fell to $16. Coleco acknowledged that it would ship only 125,000 Adams before the end of the year, one-quarter of its original estimate. (The final count was worse, about 95,000).

A prime reason for Coleco's violent swings in the market was the enthusiasm the president generated by his extravagant prognostications. When his prophecies failed, the company's credibility suffered. A severe negative reaction by the investment community to the company's hyperbole depressed the stock, perhaps sending it further south than justified.

Hype is no help. Though a sense of transcendence can be generated by the thrill of extravagant predictions, the excitement is soon over. Reality congruence (see Chapter 4) must in the long run destroy any transcendent gains in the short run. Unrealistic predictions do a terrible disservice to excellent companies. Expectations are created that often can never be fulfilled, so that when the prophecies fail both investors and employees become disillusioned, some permanently.

PEOPLE AS ASSETS

Several churches consider people their most valuable assets. Members are taught to respect and appreciate one another since, according to their beliefs, the members will be together eternally in the kingdom of God. (It's pretty serious, then, if you can't get along.)

Similarly, it's not enough for management to be "nice" to employees. Executives who run companies and managers who run departments must come to recognize that people are important. That's bottom line importance, the number on which bonuses are determined.

Some companies see people as burdens, as expense items that leach out profits from the income statement. Other companies, more enlightened, see people as genuine assets, more valuable than the physical and financial items enumerated on the balance sheet. How can a company change from a people-expense culture to a people-asset culture? After all, the people-asset attitude is the best breeding ground for commitment.

Some of the answer lies in the approach of top management; another part is founded in information. A number of major organizations are currently experimenting with a developing technology called "human resource accounting"[6] which puts numbers on people, numbers with dollar signs.

What changes in organizational culture can be brought about by providing information on the numerical value of personnel? If a manager knows that it costs the company $50,000 to bring an employee to a certain position, then that employee may be treated in a different manner. (The U.S. Navy is currently conducting research on the change in managerial attitude when human resource cost information is provided. Other organizations are doing studies in valuing the economic component of human assets for use in acquisition analysis[7]).

Of course, even apart from numbers, people are important for companies. Some organizations do not need to look at cost or value data to change their attitudes concerning the importance of human resources. But for the many companies that still do not view people as assets, the technology of human resource accounting can help.

BENEFITS ABOUND

Pulling together brings its own rewards. Common efforts increase the likelihood of group success — and more too. When human beings expend collective energies, there is something fresh fed back to each individual.

It's as if group effort generates its own power supply, and by helping on the supply side, one also shares on the receive side. The game is not zero sum. What one gives and what one gets may differ, and the difference may relate to position on the commitment scale. The higher one's commitment — that is, the more one's commitment reaches toward pure core — the greater one gets relative to what one gives.

Commitment is better than a renewable resource; the more one uses it, the more one has it. It is both energizing and infectious, benefiting the person while building the group.

MEMORIES LIGHT THE CORNER OF MY MIND

The car was packed with suitcases. John Bissent and his family would be leaving in the morning for Florida. It was February, and this wasn't going to be your average winter vacation. The trip was the annual church convention, which took place at the same location and at the same time each year.

"John, it's past midnight and those children are still awake," mumbled John's wife Betty.

"I can't sleep, either," replied her husband, turning in bed. "I'm as keyed up as the kids. I guess we all have our annual case of 'convention fever.'"

It was not easy to attend the convention. John had to miss work; the kids had to skip school. The drive was long and the expenses were high. Perhaps the effort expended enhanced the commitment.

The convention was the peak of the church year. Members would gather for an intensive week-long seminar of inspiring and uplifting messages filling their lives with Christian purpose. Days were packed with sermons and instruction; nights were rich with fellowship and song.

Members saved all year for this event. Presents were given to children and to old friends. Luxury accommodations were booked. The convention was a time for the best, the physical reflecting the spiritual, even if the best could only last a week. The convention brought together all the prime elements of vacation, reunion, and holiday. Seasonal events that everyone anticipates anchor an organization to the passage of time. When such regular occasions connote positive expectations, group traditions are strengthened, generating feelings of permanence and stability.

A similar theme is set by some sort of "organizational boot camp," strong collective activities that everyone must undergo as part of initiation into the group. (Fraternity admission rites are in this category, as are the "secret entry procedures" of various organizations.) Such shared experiences are powerful molders of emotion. They are joints of attachment between member and group. The memories formed light and warm a corner of the mind, the corner containing commitment. The process fuels commitment with higher levels of energy, moving it up the scale toward core.

BACK FROM THE BRINK, TOGETHER

For four generations, the Brennan family ran the largest business in the small midwestern city. Employing almost 2,000 people at its peak, the company had a national reputation for manufacuturing customized machine tools and a local reputation for caring for its people. The company was the pride of the city, but now its creditors were about to take and possess. Bankruptcy was at hand.

Chester Brennan, the great-grandson of the founder, had been struggling through three years of recession. Although barely 50, he looked more than 60. Gaunt in body and sallow in skin, he alone bore responsibility and shame.

All hope seemed lost. The debts couldn't be paid and creditors were clammering for the dwindling dollars. Chapter 11 bankruptcy appeared the only alternative. A receiver would be appointed by the courts to run the company. How would he explain it to his father, no longer active at 83 but still passionately interested in the affairs of his company? How would he explain it to his children?

The story of the Brennan Manufacturing Company was not an unusual one during the worst business cycle since the Great Depression. The industrial heart of Middle America was renamed the Rust Belt as many traditional firms languished.

Brennan's customers had cut back dramatically on orders for new machines, and the carrying costs of unwanted inventory and the high overheads in plant and equipment drained cash like two gaping holes in a sinking ship. Furthermore, the inroads of Japanese (and more recently Korean) competition were putting severe pressure on margins. Even his American competitors started selling below cost. Generating cash was the name of the game, the game of survival.

Chester Brennan was loath to fire any employees. He had long stated that the family had a "moral contract" with the community, and he backed up his own commitment with his own money. The company sustained huge losses before making its first layoffs in 50 years, and then only did so at the insistence of the newly organized committee of creditors.

Brennan, however, still refused to eliminate company civic programs. It ran two daycare centers and sponsored numerous sporting events. The entire Little League was a Brennan project. Not only did the company donate cash, it also gave work credit to any employee doing the coaching. Unions never even wasted their time trying to organize around here.

Though the firings numbered over 400, Chester insisted on speaking to each individual personally. It took him the better part of two weeks. Many of the hardship cases he gave cash from his own pocket, a resource evaporating as quickly as the company treasury.

The family had taken little money out of the company over the years, preferring to keep the balance sheet strong. The decision might have been a foolish one for the family, but it was providential for the firm. The only reason it had not folded long ago, as had many similar companies, was its strong equity position.

It was, for Chester, like having terminally ill parents, with all employees as family. Every day at lunch, managers and workers alike would come over and embrace him, offering their consolation and support. (He always ate in the cafeteria, though companies half the size had executive dining rooms.)

With only days remaining before the formal meeting of the creditors and the push into bankruptcy, one employee, a long-time foreman from the plant floor, came up with an idea.

"We owe you, Chester, and your daddy. You've been good to us, and the company's been getting its brains knocked in. Some of us have been talking. Now it's time to stop talking and start doing. We'll cut our pay 50 percent. We'll work 20 percent longer hours. We'll do whatever it takes!"

The proposal, hurriedly put to secret ballot, was ratified by over 90 percent of the employees. And that was *before* Chester made *his* proposal.

"In return for the loyalty and extraordinary sacrifice of our people," Chester announced in a special meeting of all employees, "the Brennan family will give 50 percent of the company to a newly formed employee trust. You were always part of our family. Now we are going to make it official."

The story ends well. Creditors, although skeptical, couldn't help but be impressed and gave a moratorium of six months. The time was sufficient. Increased productivity and greatly reduced costs were aided, as if by design, by an upswing in the economy.

The Brennan Manufacturing Company had turned the corner and was heading back to prosperity. The road would be long and the tasks hard, but success would come because the mutual commitment between company and employees was all core.

THE CONCLUSION OF THE MATTER

We come back to basics. Commitment links personal meaning and company mission, and as such plays a major role in both. It is the foundation on which the modern business enterprise is established.

Our interest is practical: How can organizations benefit by building the collective commitment of its members? Our interest is also personal: How can human beings maximize individual satisfaction in their work?

The answers turn together. They are complementary not competitive and reinforce each other with positive feedback. The answers are found along the same continuum: the commitment scale.

We began by flouting the admonition "don't mix business with religion." We took the risk in order to refresh both. Though the direct objective has been to understand commitment in religion and apply it to business, the process can be reversed. Religious organizations can learn from business corporations as well. The learning should be mutual with benefits flowing in all directions.

Business and religion are primary institutions of mankind; they are present in every human society — the former the prime supplier of material development, the latter the prime provider of spiritual sustenance. Each constitutes separate spheres of influence in the social structure, yet together they compose a common environment for individual expression and personal fulfillment.

Whether in business or religion, the firm bond of commitment is formed by linking personal meaning and organizational mission. And in another sense, as they build and reinforce each other, business and religion can form their own firm bond.

NOTES

PREFACE

1. The concept of a "special lens" with which to view selectively certain phenomena is derived from Allison's "conceptual lens," which is his way of describing different "frames of reference" or models used to explain processes of complex decision making. He writes that "by comparing and contrasting the three frameworks [which he used to explain the Cuban Missle Crisis], we see what each magnifies, highlights, and reveals as well as what each blurs or neglects." See Graham Allison, *Essence of Decision* (Boston: Little, Brown, 1971).

2. Is commitment "distinctly human"? Animals band together for physical protection and social sustenance. Are such "organizations" a single step down from the gathering together of human beings for physical comfort and social satisfaction? Sociobiologists would say yes, declaring the genetic determination of human behavior. Theologians would say no, propounding the higher calling of human beings. The debate, for our purposes, becomes moot, since we search commitment's components and applications, not its interspecies distinctions and implications. We seek the deep structure of group association, the pillars of human society.

CHAPTER 1

1. For a summary of alternative research definitions of commitment, see Bruce Buchanan II, "Building Organizational Commitment: The Socialization of Managers in Work Organizations," *Administrative Science Quarterly* 1974, 19: 533-46.

2. Erving Goffman used the term "total organizations" to characterize institutions that place a barrier to social intercourse with the outside world. See Goffman, *Asylums* (Garden City, N.Y.: Anchor Books, 1961). Our use of the term "total" involves organizations that deal with ultimate or ideal purposes in addition to constructing such barriers.

CHAPTER 2

1. "Psychosocial foreclosure" is a term used by Eric Erikson to describe an individual who is committed to his or her goals largely as a result of parental or other influence. See Erikson, "The Problems of Ego Identity," *Journal of the American Psychoanalytic Association* 1956, 4: 56-121.

2. Daniel Levinson has popularized the concept of "BOOM" (Becoming One's Own Man) as a distinctive midlife phase where the desire to have a greater measure of self-authority emerges. See Levinson, *The Seasons of A Man's Life* (New York: Knopf, 1978).

3. The importance of distinguishing between higher-order (which we dub meaning-related) and lower-order (security-related) needs in analyzing organizational identificaiton is suggested in Douglas T. Hall et al., "Personal Factors in Organizational Identification." *Administrative Science Quarterly* 1970, 15: 176–89.

4. See Richard M. Steers, "Antecedents and Outcomes of Organizational Commitment," *Administrative Science Quarterly* 1977, 22: 46–56, for a discussion of the influence of educational level on commitment.

5. For a discussion of the importance of generalized loyalty in determining commitment, see Yoash Wiener, "Commitment in Organizations: A Normative View," *Academy of Management Review* 1982, 7: 418–26.

6. Julian Rotter has been largely responsible for developing the internal/external locus of control metaphor. See Rotter, *Social Learning and Clinical Psychology* (New York: Prentice-Hall, 1954), or *The Development and Application of Social Learning Theory* (New York: Praeger, 1982). For a discussion of the pawn/origin dyad, see R. de Charms, *Personal Causation: The Internal Affective Determinants of Behavior* (New York: Academic Press, 1968).

7. There are no dearth of other personal variables that could be included. Following are three:

Physical and Sensual: The enjoyment of physical sensation; the care and feeding of appetites and drives. Examples include the gourmets and gourmands, and those who are addicted to tobacco, alcohol, and drugs. Other people, runners in particular, have become devotees of physical fitness; they would rather miss a major company meeting than not complete their self-assigned miles. Sexual desire is included here; while most people enjoy the physical act of love, some people are consumed by it.

Love and Affection: The magnetic attraction and personal compulsion to be with another person or persons; the reciprocal love of men and women; the love of parents for children. This is high on everyone's priority list, but some place love higher than others. Men turn down promotions if their wives do not want to move; women will refuse jobs if their husbands' careers come first.

Aesthetic and Artistic: The love of beauty and the arts (music, painting, literature). Some people working in companies, unable to make a living in the arts, devote all outside energies to their avocation; the results, in many cases, are employees with weak commitment and mediocre intensity. Conversely, companies sensitive to the aesthetic sense will derive higher levels of output from their creative employees. Simple matters such as office design may set the proper mood.

CHAPTER 3

1. Try some calculations with stratospheric price/earnings ratios. In order to maintain these cosmic multiples for stock prices, the company products, whatever they are, would have to be planted everywhere on earth in a couple of decades, and everywhere in the universe in the next century.

2. For a discussion of the power of a wholistic structure in group control, see A. Etzioni, "Organizational Control Structure," *Handbook of Organizations* (Chicago: Rand McNally, 1965).

3. The impact of "boundaries and their permeability" on organizational mission is analyzed in D. Katz and R. Kahn, *The Social Psychology of Organizations* (New York: Wiley, 1966).

4. The existence of a "double standard" is virtually pandemic in religious organizations. Illana Friedrich Silber uses the term without "pejorative connotations" in her paper "Dissent Through Holiness: The Case of the Radical Renouncer in Theravada Buddhist Countries," *Numen* 1981, pp. 164–193. (Note R. J. Z. Werblowsky's use of the more neutral expression "two-tiered religiousity" in "Modernism and modernization in Buddhism" in *The Search for Absolute Values in a Changing World* 1977. San Francisco: The International Cultural Foundation). The double standard, writes Silber, "upholds a clear cut distinction between virtuoso [religious elite] and layman, but also avoids total disconnection between the two in a variety of ways. This double standard enables the layman to cope, to a certain extent, with the extreme other-worldliness [or apparent higher holiness] of the ideal of renunciation [or social position and power]. It provides a certain degree of legitimation of lay activities, while at the same time unambiguously affirming the superiority of the virtuoso's pursuit of other-worldiness. . . . The lay world, although undoubtedly deemed inferior, is allowed a significant degree of autonomy. But — and this is of crucial significance — it is never conceived as the locus of salvation."

5. See W. Kiechel III, "Wanted: Corporate Leaders," *Fortune*, May 30, 1983, for a popular discussion of the relationship between leadership and organizational purpose.

6. Herbert Simon, Richard Cyert, and James March are pioneers in new ways of thinking about the theory and practice of management. Concepts propounded include: the limits of rationality, the process of problem-driven search, the formulation of expectations, and the execution of managerial choice. Each articulates real-world relevance with sophisticated constructs. See Herbert Simon's *Administrative Behavior* (New York: Free Press, 1976); R. M. Cyert and J. G. March, *A Behavior Theory of the Firm* (Englewood Cliffs, N.J.: Prentice-Hall, 1963).

7. See J. R. P. French and B. Raven, "The Bases of Social Power," in Dorwin Cartwright, ed., *Studies in Social Power* (Ann Arbor, Mich: Institute for Social Research, 1959).

8. For a complete and fascinating discussion of how "organizational process" (and "bureaucratic politics") affect decision making, see Graham Allison's *Essence of Decision,* op. cit. Allison uses the 1962 Cuban Missle Crisis as substrate for showing how the "rational actor" model of decision making — where all decisions are made according to a logical calculus — cannot completely account for organizational decisions. Organizational units are shown to have independent existence and operate outside the linear patterns of normal logic. ("Monoliths perform large action for large reasons.") Although developed for governmental and political decision making, Allison's three models — rational actor, organizational process, and bureaucratic politics — are directly applicable to business.

CHAPTER 4

1. For a good discussion of role strain in the context of changing spousal roles over time, see W. Burr "Role Transitions: A Reformulation of Theory," *Journal of Marriage and the Family* (August 1972): 407–16.

2. Howard Becker in a classic paper analyzed the importance of "side bets" or investments in determining organizational commitment. See Becker, "Notes on the Concept of Commitment," *American Journal of Sociology* 1960, 66: 32–40.

3. See L. Festinger, *A Theory of Cognitive Dissonance* (Evanston, Ill.: Row and Peterson, 1957).

4. L. Festinger, H. Riecken and S. Schacter, *When Prophecy Fails.* (Minneapolis: University of Minnesota Press, 1956).

CHAPTER 5

1. "Valence" is a term used to embody this commitment strength, drawing the analogy from the relative power of ions, charged molecules, to react in chemical combinations. A high valence is indicative of high commitment strength either positive or negative, a low valence of low commitment strength. For example, the term "valence" has been used by Victor Vroom in his valence-expectancy theory to describe the strength of an individual's preference for an outcome. See his *Work and Motivation* (New York: Wiley, 1964).

2. The term "calculative commitment" was used to describe a commitment type by A. Kidron, "Work Values and Organizational Commitment," *Academy of Management Journal* 1978, 21: 239–46. "Normative" commitment was used to describe another commitment type by the author.

3. For the remainder of the book, the words "core," "calculative," or "cog" when used alone will imply core(+), calculative(+), or cog(+), respectively. Also, when the word "commitment" is used by itself it usually means core(+).

4. Our three elements used to determine "mission contribution" roughly parallel aspects of the Porter-Lawler model of motivation (used to predict performance accomplishment). See Lyman Porter and Edward Lawler III, *Managerial Attitudes and Performance* (Homewood, Ill.: Irwin, 1968).

CHAPTER 6

1. For a complete analysis of human achievement, see the works of David C. McClelland. Primary themes include: the need for achievement; the use of fantasy to assess achievement; the distinction between power and achievement; achievement as an entrepreneurial characteristic; achievement in different socioeconomic situations; motivational training for achievement. D. McClelland, *The Achieving Society* (New York: Van Nostrand Reinhold, 1961). D. McClelland and D. Winter, *Motivating Economic Development* (New York: Free Press, 1969). D. McClelland, J. Atkinson, R. Clark, and E. Lowell, *The Achievement Motive* (New York: Appleton-Century-Crofts, 1953). D. McClelland *Motivational Trends in Society* (Morristown, N.J.: General Learning Press, 1971).

CHAPTER 7

1. The five commitment breakers correlate well with Seeman's 1972 summary of alienation research. He proposed that alienation is founded on one or more of the following feelings about one's internal self and the external world: powerlessness, meaninglessness, normlessness, social isolation, value isolation, self-estrangement. M. Seeman, "Alienation and Engagement," in A. Campbell and P. E. Converse eds., *The Human Meaning of Social Change* (New York: Russell Sage Foundation, 1972).

2. Viktor E. Frankl, *Man's Search for Meaning: An Introduction to Logo Therapy.* Boston: Beacon Press, 1962. Paperback edition, New York: Washington Square Press, 1963.

3. L. Festinger, *A Theory of Cognitive Dissonance,* op. cit.

CHAPTER 8

1. John Kenneth Galbraith, "Corporate Man," *The New York Times Magazine*, January 1984.

2. Raymond W. Smilor and Robert Lawrence Kuhn, *Corporate Creativity: Robust Companies and the Entrepreneurial Spirit* (New York: Praeger 1984.)

3. For a more complete discussion of the strategic framework in its normal role in formulating, evaluating, and implementing corporate strategy, see the following: R. L. Kuhn, *To Flourish Among Giants: Creative Strategies for Mid-Sized Firms* (New York: Wiley, 1984). R. L. Kuhn, *Mid-Sized Firms: Success Strategies and Methodology* (New York: Praeger, 1982). C. Hofer and D. Schendel, *Strategy Formulation: Analytical Concepts* (St. Paul, Minn.: West, 1978). K. Andrews *The Concept of Corporate Strategy* (Homewood, Ill: Irwin, 1980).

CHAPTER 9

1. The case of "The Company from Central Casting" is a classic example. A small group of professionals bid and received a healthy government contract. They were fully qualified but the government insisted on checking their facilities and resources. Well, there were *no* facilities or resources. So the enterprising fellows, as if setting up a movie set, rented a large building and filled it with furniture, drafting equipment, and unfolded blueprints. They hired several dozen "extras," gave them an hour's lesson in looking the part, and then put the show on the road. No only was the charade successful, but the wily entrepreneurs fulfilled the contract and went on to build a large company.

2. As a point of limited interest, one of Rabbi Mandlebaum's young servants, a scholar of minor note, had been asked by the leading associate rabbis

(including the son of the chief rabbi) to prepare an organized outline of the movement's teachings of Torah. He was instructed to be sure to present each doctrine in the best possible manner. The need had arisen because of growing media interest in the beliefs of the group, and consequent scrutiny by antagonistic sects both within Judaism and without. The rabbi's teachings had to be given proper scriptural support. Logic and accurate interpretation were essential. But little did the minor servant realize, he was sowing the seeds of his own destruction. For the more successful this systematic theology would become, the more jealousy the project would provoke. For who was this minor servant? Not even a rabbi. Not even an assistant rabbi!

Nonetheless the minor servant set about his task with fear and fervor, seeking, however naively, total cooperation of clergy and older scholars — though he would write all the words himself. He did have, he would later admit, some ulterior motivations in the preparation of the project, a hidden agenda that he kept secret from superior scholars and rabbis.

He was worried. Rabbi Mandlebaum was elderly and had been taken ill; and some associate rabbis to whom authority would eventually pass were contentious and fractious with limited knowledge or interest in doctrine. The minor servant was worried that the sanctity of the rabbi's teachings might be corrupted. Several of the rabbi's important teachings were already coming under quiet attack. One, for example, was his teaching that although man had some nonphysical essence, some "spirit," that it was not an immortal soul. The minor servant sought to solidify this truth, among other similar truths, in his massive project. Though warned by friends about minefields and icebergs, he pushed forward with full steam, oblivious to approaching disaster.

Most important to him was the proper positioning of the Torah's essential message. What must be emphasized were not peripheral points of grooming and dress, but central doctrines of meaning and purpose. Stress must be put where stress should be found: on the overwhelming teachings about God, man, earth, and universe; on the laws and precepts for spiritual and moral obedience; on the history and prophecy of Israel. Movement teachings, wrote the minor servant, must reflect the scriptures in relative importance as well as absolute substance.

Some of the lesser rabbis, the minor servant had observed, could not follow the chief rabbi's vision; his most profound truths were not being accurately understood nor properly appreciated. The essential core of doctrinal teaching — the spiritual meaning of mankind — too quickly bored the junior rabbis, and the "twiggy," outlying doctrines too easily infatuated them. These younger men loved speaking on the physical things of the world — behavioral directions for daily living — codified instructions of do's and don'ts — all the ritual that the chief rabbi had always put in proper perspective. The purity of Torah must be trumpeted, the complexity of interpreters muted!

Truth to be truth, believed the minor servant, must be accurate in content, style, and relative weight. What must be highlighted is the doctrinal core of God and the ultimate purpose of human life. We must magnify, he later wrote, the spiritual teachings of scripture, and not let the barnacles of physical traditions hide and encumber them. Man is created in the image and likeness of God, and has incredible spiritual potential. The God of Israel is the Almighty Creator and His Plan shall encompass the universe.

200

3. Rosebeth Moss Kanter. *The Change Master.* (New York: Simon and Schuster, 1983).

4. One would think that the fabricators of dated and convoluted prophecies, so easily falsified, would fear embarrassing the God who made them. A desire to know the future is a uniquely human aspiration, and all forms of forecasting, from astrology and the occult to expert opinion and computer projections, are available in abundance in modern society.

Biblical prophecy, however, is different. It is a singular class of prognostication, written for different reasons, preserved for different purposes. The God who speaks through the Bible, the Being who claims to be Creator of heavens and earth, proclaims prophecy as proof of His existence: "I am the Lord: that is my name. . . . Behold, the former things are come to pass, and new things do I declare: before they spring forth I tell you of them . . . for I am God, and there is none else . . . Declaring the end from the beginning, and from ancient times the things that are not yet done . . . I have spoken it, I will also bring it to pass; I have purposed it, I will also do it." (Isaiah 42:8-9; 46:9-11.) (All who claim "special knowledge" of prophecy would be well advised to ponder Isaiah 41:22-24.)

5. See Thomas B. Rosenstiel, "Coleco's Fortunes Take a Roller-Coaster Ride," *Los Angeles Times*, December 5, 1983, for more details of this account.

6. Two pioneers in the field of human resource accounting have been Rensis Likert and Eric Flamholtz. See R. Likert, *The Human Organization: Its Management and Value* (New York: McGraw-Hill, 1963). See also E. Flamholtz, *Human Resource Accounting* (Encino, Calif.: Dickenson, 1974).

7. An example of human resource valuation in the acquisition of a security brokerage firm and the tax implications of such a valuation is reported in E. Flamholtz, G. Geis, and R. Perle, "A Markovian Model for the Valuation of Human Assets Acquired by an Organizational Purchase," *Interfaces*, in press.

BIBLIOGRAPHY

Argyris, Chris. *Integrating the Individual and the Organization*. New York: Wiley, 1964.

Chandler, Alfred D., Jr. *Strategy and Structure*. Garden City, N.Y.: Doubleday-Anchor, 1966.

Etzioni, Amitai. "Organizational Control Structure." In *Handbook of Organizations*, ed. J. G. March. Chicago: Rand-McNally, 1965.

Festinger, Leon. *A Theory of Cognitive Dissonance*. Stanford, Calif.: Stanford University Press, 1957.

Flamholtz, Eric. *Human Resource Accounting*. Encino, Calif.: Dickenson, 1974.

Frankl, Viktor E. *Man's Search for Meaning: An Introduction to Logotherapy*. Boston: Beacon Press, 1962. Paperback edition, New York: Washington Square Press, 1963.

Kantor, Rosebeth Moss. *Commitment and Community*. Cambridge: Harvard University Press, 1972.

_____ . *The Change Masters*. New York: Simon and Schuster, 1983.

Katz, D., and Kahn, R. *The Social Psychology of Organizations*. New York: Wiley, 1966.

Kuhn, Robert Lawrence. *To Flourish Among Giants: Creative Management for Mid-Sized Firms*. New York: Wiley, 1984.

Levinson, Daniel. *The Seasons of a Man's Life*. New York: Knopf, 1978.

Likert, Rensis. *The Human Organization: Its Management and Value*. New York: McGraw-Hill, 1963.

Maslow, Abraham. *Motivation and Personality*. New York: Harper & Row, 1954.

Porter, Lyman, and Lawler, Edward III. *Managerial Attitudes and Performance*. Homewood, Ill.: Irwin, 1968.

Smilor, Raymond W., and Kuhn, Robert Lawrence. *Corporate Creativity: Robust Companies and the Entrapreneurial Spirit*. New York: Praeger, 1984.

INDEX

ABOUT THE AUTHORS

ROBERT LAWRENCE KUHN is a scientist, strategist, scholar and author at home in the complementary worlds of business and academia. He is Senior Fellow in Creative and Innovative Management at the IC² Institute at the University of Texas at Austin, and is an adjunct professor of corporate strategy in the Department of Management and Organizational Behavior of New York University.

Dr. Kuhn is actively involved with several high technology ventures and investment groups. He specializes in new enterprises, financial transactions, and mergers and acquisitions. (He is noted for his restructuring of Eagle Clothes.) He works with ventures, technologies and government in Israel.

Dr. Kuhn holds a B. A. (Phi Beta Kappa) in Human Biology from Johns Hopkins University; a Ph. D. in Neurophysiology from the Department of Anatomy and Brain Research Institute of the University of California at Los Angeles; and an M. S. (Sloan Fellow) in Management from the Massachusetts Institute of Technology where he was also a research affiliate in Psychology.

Recent books include: *To Flourish Among Giants: Creative Management for Mid-Sized Firms* (Wiley); *Commercializing Defense-Related Technology* (Praeger); and *Corporate Creativity: Robust Companies and the Entrepreneurial Spirit* (Praeger). He is Senior Editor of *Texas Business* magazine, and is a contributing editor to the *Journal of Business Strategy*. He is Editor-in-Chief of a forthcoming *Handbook for Creative and Innovative Managers* (McGraw-Hill).

GEORGE T. GEIS is a professor of business administration, researcher, management consultant and author. He has served on the faculty of several colleges and universities and is Research Coordinator at the Center for Human Resource Management, Institute of Industrial Relations, the University of California at Los Angeles.

Dr. Geis received a B. S. in Mathematics (summa cum laude) from Purdue University, a Ph. D. in Educational Psychology from the University of Southern California, and an M. B. A. from the Graduate School of Management at UCLA, where he was also a Postdoctoral Scholar. His book/disk package on personal financial management is published by Ashton-Tate.

3